D1293527

THE ENGLISH MIND

THE
ENGLISH
MIND

STUDIES IN THE ENGLISH MORALISTS
PRESENTED TO
BASIL WILLEY

EDITED BY HUGH SYKES DAVIES AND
GEORGE WATSON

CAMBRIDGE
AT THE UNIVERSITY PRESS
1964

PUBLISHED BY
THE SYNDICS OF THE CAMBRIDGE UNIVERSITY PRESS

Bentley House, 200 Euston Road, London, N.W.1
American Branch: 32 East 57th Street, New York 22, N.Y.
West African Office: P.O. Box 33, Ibadan, Nigeria

©

CAMBRIDGE UNIVERSITY PRESS
1964

B
1111
D3

WHEATON COLLEGE LIBRARY
NORTON, MASS.

*Printed in Great Britain by
Spottiswoode, Ballantyne & Co. Ltd.
London and Colchester*

124476

THE CONTRIBUTORS

NOEL ANNAN *is Provost of King's College, Cambridge, and a lecturer in Politics.*

JOHN BEER *is a lecturer in English at Manchester University.*

R. L. BRETT *is professor of English at the University of Hull.*

J. B. BROADBENT *is a Fellow of King's College, Cambridge, and a lecturer in English.*

HERBERT BUTTERFIELD *is Master of Peterhouse, Cambridge, and Regius Professor of History.*

DONALD DAVIE *is professor of Literature at the University of Essex, Colchester.*

HUGH SYKES DAVIES *is a Fellow of St John's College, Cambridge, and a lecturer in English.*

MATTHEW HODGART *is a Fellow of Pembroke College, Cambridge, and a lecturer in English.*

JOHN HOLLOWAY *is a Fellow of Queens' College, Cambridge, and a lecturer in English.*

GRAHAM HOUGH *is a Fellow of Christ's College, Cambridge, and a lecturer in English.*

THEODORE REDPATH *is a Fellow of Trinity College, Cambridge, and a lecturer in English.*

ANNE RIGHTER *is a Fellow of Girton College, Cambridge, and a lecturer in English.*

HEINRICH STRAUMANN *is professor of English at the University of Zürich.*

GEORGE WATSON *is a Fellow of St John's College, Cambridge, and a lecturer in English.*

IAN WATT *is professor of English at the University of East Anglia, Norwich.*

RAYMOND WILLIAMS *is a Fellow of Jesus College, Cambridge, and a lecturer in English.*

CONTENTS

BASIL WILLEY

KING EDWARD VII PROFESSOR OF ENGLISH LITERATURE
IN THE UNIVERSITY OF CAMBRIDGE, 1946–1964

A TRIBUTE BY HERBERT BUTTERFIELD

In January 1919 Basil Willey, who three years before had been admitted to Peterhouse as an Entrance Scholar in History, came into residence in Cambridge to work for Part II of the Historical Tripos. The effects seem to have built themselves into the structure of his mind; for when he became Edward VII Professor of English Literature in 1946, he hinted at the idea of a 'Cambridge Modern Greats', and pointed out that 'the Tripos has always been the English Tripos, not the English Literature Tripos'; and he identified himself with the view of G. M. Trevelyan—'Literature and History are twin sisters, inseparable.' He tells us in his Inaugural Lecture that 'a closer interchange between "English" and "History" in particular is what I should like to see'.

We are accustomed now to connect literature with life, not so much by linking books with their authors as by viewing them in their historical setting, in relation to their social or intellectual . . . 'background'. Literary movements . . . cannot fully be explained without reference to forces at work outside the field of literature itself.[1]

From the nature of his original training, it might have been inferred that when he moved to the study and teaching of literature he would hold a distinctive place in the English Faculty at Cambridge. It happened that the Faculty was preparing to receive him; for before he had come into residence we catch the first hints of what was to be the opportunity that helped to shape his career. E. M. W. Tillyard, in *The Muse Unchained*, has described how Quiller-Couch had been working hard in 1917 to secure that a paper on the English Moralists should be introduced into the English Tripos. Q had been defeated on that occasion, chiefly by H. M. Chadwick and the

---

[1] *The Q Tradition* (Cambridge, 1946), p. 26; cf. pp. 27 and 29.

Rev. H. F. Stewart; but nearly ten years later, a movement for the reform of the Tripos gave him the opportunity for a further campaign.

Although Q disliked giving his attention to Tripos reform, there was one possibility he greatly minded about: that of introducing a paper on the English Moralists. . . . No one else believed in the wisdom of inserting such a paper in the literary sections of the Tripos, where it seemed an intruder; and Q himself was so elusive, if you asked him what exactly he meant by the English Moralists, . . . that our distrust did not lessen. His usual retort to a question was a lyrical outburst on the glories of their writings issuing into a roll-call of the great names: 'Hooker—Hobbes—Locke—Berkeley—Hume'; and ending with an exhausted 'my God', as emotion got the better of him. . . . Q's most tangible service to the Cambridge English School was in being the only begetter of the paper on the English Moralists.[1]

The very fact that the new subject had eluded definition carried the consequence that its establishment would provide somebody with a creative opportunity. Tillyard tells us that the adoption of the Moralists paper had the effect of producing a new teaching need and quickly rendered indispensable the services of Basil Willey, who became a full University Lecturer in 1934 and a Fellow of Pembroke in 1935. He says that 'Willey made the Moralists paper and . . . the Moralists paper made him'; and there is probably some truth and some exaggeration in both these statements. Yet if we measure Willey's achievement by the main body of his published work, we cannot escape the view that something in his mentality, and something in his way of experiencing life, have been almost permanent characteristics of the man—anterior to the accidents of his teaching career. And these are the things which have governed both his choice and his treatment of the writers he has studied. His handling of the Moralists paper has been his own.

  He has changed little in the course of his life, and when he was a young man at Peterhouse he was already somewhat gentle, somewhat remote—on the way perhaps to becoming benignant—though one learned to detect inside him a fire and a passion that were kept controlled. One was primarily impressed by the sensitiveness of his whole structure; but though

[1] E. M. W. Tillyard, *The Muse Unchained* (London, 1958), pp. 108, 118.

one saw only the charm of a meditative man when one looked him in the face, the profile was strong even then, becoming more pointed and more weather-scarred by the passage of time, but always cutting the air in a rather determined manner. From his youth his academic interests have been combined with a love of music and skill at the piano; and it has been a matter of permanent significance in his intellectual development that to him the arts are intimately associated with the innermost parts of the personality; for him they have always answered to something important in human experience; he could not feel that a man was a complete human being without them. He has been a Methodist too, still in the tradition of liberal non-conformity—ready as a thinker to take his stand on the validity of religious experience, but determined, in spite of the depth of the feelings involved, to confront with relentless honesty the intellectual problems that Christianity presents. Similarly, he has always had that feeling for nature which is illustrated at a later date by his praise for Thomas Arnold and the Lake District:

the whole course of English thought and letters in the nineteenth century would have been different if this island had not contained the mountain paradise of Westmorland and Cumberland. The Lake District was part of its religious creed; as Mr Aldous Huxley has said, for good Wordsworthians a tour through Westmorland was 'as good as a visit to Jerusalem'. The Alps, indeed, offered their rarer ecstasies to the leisured and adventurous, but the Lakeland mountains, linking heaven with home, spoke more healingly and intimately to the heart.

And he adds: 'Mountain joy can be sacred, not profane.'[1]

Much the greater part of Willey's work lies in the realm of 'the history of ideas'; but as he moves over the successive centuries it becomes clear that he is following a path of his own. There is a remarkable uniformity and continuity in the main series of his writings. The books marshal themselves into a great historical theme; and their internal variety makes for comprehensiveness in Willey's treatment of the theme. His first publication, a prize essay on *Tendencies in Renaissance Literary Theory*, appeared in 1922, before the paper on the Moralists

[1] *Nineteenth Century Studies* (London, 1949), pp. 69-71.

had been established in the English Tripos. In its early pages however, there is a passage which links even this booklet with the main body of his published work. His treatment of an imaginary dialogue between Petrarch and St Augustine leads to a discussion of the decline of the medieval idea that 'aesthetic gratification is a sensual sin'. In this passage some of the tones of the later Willey are already audible. In a way that he can hardly have realized at the time, it was a premonition of the programme that he was to carry out.

The work which made his name in 1934, *The Seventeenth Century Background*, deals with a larger aspect of the transition from the medieval to the modern mentality. It opens with a chapter on 'The Rejection of Scholasticism' and describes the changing climate of opinion in the age of the scientific revolution. Willey is interested in the effect of the change on poetry, and still more on the religious outlook—the effect on man's general feeling about the world. For him the matter is not merely a question of scholarship but an issue of real life; and he addresses 'not professional philosophers, but students of literature, and not professional students merely but all to whom poetry, and religion, and their relation to the business of living, are matters of importance'. Previously he had discussed 'aesthetic gratification', but now it is the problem of Truth that is at the centre of the picture. He sets out to show the kind of Truth that the new scientific age required. But the main theme is continued in another book, dealing with the eighteenth century—a further study of a transition that affects both poetry and religion, because it alters man's feelings about life and the universe. Attention is now focussed on 'the idea of Nature'. In the eighteenth century, we learn:

Nature was the grand alternative to all that man had made of man; upon her solid ground therefore—upon the *tabula rasa* prepared by the true philosophy—must all the religion, the ethics, the politics, the law and the art of the future be constructed. . . . It was not the ambiguity of 'Nature' which people felt most strongly; it was rather the clarity, the authority, and the universal acceptability of Nature and Nature's laws.[1]

These two volumes both ended in chapters on Wordsworth,

[1] *The Eighteenth Century Background* (London, 1940), p. 2.

and the first of the two volumes of *Nineteenth Century Studies*
(1949–56) opens with an important account of Coleridge as a
thinker. In the discussion of the writings of these two men—
the poetry in the one case, the philosophy in the other, but in
both cases the treatment of human experience at something like
the religious level—Willey's historical work seems to find its
culmination. If J. S. Mill, writing in 1838 about Bentham and
Coleridge, could say that 'there is hardly to be found in
England an individual of any importance in the world of mind
who did not first learn to think from one of these two', there
can be no doubt that Willey—himself one of the lovers of the
Lakeland—found Coleridge the one who touched his sympathies. This is apparent in the two volumes of *Nineteenth
Century Studies*, which deal more directly with the conflict between science and traditional religion. Of the second volume
we are told in the Preface: 'Its central theme is "the loss of
faith", or . . . the reinterpretation of current orthodoxy in the
light of nineteenth century canons of historical and scientific
criticism.'

Predominant therefore throughout Willey's main work is the
question of the confrontation of Christianity with modern
thought since the Renaissance, and particularly since the rise
of modern science. The same issues are treated in a more
general way—and from an avowedly personal angle—in
Christianity Past and Present, which appeared in 1952. Here is no
mere question of the past seen at a distance and examined
impersonally—dissected in cold blood. The works of Willey
are not merely books about books: they are studies of a whole
aspect of modern experience by a man who has traversed and
re-traversed the field in his own life. He recaptures some of the
momentousness which the conflicts had for people intimately
concerned in them. He has the right imaginative sympathy
for the men who just missed being Christian or, while retaining
their faith, conducted a lonely campaign against orthodoxy.
He deals with *In Memoriam* because 'it goes behind Christianity,
confronting the preliminary question which besets the natural
man, the question whether there can be any religious interpretation of life at all'. And constantly his own ideas break
through as he makes his comments on the successive writers

whom he discusses. It is reported that Tennyson, when he saw the wonders disclosed by the microscope, said: 'Strange that these wonders should draw some men to God and repel others. No more reason in the one than in the other.' Willey's comment on this remark is interesting; he says: 'I suspect it was at variance with his [Tennyson's] own subconscious feeling.'

He has moved with modesty in a world of scholars, and has quietly pursued an independent course. As a lecturer he is helped by happy phrases and an eye that twinkles; by a gift for quiet irony and a touch of humour. He has never been greatly interested in administration and prefers to avoid controversy that he cannot pacify by the exercise and example of charity. And so he achieves a certain remoteness, but avoids giving the impression that it is unsympathetic. Nothing could exceed in warmth the encouragement he has given to young scholars and the help he has brought to teachers of English in other universities. Some lively works in the study of the English Moralists—John Holloway's *The Victorian Sage* (1953), Raymond Williams's *Culture and Society 1780–1950* (1958) and Dorothea Krook's *Three Traditions of Moral Thought* (1959)—have owed much to him. It was peculiarly fitting that he should be invited to work with the panel of English language experts who helped in the New English Bible. Those who have contributed to the present volume rejoice to have the opportunity of expressing their admiration and their indebtedness.

1

FRANCIS BACON

BY ANNE RIGHTER

It was the fate of the Roman Colosseum to serve for many centuries as a quarry. Innumerable tons of stone were carted away to be incorporated into later and quite diverse structures, to support the roofs, comprise the walls, or be lost to sight among the foundations of buildings whose purpose, scale and form were utterly different from those of Vespasian's amphitheatre. That the relentless pillaging of ages should nevertheless leave standing a wreck so gigantic, and essentially so coherent, testifies eloquently both to the magnitude of the original, and to the diminished aspirations of later men. There is a sense in which the work of Francis Bacon (1561–1626) also has served the centuries as a quarry. One piece is mortised into the Royal Society. Others help to compose the post-medieval structure of English prose, of English historiography, of English law. Fragments of Baconian architecture turn up on all sides: in Hobbes and in Locke, Descartes, Leibniz, Voltaire, Mill, Kant, Shelley, Coleridge and Marx. Technology, the experimental method, inductive reasoning, linguistic analysis, psychology: all of them appear to incorporate some elements of Bacon's thought, although it is usually difficult to identify these elements precisely, or to determine their real importance. Equally tenacious is the transferred life of those Baconian phrases in which, miraculously, abstract ideas become available to the senses without relinquishing their basic character and precision: the clear and equal glass, the idols of cave, tribe, market-place and theatre, the instances of the lamp, the doctrine of scattered occasions, the branching candlestick of lights. Separated from their original context, they continue not only to live, but to articulate hypotheses and discoveries of which Bacon himself never dreamed.

This gradual dismemberment of the *Instauratio magna*, and

of the works clustered around it, is nothing to which Bacon, in principle at least, would have objected. In fact, he had foreseen it. Over and over again he refers the ultimate realization of his thought to the future. His published work is a bell to call other wits together, a collection of sparks flying out in all directions to kindle a general conflagration or, most memorably of all, an instrument which the craftsman can tune but upon which he cannot perform.

And being now at some pause, looking back into that I have passed through, this writing seemeth to me (*si nunquam fallit imago*), as far as a man can judge of his own work, not much better than that noise or sound which musicians make while they are in tuning their instruments: which is nothing pleasant to hear, but yet is a cause why the music is sweeter afterwards. So have I been content to tune the instruments of the Muses, that they may play that have better hands.[1]

Whether Bacon ever suspected that the music of the future, indebted to him as it is in so many ways, would nevertheless reject that unifying Method by which he set such store is hard to determine. There were moments in which he himself seemed troubled by the fact that his marvellous mechanism for discovery seemed disinclined to desert 'the braver gate (of ivory)' for the practical gate of horn. Certainly, however, he was aware that his ideas in general were incomplete, as abbreviated and hastily roughed out as most of the writings in which they were embodied. Time was short; it was a question of indicating directions and, perhaps even more important, of persuading posterity to try.

What would have appalled Bacon is the extent to which his influence has been seen as pernicious. He could never have guessed that his efforts to establish the Kingdom of Man would come to be regarded as destructive by precisely those generations which at last inhabit it. Like the father of Salomon's House in the *New Atlantis* (1627), Bacon genuinely 'pitied men'; that he should be regarded—frequently by writers also concerned to deny his positive contributions—as the architect of the dilemmas of the twentieth century, the man who effected

[1] *The Advancement of Learning* (London, 1605), II, xxiv. Future numerical references are to this work.

an unholy and lasting divorce between science and poetry, reason and the imagination, Christian ethics and the way of the world, is a species of tragic irony. Yet Bacon has persistently appeared for our time in the role of false prophet, a Moses who leads not to the Promised Land of Cowley's adulatory poem, but to the wilderness of materialism. He is the villain of that moment of indecision between the medieval and the modern worlds, which other artists (Donne, Ralegh, Marlowe, or even Leonardo da Vinci) have been praised for reflecting; the man who cut through and reduced a fertile richness of choice and ambiguity to what C. S. Lewis (speaking of the *Essayes*) has described as a metallic-looking cactus raised on the edge of a desert, 'sterile, inedible, cold and hard to the touch'.[1]

It is a commonplace of Bacon criticism to refer to his inconsistency, and to the astonishing measure of disagreement which exists among his commentators. On a personal level there is the disparity between Spedding's misunderstood man of integrity and feeling, and the more popular image of the 'meanest of mankind'. As for conflicting interpretations of the work and its influence, they are so numerous that it sometimes seems impossible to find out the truth at all.[2] Certainly Bacon was a complicated man, given to self-contradiction. Considering the scope of his thought, together with its emphasis upon continuous growth and correction, these inconsistencies are scarcely surprising. Even more important, however, is the fundamental fact that Bacon's work is not only unfinished: it was by its very nature impossible to finish. Moving from one fragmentary statement to another with a kind of desperate urgency, he himself clearly thought that time, isolation and his civil employments were the impediments, the *remorae* of his beloved image, that kept the great ship from sailing. It does not seem to have occurred to him that the task itself was impractical: basically contradictory in that it lay beyond any single man's accomplishment, yet utterly dependent as a whole upon his own creating imagination. It is, perhaps, only with the triumph of modern science

---

[1] *English Literature in the Sixteenth Century, Excluding Drama* (Oxford, 1954), p. 538.
[2] An amusing balance-sheet of opinion on Bacon can be found in Rudolph Metz, 'Bacon's Part in the Intellectual Movement of his Time', in *Seventeenth-Century Studies Presented to Sir Herbert Grierson* (Oxford, 1938) and in Elizabeth Sewell *The Orphic Voice* (London, 1960), pp. 59–60.

that it has become possible to see how Faustian a figure Bacon was and how paradoxical the plan of the *Instauratio magna*. Despite his insistence upon the anonymity of science, the independence of the Method from the special abilities and characteristics of those who employ it, this is an intensely individual dream. The unity of the *Instauratio magna*, its true form, is that of a various, enormously inclusive but nevertheless particular mind. One is brought back to it at every step. Whatever the practical consequences of those pieces of Bacon's work which have been taken up by later men, the architecture of the whole is that of the imagination, not of fact: the unfinished cathedral at Beauvais rather than the Colosseum. What is attempted outreaches the capacities of the material, the form, and the creator by whom they are utilized. It is a strange situation, and one which should condition response to the prose as inevitably as it does the reaction to that fantastic choir and transept without a nave which is all of Beauvais that could be made to stand. It is also perhaps more promising than that weary discussion about the treatment of the imagination in the *De Augmentis* (1623) and *The Advancement of Learning* (1605) as a way into the consideration of Bacon as an artist.

'Lord Bacon', Shelley declared firmly in the *Defence of Poetry*, 'was a poet.' The remark is all too familiar. What is usually forgotten is that Shelley went on to explain precisely why.

His language has a sweet and majestic rhythm, which satisfies the sense, no less than the almost super-human wisdom of his philosophy satisfies the intellect; it is a strain which distends, and then bursts the circumference of the reader's mind, and pours itself forth together with it into the universal element with which it has perpetual sympathy.

There is much in the expression of this with which it is fashionable, or has been until recently, to find fault. Yet Shelley is neither indulging here in that woolly, uncritical thinking of which he has so often been accused, nor is he simply referring vaguely to the splendours of Bacon's prose. He is saying something about Bacon's qualities as a writer which is both intelligent and perceptive. Bacon's prose succeeds for Shelley not merely in gratifying both the intellect and the senses, but in bringing them together for a purpose. His is a style of persuasion

which forces a kind of greatness upon the mind of the reader,
an enlargement which, working through mind and emotions
both, enables the reader to break through his ordinary attitudes
and comprehend that Truth which Bacon's language serves.

Shelley's claims for Bacon are large ones, but no greater than
those of Coleridge. For Coleridge, Bacon was one of the four
great English geniuses, and he expended considerable effort in
an attempt to prove that 'the Athenian Verulam and the
British Plato', as he called them, were twinned and kindred
spirits. Coleridge is less concerned than Shelley with Bacon's
language, and more with the extractable core of his thought.
He does, however, note at one point that

> faulty verbal antitheses [are] not unfrequent in Lord Bacon's
> writings. Pungent antitheses, and the analogies of wit in which the
> resemblance is too often more indebted to the double or equivocal
> sense of a word than to any real conformity in the thing or image,
> form the *dulcia vitia* of his style, the Dalilahs of our philosophical
> Samson.[1]

In a note, Coleridge offers an example taken from *The Advancement of Learning*: 'As for the philosophers, they make imaginary
laws for imaginary commonwealths, and their discourses are as
the stars, which give little light because they are so high' (II,
xxiii, 49). Coleridge's objection to this sentence is based upon
his observation that the word 'high' means 'deep or sublime'
in the one case, and 'distant' in the other. He concedes that
Bacon's meaning is clear and evident; nevertheless he is offended
by the play on words. Conditioned as we are by 'metaphysical'
poetry, by the serious and sympathetic approach to Donne and
his school, it is hard to agree with Coleridge. We no longer
believe that Shakespeare threw away the world for a quibble.
Similarly, the multiple meanings involved in Bacon's word
'high' justify themselves not only because they are perfectly
controlled, but because they demand to be seen as an integral
part of the economy and vitality of the sentence. Bacon *intends*
to marry the two ideas of remoteness and of depth and sublimity. The star image allows him tersely and suggestively to
do so. He is not exercising his wit at the expense of the thing
he has to say, as Coleridge thought: he is saying exactly what

[1] *The Friend* (London, 1818), section II, essay viii.

he means in a fashion which associates his prose with some of the techniques of seventeenth-century poetry.

The ambiguities and misunderstandings of Baconian criticism can perhaps be illustrated nowhere more clearly than in the fact that this very sentence from *The Advancement of Learning*, which Coleridge castigates for its 'metaphysical' qualities, forms part of Professor L. C. Knights' attack upon Bacon as the early representative and guiding spirit of that 'dissociation of sensibility' under which we still labour but from which 'metaphysical' poetry of course, and the great Elizabethans, were blissfully free:

> The great majority of his figures of speech are simple *illustrations* of the ideas that he wishes to convey . . . the function of the images is not to intensify the meaning, to make it deeper or richer, but simply to make more effective a meaning that was already fully formed before the application of the illustrative device.[1]

And Knights goes on to assert that Bacon uses language like a lawyer, for narrowly forensic purposes, rather than as a complex means of expression. For him, that comparison of the philosophers of imaginary commonwealths with the stars, which Coleridge found insufficiently direct and referential, is an example of imagery introduced into the sentence mechanically, to prove a point, and thereby debased. Coleridge complains that the wit and detachable life of Bacon's image detract from the clarity and logic of the point being made: Knights that it is a dead figure of speech, introduced solely as an illustration of the argument. Both views seem to do Bacon less than justice. It would be more accurate to say, surely, that the star image is employed in the sentence neither as a bit of verbal gymnastics, nor as a legal rhetorician's means of expressing contempt for the witness. The philosophers of Utopia are to be sent away, but sadly, like Plato's poets. The association with the stars deliberately confers upon them a dignity and splendour which is as much a part of Bacon's judgement as his rejection—a rejection which proceeds from the fact that they are too far from the earth to light it. After all, Bacon himself did not

---

[1] 'Bacon and the Seventeenth-Century Dissociation of Sensibility', in Knights, *Explorations* (London, 1946), pp. 98–9.

despise the task of framing imaginary laws for an imaginary commonwealth, even though he felt obliged in the end to leave the *New Atlantis* unfinished in favour of the weary but (as he saw it) more necessary task of collecting data for a natural history.

Knights is of course as aware as Coleridge that Bacon sometimes plays on the multiple meanings of words, although he cannot approve of the way in which, as it seems to him, it is done. 'For the truth is, that time seemeth to be of the nature of a river or stream, which carrieth down to us that which is light and blown up, and sinketh and drowneth that which is weighty and solid' (I, v, 3). It is one of Bacon's favourite images, the visual formulation of an idea which appears over and over again in his work with little verbal change. For Knights, this play upon 'light' and 'solid' is illegitimate and the image deceitful, because 'although the analogy appears to clinch the argument, it does not in fact prove anything. The comparison is *imposed*, and instead of possessing the validity that comes from the perception of similarity, it is simply a rhetorical trick.' It is not easy to see why Bacon's river is any more *imposed* than Donne's in that beautiful analogy beginning 'As streames are, Power is' with which the argument of the 'Third Satyre' concludes. Both in fact are attempts to embody a thoroughly abstract and at the same time very particular idea in physical terms. As for that false clinching of the argument which makes Knights indignant, as though he were listening to the sophistries of some smooth-tongued lawyer defending a dubious cause, Bacon might have replied that he was scarcely more interested in *proving* anything by his analogy than Donne in his 'Third Satyre', or his good friend George Herbert in 'The Pulley'. He would not have denied that he intended to *persuade*, in a sense by no means alien to the poetry either of Herbert or of Donne. Here the work done in recent years on Bacon's view of rhetoric and the imagination speaks against Knights.[1] Bacon did not, as Knights affirms, regard rhetoric as fundamentally a 'deceitful art'. That it could be such, and

---

[1] Cf. Karl R. Wallace, *Francis Bacon on Communication and Rhetoric* (Chapel Hill, N.C., 1943); John L. Harrison, 'Bacon's View of Rhetoric, Poetry and the Imagination', *Huntington Library Quarterly*, XX (1957).

all too often was, he was as well aware as Plato in the *Gorgias*; Bacon's own work entitled *Of the Coulers of Good and Evill* (1597) was intended as a touchstone in this respect, a means of arming the listener or reader against the legerdemain of language used in the service of specious proof. Both by precept and example, he was concerned to advance an idea of rhetoric as a marriage between reason and the imagination for the purpose of moving the will, which was strictly bound to the service of truth and right action. Emblems, fables, similitudes and other figures of speech are for Bacon anything but mechanically imposed ornaments: they are the indispensable means of transforming 'conceits intellectual to images sensible, which strike the memory more' (II, xv, 3), becoming more vivid and available to the understanding precisely because they appeal to the whole man, not simply to his intellect. Certainly, Bacon does not believe that he is proving a point when he says that in the river of Time things of worth are known to sink and be lost to sight, while the trivial floats and eddies with the current. He is trying essentially to persuade his reader to break through that crippling subservience to tradition which venerates Aristotle and passes over Heraclitus, imitates Cicero and forgets about Tacitus, simply in accord with the valuation placed upon these writers by the past. He is, as Shelley understood, concerned to kindle the imagination of his audience in order to enlarge the circumference of its mind, to shatter barriers and conventional attitudes with an individual combination of reason and poetry which enfranchises rather than restricts. Here, as in that great passage about the spiderous nature of scholasticism—the dangers of knowledge divorced from objective reality—which Knights links with the 'river of Time' sentence in his attack, Bacon is employing imagery neither in the service of false argument, nor simply for decoration: it is a precise and subtle means of expression linked tightly to the great English tradition of imaginative prose.

Knights further insists that Bacon's images, as mere demonstrations or supports for arguments, display none of that 'vivid feeling for *both* sides of the analogy such as we find in more representative Elizabethans'. This poverty of response, he implies, betrays itself particularly in Bacon's references to the natural world. Only in one isolated passage is he able to feel any consciousness in Bacon of 'the creative life behind the natural phenomena that he observes'. Otherwise, in his view, we are face to face with a wholly pragmatic and insensitive observer. J. B. Leishman, in *The Monarch of Wit* (1951), has queried Knights' 'both sides of the analogy', not merely with respect to Bacon's alleged insufficiency but in itself, as a doubtful characteristic of seventeenth-century poetry. As for Bacon's indifference to the non-human life of nature, one does not need to go as far as Spedding (who found in Bacon's translation of the Psalmist's fatalism,

> Or as the grass, that cannot term obtain
> To see the Summer come about again,

a tenderness of expression and sensitive sympathy with nature tantamount to a 'poet's faith') to feel that Knights' observation is unjust. Professor D. G. James has pointed out how instinctively Bacon's mind recoiled from that colourless, mechanistic world which at one point it approached, taking refuge instead in an outworn vitalism which bestowed 'perception' and 'election' upon objects in a fashion familiar to us in the poetry of Shakespeare.[1] Even when Bacon happens to be arguing for the reconstitution of First Philosophy, for the recognition of unity in diversity, his prose preserves both the individuality of the things he is concerned to link, and his own delight in their separate natures:

Is not the precept of a musician, to fall from a discord or harsh accord upon a concord or sweet accord, alike true in affection? Is not the trope of music, to avoid or slide from the close or cadence, common with the trope of rhetoric of deceiving expectation? Is not the delight of the quavering upon a stop in music the same with the playing of light upon the water? *Splendet tremulo sub lumine pontus.* Are not the organs of the senses of one kind with the organs of reflection, the eye with a glass, the ear with a cave or strait, determined and bounded? Neither are these only similitudes, as men of narrow observation may conceive them to be, but the same footsteps of nature, treading or printing upon several subjects or matters. (II, v, 3)

---

[1] *The Dream of Learning* (Oxford, 1951), p. 18.

This passage from the second book of *The Advancement of Learning* is of further interest in that it seems flatly to contradict Knights' assertion that 'although the *Advancement*, like the *Essays*, is studded with literary quotations and allusions, their purpose is invariably to point a moral or illustrate an argument: there is never any indication that Bacon has been *moved* by poetry'. No one could say, surely, that the lovely line from the *Aeneid* which Bacon has set in the midst of his own prose was introduced either to point a moral or to illustrate an argument. It is useless for either purpose. Nor is it the kind of line which anyone remembers in the first place, or enters into a commonplace book with an eye to such future service. This Virgilian glittering of light on the sea must be valued for itself or not at all. As for its presence in Bacon's mind, and on his page at this particular moment, it has clearly been evoked by that sensuous procession of love, music, the arts of language, and the beauty of the natural world which it crowns. Whatever his critics (the 'brushers of noblemen's clothes', as he liked to call them) may say, the senses were always for Bacon far more than a simple mechanism for perceiving, in order to master, facts. They were also, in his own experience, the points at which the abstract and the palpable, the intellect and the responses of the body, met and gave delight. One may search in vain through Bacon's work for any shamefaced confession of emotion of the sort that Sidney has given us with regard to the old ballad of Percy and Douglas, but this scarcely means that he was insensitive to poetry. No man who was could have summoned up that line of Virgil in those circumstances, nor felt impelled at that precise moment to pass from highly charged prose to verse.

Knights' account of Bacon's actual statements about the role of poetry and the value to be placed upon the activity of the imagination has been so well and convincingly amended that it is needless to refer to the issue more than briefly. If Bacon's discussion of poetry in *The Advancement of Learning* is brief and unimportant by comparison with the time he devotes to other matters, there is a good and valid reason for such summary treatment. Poetry, as Bacon is at pains to affirm, is not one of the 'deficient arts' which his book aims to rescue from neglect.

It is, in fact, flourishing. (*The Advancement of Learning* was published in 1605; considering the verse, both dramatic and non-dramatic, produced just before that time, and what was still to come, it would be hard to contest Bacon's judgement.) Bacon was a man able to foresee the problems which poets would encounter in that world of the future in which science should finally have come into its own. It was in order to save poetry from dismissal, once that whole medieval-Renaissance conception of the micro-macrocosm to which it was bound had crashed into pieces, that Bacon handled it as he did:

If man is incapable of the true 'image of the universal world', then he can no longer be regarded as a microcosm any more than nature can be proved a macrocosm, and the poet cannot mirror this fractured world; it is not his function to deal with irreconcilables. Bacon's answer was definite and final: he cannot. Therefore discard the pretense that the poet is a mirror of nature, cry aloud that he is not and never can be the world's philosopher (in the Baconian sense), and define his task anew in terms of fashioning for the delectation and profit of man 'a more ample greatness, a more exact goodness, and a more absolute variety, than can be found in the nature of things' (*The Advancement of Learning*, ii, 88). The poet can no longer pretend to mirror the scientists' world-as-it-is; accept the dualism and save poetry as a mirror of reality-as-moral/aesthetic pattern. Alas that the misinterpretation of doctrine should have resulted in the parochialisms of Davenant's epics of manners.[1]

Harrison claims that Bacon's separation of poetry from philosophical knowledge gave poetry a credit different in kind, not merely in degree, from science. Also, that his treatment of the imagination authorized its importance in political and ethical matters, while in his respect for and understanding of allegory and myth he anticipated some important modern attitudes.

Knights often seems to castigate Bacon unfairly for beliefs which scarcely represented any special pragmatic wickedness of his own, but were the common coin of the period. Bacon's immersion in his historical moment, the Elizabethan quality of his mind, is at least as striking as the extent to which his individuality separated itself from the beaten paths of the age. Much of what Bacon says about poetry as illustration or moral

---

[1] Harrison, *op. cit.* p. 119.

guide can be paralleled in Sidney. Between Bacon's assertion that poetry has 'some participation of divineness, because it doth raise and erect the mind, by submitting the shows of things to the desires of the mind; whereas reason doth buckle and bow the mind unto the nature of things' (II, iv, 2), and Sidney's famous distinction between the golden world of poetry and the brazen world of fact, there would seem to be little difference. As for Bacon's failure to perceive the value of poetry as a means 'of deepening and refining the emotions', such a perception would have been a surprising part of any Elizabethan aesthetic. Writers like Sidney, Jonson, or Montaigne— whose sensibilities presumably were not 'dissociated'—do not approach such an evaluation any more clearly than Bacon. For Knights, however, Bacon's whole attitude towards the emotions is repressive, inadequate, and 'makes against wholeness of living'. Here again, it is hard to see how Bacon's belief that a man should not be 'passion's slave', but should keep his emotions under the control of his reason, or noblest faculty, sets him apart from his contemporaries. It is true that Elizabethan tragedy presents us with a whole gallery of heroes who fail to act in accordance with this principle, but then the behaviour of Hamlet, Lear, Brachiano, Hieronymo or Vindice is scarcely for imitation in any off-stage world. As for Bacon's treatment of the dangers of love, in a work intended for the guidance of statesmen and princes, it seems neither as pernicious as Knights suggests, nor as far from the meditations of a man like Burton on the same subject. 'They do best, who if they cannot but admit love, yet make it keep quarter, and sever it wholly from their serious affairs and actions of life, for if it check once with business, it troubleth man's fortunes.' This sentence from the essay 'Of Love' which Knights singles out for special opprobrium is, of course, simply a conventional Renaissance prudential counsel, and one perhaps as relevant to the Cabinet Ministers of the present day as to those of Bacon's own time.

That Knights' final plea for a reason that 'recognizes the claims of the sensibility as a whole and tries to work in harmony with it' is moving and urgent, no one could deny. He speaks eloquently about the inner schism of the twentieth century, the emotional poverty that has been the unexpected companion of Bacon's Kingdom of Man. One is led to disagree with him only in his assessment of Bacon himself as the villain of the piece, and in the distortion of Bacon's prose so as to make it the progenitor of our most serious modern ills. In point of fact, Eliot's phrase 'dissociation of sensibility' is inescapably modern, and describes a modern dilemma—one from which Knights himself (and all of us, in that we belong to the age we do) cannot completely escape. But it is a mistake to project this dilemma on to the past, particularly when by doing so the real nature of thought and writing which might be of inestimable service is obscured and falsified. Bacon is by no means a negative figure, a disintegrator and destroyer. More accurately, he is a man who foresaw both some of the achievements and some of the ills of the future, and whose wholeness of thought, a welding together of reason and the imagination, the individual and the impersonal, the abstract and the sensuous, still possesses a positive power.

In his essay on 'Style', Pater speaks of the delicate line separating mere fact from something which must be recognized as different in quality and degree:

In Pascal, for instance, in the persuasive writers generally, how difficult to define the point where, from time to time, argument which, if it is to be worth anything at all, must consist of facts or groups of facts, becomes a pleading—a theorem no longer, but essentially an appeal to the reader to catch the writer's spirit, to think with him, if one can or will—an expression no longer of fact but of his sense of it, his peculiar intuition of a world, prospective, or discerned below the faulty conditions of the present, in either case changed somewhat from the actual world.

It might be a description of *The Advancement of Learning*, or indeed of Bacon's work as a whole. It is for his *sense* of fact, the colours and the peculiar unity of a single mind mirrored in a prose responsive to the slightest demands made upon it that Bacon must be regarded, in Shelley's sense, as a poet. He may have believed in his own famous image of man's mind as a clear and equal glass, lending no dimension or colour of its own to that external reality which it reflected: he himself was fortun-

ately incapable of such impersonality. Even in the 'scientific'
collections of data, the *Historia Vitae et Mortis*, or the *Historia
Densi et Rari*, the presence everywhere of an individual shaping
mind preserves some value in the work for an age scarcely able
to separate Bacon's supposition that lions lose their teeth
because their breaths are so strong from the fantastic lore of
medieval bestiaries, or to ponder seriously over his announce-
ment that 'Wine and beer in frost lose their vigour; yet in
thaws and south winds they revive, relax, and as it were ferment
again'. The strange animism of this latter remark, in which
the single technical term is handled far more diffidently than
those which seem to endow the inanimate with a soul, is altogether characteristic of Bacon, and worlds away from what we
ordinarily regard as dispassionate, scientific observation.

The astonishing variety of Bacon's prose has often been
remarked, even Knights pointing with approval to passages in
the *Historie of the Raigne of Henry VII* (1622) which, he claims,
might have been written by Nashe. In accordance with his own
rhetorical precepts, Bacon seems to have adjusted his English
style anew in every major work, fitting it as perfectly as possible
to the subject-matter, the purpose and the audience addressed.
The masques and entertainments, the great parliamentary and
legal speeches, the historical work, *The Advancement of Learning*,
New Atlantis and *Essayes* have each a manner appropriate to
them. Yet all are bound together by a common concern for
the inseparability of thought and expression which involves
more than a simple reaction against the verbal excesses of
Ciceronian style. All of them, in their different ways, appeal
to the reader to catch not simply fact but that peculiar and
individual *sense* of fact of which Pater speaks. It is in this
manner, rather than as the fountainhead of Royal Society
plain prose of the last quarter of the seventeenth century, that
Rawley's account of Bacon's belief that words should be
'subservient or ministerial to matter, and not the principle'
asks to be understood. What he was enunciating is a principle
of good prose in any period, whether it is that of Sir Thomas
Browne at his best, or of Flaubert.

It would be hard to deny that when he picked up his pen,
Bacon himself was probably unconscious of the degree to which

he reflected his own inner landscape, as well as that of the external world. It was certainly not his purpose to do so. Nothing, in fact, is more obvious than the care with which he avoids introducing any of those 'personal' touches in his writing which make other Elizabethans so much more immediately appealing. At least four factors, however, worked to make him an artist in spite of himself: his isolation, the need to persuade, a sense of devouring time, and the fact that abstract ideas stubbornly presented themselves to him through the medium of the senses. 'I may truly say, my soul hath been a stranger in the course of my pilgrimage', Bacon wrote sadly in his old age. It is a point that he touches upon more than once, in private meditations and in those Latin appeals to various European scholars through which he hoped, vainly, to gather support beyond England for his great work. All his life Bacon was surrounded by people (from Ben Jonson to the unhappy Essex) who genuinely admired him and held his friendship in high regard. Yet there was no one really to comprehend his thought and aims. James I accepted the dedication of *The Advancement of Learning*, but remarked privately that Bacon's work was like the peace of God, that passeth all understanding. Harvey, Bacon's personal physician, appears to have thought highly of his employer's wit and style. For the plans and conclusions of Bacon the philosopher-scientist, on the other hand, the true man of science had only the slightest respect. From the very beginning, Bacon faced a unique problem of communication:

For that knowledge which is new, and foreign from opinions received, is to be delivered in another form than that that is agreeable and familiar; and therefore Aristotle, when he thinks to tax Democritus, doth in truth commend him, where he saith, 'If we shall indeed dispute, and not follow after similitudes, &c.' For those whose conceits are seated in popular opinions, need only but to prove or dispute; but those whose conceits are beyond popular opinions, have a double labour; the one to make themselves conceived, and the other to prove and demonstrate. So that it is of necessity with them to have recourse to similitudes and translations to express themselves. And therefore in the infancy of learning, and in rude times, when those conceits which are now trivial were then new, the world was full of parables and similitudes; for else would men either have passed over without mark, or else rejected for paradoxes that which was offered, before they had understood or judged. (II, xvii, 10)

It is, in effect, Bacon's explanation of the nature of his own prose. His thought was both complicated and unfamiliar; its expression was not easy. Furthermore—although here we reach the borders of a region where Bacon's own judgement and self-awareness cannot be relied upon—it was to a very large extent the child of the imagination, a 'dream of learning', and therefore asked naturally for the services of the imagination in order to declare itself.

Bacon needed desperately to persuade. He had to make a whole series of ideas and convictions not merely clear but convincing to a world which seemed slow and reluctant to think, but whose co-operation was nevertheless essential to the success of his enterprise. Even had he really wanted, he could not have used the mechanical, impersonal prose of later scientists. Moreover, he was pressed by mortality. 'Time groweth precious with me', he was writing even in 1606. Bacon was as obsessed with the brevity of human life as Shakespeare, by the bitter contradiction between man's potentialities and the span of time allotted for their realization. This is the urgency which drives so many of his sentences to a conclusion in which the claims of emotion, of the footsteps treading behind, and of reason (man's mind as a clear and equal glass) achieve a balance by no means alien to Elizabethan tragedy, yet peculiarly Bacon's own. For 'it is the duty and virtue of all knowledge to abridge the infinity of individual experience, as much as the conception of truth will permit, and to remedy the complaint of *vita brevis, ars longa*' (II, vii, 6).

Bacon, as Caroline Spurgeon once noted, tended to represent all good things, and in particular all desirable forms of mental activity, under the form of light.[1] The light and darkness patterns in his work are everywhere visible, and almost invariably charged with an emotion which seems to spring equally from the idea expressed by the individual passage, and from Bacon's curious sensitivity to varying degrees of obscurity and

[1] Caroline F. E. Spurgeon, *Shakespeare's Imagery and What It Tells Us* (Cambridge, 1935), pp. 16–29.

brilliance. Miss Spurgeon's account of Bacon's imagery was primarily concerned to distinguish it from Shakespeare's, and it was not perhaps altogether fair to Bacon. Certainly she was right in pointing out the extent to which he relied upon Biblical reference. But then his dependence upon myth, anecdote of the kind collected in his *Apophthegms*, and fantastic natural history of the sort that the writer knows to be false in itself, is equally striking. He was fond of many comparisons which proclaim him a man of his period—the world as a stage or a garden, man's life as a journey, analogies with music, and the like—but it is particularly noticeable how many of his most characteristic similitudes and metaphors are concerned not merely to render the abstract palpable to the senses, but to suggest that like the things of the green and growing world, these abstract ideas partake somehow of those organic principles of growth and change which we associate with trees, plants, and the development of streams from their source to the sea.

This characteristic of Bacon's imagery suggests a comparison with Elizabethan drama. That Bacon was interested in the stage is apparent from the frequency with which he refers to it and invokes its terminology. He was well aware that men react differently—and often more strikingly—as part of a theatre audience and as individuals, aware also that the evil which comes upon a man from his own fault, and not simply from fortune, 'strikes deadly inwards' and is essential to tragedy. It is true that he also believed these facts had been insufficiently exploited owing to what he described as the plain neglect of drama as a discipline in his own time. He was not, however, the only Elizabethan who suffered from a neoclassical blindness; his failure to recognize what was directly in front of him does not mean that he was unable to understand what the theatre was all about. Certainly, there would seem to be a profound and subtle relationship between Shakespearian drama and Bacon's attitude towards Truth.

Professor Basil Willey has observed how genuinely Bacon seems at times to approach the spirit of Keats' 'negative capability'. 'Nothing', he writes, 'is more characteristic of Bacon than his distrust of the "meddling intellect", which interposes too soon with its abstractions and distorts nature instead of explaining her.'[1] A double impulse, a need to discover and establish Truth on the one hand, and to prevent thought from settling and assuming a fixed form on the other, lies at the heart of all of Bacon's work. It is a measure, perhaps, not only of his greatness but also of his weakness as a practical man of science. Even as he could never sacrifice, as Gilbert or Harvey did, the wholeness and impossible scope of his thought in favour of some small area of knowledge which could have been mastered, so he could not resolve the contradication involved in his desire both for Truth and for a state of continuous potentiality, except by imaginative means. It is on some such rock that the Method, with its insistence upon a complicated double movement between experiment and axiom, particular and general idea, foundered. Despite all of Bacon's hopes, it must always have looked more like Richard II's flight of fancy about the two buckets filling one another than a genuinely utilitarian process. It is the imagination in the end, an imagination clandestinely escaped from the place to which Bacon assigned it, and not reason, which cements together the structure of his thought.

Hence the importance of those image patterns referred to earlier, in which abstract ideas are expressed by means of similitudes in which possibilities of growth and change are implicit. The favourite idea of light as a form or symbol for Truth also explains itself in these terms. Fluid, changing, measurably present and yet impossible to circumscribe, light is the obvious imaginative guise under which the contradictions of Bacon's twin impulses could be caught up and resolved. Imagery however, could scarcely bear the entire burden. In *Henry VII* Bacon can be observed working on his material in such a way that the structure of the book as a whole declares the quality of its author's mind. A delicate balance between facts and events in all their complexity and essential irrationality, and the degree of order imposed upon them by a mind concerned to create some significant form of Truth—without limiting the material falsely, or reducing it to the deadness of paraphrasable content—makes the account not only a complete success of its kind, but also the blood-brother of Shakespeare's history plays. Bacon's *Henry VII* stands brilliantly between the

[1] *The Seventeenth Century Background* (London, 1934), p. 36.

shapeless, helter-skelter records of the chroniclers, and that medieval impoverishment of history which reduced it to man's idea of God's will. It is exactly the position that Shakespeare's *Henry V* occupies between the inconsequential jumble of the anonymous *Famous Victories of Henry V* (a play that might have been written by Bardolph and Pistol) and the relentless historical propagandizing of Bale's *King John*. These two works by Bacon and Shakespeare are, despite difference of genre, fundamentally alike in their reconciliation by means of the imagination of an idea of order with the natural heterogeneity of experience.

Historical writing obviously presents a special problem, and also a special means of solution. It is a definable form, as most of the rest of Bacon's writing was not, possessed of both ancient and Italian, if not of English, models. Also, it is inevitably limited by what has happened to survive as record of the past, and by the judgement of the individual observer. Timeless, inhuman nature, on the other hand, recognizes no such limits. Even human nature, once divorced from specific instance and circumstance, or from the frank bias and experience of the writer, becomes difficult to discuss in any way that escapes both the vague and the dogmatic. It was in these two areas, however, that Bacon felt his major task of interpretation lay. Not surprisingly, he felt the need of some instrument for both discovery and continuous search—and found it in the aphorism:

As young men, when they knit and shape perfectly, do seldom grow to a further stature; so knowledge, while it is in aphorisms and observations, it is in growth; but when once it is comprehended in exact methods, it may perchance be further polished and illustrate and accommodated for use and practice; but it increaseth no more in bulk and substance. (I, v, 4)

Aphorisms, he remarked elsewhere, 'representing a knowledge broken, do invite men to inquire further; whereas methods, carrying the show of a total, do secure men, as if they were at furthest' (II, xvii, 7). Given his peculiar dilemma between the desire for truth and the distrust of certainty, the need to generalize and abridge and the fear of violating the individuality of facts, no form could have suited him better.

At the moment, Bacon's *Essayes*, the single English work in which his conception of the aphorism can be adequately studied, seems to be generally undervalued. Knights finds the traditional reputation of the book exaggerated; Lewis quotes with approval Professor Douglas Bush's remark that 'everyone has read them, but no one is ever found reading them'.[1] In point of fact, that cosy image of short, discursive pieces full of their author's personal charm, reading suitable for drowsy winter evenings beside the fire, which Lamb and other nineteenth-century writers have succeeded in imposing upon the form, is the worst possible approach to Bacon's essays. Equally disserviceable is the habit of referring to them as though they formed an homogeneous whole. Everyone knows about the way in which the essays gradually increased in number from the ten of the original 1597 edition to the fifty-eight of the 1625 version; and about both the stylistic change involved and the position of the work with regard to Bacon's plea in *The Advancement of Learning* for a collection of civil and moral knowledge. Yet the 1625 edition is not a tidy knitting together of various ideas which interested Bacon; it is an accumulation of disparate pieces as difficult to generalize about, or to connect internally, as Donne's *Songs and Sonets*, and it is to be read in a not dissimilar fashion. No one would attempt to talk about Donne's *jeu d'esprit* 'The Bait', or 'The Flea', in the same language, and as though they were poems quite compatible in quality and intent with 'The Extacie' or 'A Valediction, Forbidding Mourning'. Yet essays as dissimilar as those 'Of Gardens', 'Of Seditions' and 'Of Truth' are commonly blanketed under the same generalizations, described in the same terms, as though there were not all the difference in the world between them.

In general, Bacon's essays fall into three classes. The first is concerned to give straightforward advice in the most economical and memorable form possible, whether for the building of houses, the planning of masques and gardens, or the proper attitude towards studies. They are characteristically terse, but on the whole can be read much as one reads ordinary prose. The second group weaves together a series of shrewd observa-

---

[1] Bush, *English Literature in the Earlier Seventeenth Century* (Oxford, 1962) (revised), p. 197.

tions, examples from the past, and hints of general principles in such a way as to indicate directions and provide materials for assessing individual situations without assuming any form or point of view which could be considered as final, complete, and beyond further growth. An essay like 'Of Dispatch', or 'Of Empire', demands a more active co-operation from the reader than those of the first group, a combined effort of reason and imagination based upon the realization that what Bacon has provided on the page is a series of interacting half-statements, rather than a conclusion. By far the most interesting, however, are those pieces in which, characteristically, the need to realize and yet not to inhibit certain abstract ideas forces Bacon to the limit of his powers, and to a use of the aphorism in which prose approaches perhaps as closely as is possible in its compression and suggestiveness to the condition of poetry:

Since aphorisms (unlike maxims or reflections) are not simply true or untrue, but illuminate reality in an indirect way: since, in other words, they always mean what they 'mean' *and* something more . . . it follows that even if a number of aphorisms could be grouped in such a way that from one set of meanings a coherent system might be constructed, yet their second (equally important) meanings would still remain defiant of system, each pointing in a different direction.[1]

Dr Stern is here thinking primarily of the aphorisms of Lichtenberg, but his words are equally appropriate to the collections of aphorisms which make up the greater part of the essays in this third group.

An essay like 'Of Truth' asks to be read partly as a 'metaphysical' poem is read, and partly in a peculiar fashion imposed upon it by the aphorism as a form. 'What is Truth; said jesting Pilate; And would not stay for an Answer.' The rifle-shot of this opening, the little imaginative explosion, is a familiar Baconian technique and frequently imitated. Less imitable however, is the curious configuration of the space which separates this first sentence from the one which follows. 'Certainly there be, that delight in Giddinesse; And count it a Bondage, to fix a Beleefe; Affecting Free-Will in Thinking, as well as in

[1] J. P. Stern, *Lichtenberg: a Doctrine of Scattered Occasions* (Bloomington, Ind., 1959), pp. 262–3.

Acting.' It is not merely that these are two sentences of a markedly different kind: the second simply does not move forward from the first in any fashion which we normally associate with the logic of prose. The movement performed is deliberately oblique in a way that forces the reader in part to create the link himself. A passive attitude here, or even a very rapid perusal of the page, is fatal to the essay. The sentences will indeed seem, as they have to one of Bacon's critics, to lie together end to end as stiffly as logs. Agree to the special demands of Bacon's prose on the other hand, here and throughout the essay, and a vast and complex building—the joint creation of author and reader, of reason and the imagination, completely individual and yet never either exhausted or quite the same twice—begins to arise from the sentences.

It is the nature of the aphorism to mean more than one thing. In the words themselves, not merely in the progression of the sentences, Bacon contrives to gather together a whole series of different and sometimes contradictory meanings and emotions; to hold them in suspension in such a way that they react upon one another; and to explore without dictating. It is characteristic of Bacon, for instance, that his value of Truth does not exclude a sense of the splendour of illusion, and that he can manage to pay 'the lie' a handsome tribute with the very same words which on another level are concerned to emphasize its failings.

This same truth, is a Naked, and Open day light, that doth not shew, the Masques, and Mummeries, and Triumphs of the world, halfe so Stately, and daintily, as Candlelights. Truth may perhaps come to the price of a Pearle, that sheweth best by day: But it will not rise, to the price of a Diamond, or Carbuncle, that sheweth best in varied lights.

The man who wrote those sentences not only had a feeling for both sides of the analogy: he was capable of recognizing and expressing a complexity of experience which only Shakespeare perhaps among his contemporaries handled with greater skill. And Bacon did not have, as Shakespeare did, the services of actors, stage, and drama as a form to help him illuminate ideas from many sides simultaneously.

All things considered, it is remarkable how frequently Bacon's language approaches that of the contemporary stage. From the point of view of verbal similarities, the wonder is not so much that the Bacon-Shakespeare controversy has never ended, as that it has not been found necessary to prove that he was not Webster, Marlowe, Chapman, Marston, nor yet the unknown author of the interpolations in *The Spanish Tragedy*. The very terseness and pointed quality of his sentences, particularly in the *Essayes*, doubtless has something to do with this. His is a much less elaborate and implacably *written* style than many of the period, and it possesses some of the directness and immediacy of dramatic speech:

And therefore Velleius the Epicurean needed not to have asked, why God should have adorned the heavens with stars, as if he had been an *aedilis*, one that should have set forth some magnificent shows or plays. For if that great work-master had been of an human disposition, he would have cast the stars into some pleasant and beautiful works and orders, like the frets in the roofs of houses; whereas one can scarce find a posture in square, or triangle, or straight line, amongst such an infinite number; so different a harmony there is between the spirit of man and the spirit of nature. (II, xiv, 9)

Even in a passage like this, where Bacon is concerned to tear down the whole fabric of the Elizabethan world picture, to say something exactly opposite from Shakespeare, his means of expression are so closely allied as to make it seem as though some ghostly anti-Hamlet were speaking. Reason still requires the services of the imagination in order to express itself: the new and the old stand together for a last moment on the brink of a world which Bacon had in some measure foreseen, but in which he would have remained a stranger.

2

THOMAS HOBBES

BY R. L. BRETT

At the heart of the philosophy of Thomas Hobbes (1588–1679) lies his combination of strict empiricism with a rationalist and deductive method. His epistemology and psychology rest upon the conviction that all our knowledge ultimately derives from sense experience, for as he writes in the opening chapter of *Leviathan* (1651), '. . . there is no conception in a man's mind, which hath not at first, totally, or by parts, been begotten upon the organs of sense. The rest are derived from that original' (I, i).[1] Hobbes also argues that we can only obtain knowledge which is universally true by proceeding deductively from exact definitions, and by a process of reasoning, to link these in a logically necessary chain of argument. Philosophy, for Hobbes, is no other than reasoning.

This kind of logical empiricism leads in Hobbes to a dualism in knowledge itself.

There are of KNOWLEDGE two kinds; whereof one is *knowledge of fact*: the other *knowledge of the consequence of one affirmation to another*. The former is nothing else, but sense and memory, and is *absolute knowledge*; as when we see a fact doing, or remember it done: and this is the knowledge required in a witness. The latter is called *science* [i.e. exact and universally valid knowledge]; and is *conditional*; as when we know, that, *if the figure shown be a circle, then any straight line through the centre shall divide it into two equal parts*. And this is the knowledge required in a philosopher; that is to say, of him that pretends to reasoning. (I, ix)

The first kind of knowledge is entirely of particulars; it is an absolute knowledge, for facts are neither true nor false but simply facts. Even history is only a record of particular facts, and according to Hobbes a study of it cannot lead to general-

---

[1] *Leviathan*, ed. Michael Oakeshott (Oxford, 1946), p. 7. All quotations from *Leviathan* are from this edition.

izations which are necessarily true. No doubt a study of history will give a man wisdom, and past experience will enable him to look to the future with some 'foresight'; it will give him what Hobbes calls 'prudence'. But 'experience concludeth nothing universally',[1] and history and prudence are not knowledge as understood by the philosopher.

Nor does science (in the modern sense that is, and not as used by Hobbes, who equates it with philosophy) provide us with certain and universal truth. For mathematics he had a great admiration, and it was on first looking at the works of Euclid, at the age of forty, he tells us, that he 'fell in love with geometry', delighted 'not so much by the theorems as by its way of reasoning'. But for the experimental method he had no sympathy. In spite of his early and close association with Bacon, he scarcely mentions him in his writings, and his attitude to the Royal Society and all it stood for was almost contemptuous. Science when based on observation and induction cannot give us real knowledge.

But though Hobbes distinguishes between philosophical and empirical knowledge, he believes that it is the former and not the latter which is concerned with cause and effect. Experience cannot discern any causal relation between particulars; this is the result of reasoning. He defines philosophy at the beginning of *De corpore* as '. . . such knowledge of effects or appearances, as we acquire by true ratiocination from the knowledge we have first of their causes or generation: And again, of such causes or generations as may be from knowing first their effects.'[2] God is ruled out as a subject for philosophical speculation, for God, as a matter of definition, is uncaused. He does not deny the existence of God, but considers it a matter of faith and not knowledge. Knowledge then, in its philosophical sense, and as described by Hobbes, is distinct from experience, from history, from science and from theology. Its limits are very sharply drawn; its concern is with cause and effect, and as we shall see in a moment, only with these in a very special and restricted sense.

---

[1] *Discourse on Human Nature*, in *English Works of Thomas Hobbes*, ed. William Molesworth, vol. IV (London, 1840), p. 18.
[2] *English Works*, ed. Molesworth, vol. I (London, 1840), p. 3.

According to Hobbes a relationship between the two kinds of knowledge he has defined is effected by the use of language. Man, along with all the animal world, is endowed with perception, but alone among the animals he has the power of reflexion and is self-conscious. The instrument of this power is his ability to use language. Hobbes refers to language in many places in his writings and devotes an entire chapter of *Leviathan* to it. Briefly, his account of language is that it enables man to pass from a knowledge of particulars to general notions. We attach names to the images of sense-perception as an aid to memory, and then we relate these names by putting them in propositions. But language is not only a medium of thought, it is a means of communication. Hobbes distinguishes four uses of language. The first of these connects it with reason; '. . . to register what by cogitation we find to be the cause of any thing, present or past; and what we find things present or past may produce, or effect'; the second sees it as communication, 'to show to others that knowledge which we have attained'; the third considers it as persuasion, 'to make known to others our wills and purposes, that we may have the mutual help of one another'; and the fourth views it simply as a source of aesthetic pleasure; 'to please and delight ourselves and others, by playing with our words, for pleasure or ornament, innocently' (I, iv).

The power language has as a medium of thought is drastically restricted by Hobbes's nominalism. Though language enables us to pass from particulars to general notions, Hobbes does not believe that universals have any existential validity. They are simply names given to a class of individual beings as a kind of shorthand reference.

Of names, some are *proper*, and singular to one only thing, as *Peter*, *John*, *this man*, *this tree*; and some are *common* to many things, *man*, *horse*, *tree*; every of which, though but one name, is nevertheless the name of divers particular things; in respect of all which together, it is called an *universal*; there being nothing in the world universal but names; for the things named are every one of them individual and singular. (I, iv)

Reason, which is nothing more in Hobbes than reasoning, is the power of joining names together in propositions which are seen to be self-evident. But though we can transcend the particularity of brute fact and make generalizations, these are true only in a very limited sense. For generalizations are only about names and not about the real world. It was this profound scepticism that caused J. S. Mill, who admired Hobbes as 'one of the clearest and most consecutive thinkers whom this country or the world has produced', to criticize Hobbes's theory of logic.

The only propositions of which Hobbes' principle is a sufficient account are that limited and unimportant class in which both the predicate and the subject are proper names. . . . But it is a sadly inadequate theory of any others. That it should ever have been thought of as such, can be accounted for only by the fact that Hobbes, in common with the other Nominalists, bestowed little or no attention upon the *connotation* of words and sought for their meaning exclusively in what they *denote*; as if all names had been (what none but proper names really are) marks put upon individuals; and as if there were no difference between a proper and a general name, except that the first denotes only one individual and the last a greater number.[1]

It follows from Hobbes's nominalism that when he says philosophy is concerned with cause and effect, he does not mean cause and effect as they are empirically verified by physical science. Causation for him is a concept of logic, it is what is logically demonstrable and not what is empirically verifiable. Hobbes believes that he proceeds deductively from purely empirical axioms which introspection declares to be self-evident, but the identification of causality with logical entailment is a rationalist assumption which is really incompatible with his empiricism. Even body and motion, which for Hobbes are the two great principles from which he deduces his philosophical system, are not proved by observation. Sensation, which is the source of all our knowledge, demands a belief in both body and motion. Without body there could be no motion and without bodies being moved so as to act upon our sense organs there could be no sensory experience. Body and motion are pre-requisites for our having any knowledge at all.

Hobbes is equally forthright in his declaration that the knowledge gained by reasoning is only conditional and not absolute.

---

[1] *A System of Logic* (London, 1843), I, v, 2.

And therefore, when the discourse is put into speech, and begins with the definitions of words, and proceeds by connexion of the same into general affirmations, and of these again into syllogisms; the end or last sum is called the conclusion; and the thought of the mind by it signified, is that conditional knowledge, or knowledge of the consequence of words, which is commonly called SCIENCE. (I, vii)

The function of reason is to frame propositions which are analytical. Hobbes sees the work of reason as best exemplified in mathematical calculation, which starts from certain agreed premisses and arrives at its conclusions by logical necessity.

This implies that reason is concerned not with ends but means. If, for instance, men desire peace (and Hobbes thinks that everyone would be ready to accept this hypothesis), reason will indicate the means by which we can ensure it, and his *Leviathan* contains a long succession of arguments which he thinks are demonstrably true to show how this can best be done. The end itself is not dictated by reason, for value is not a matter of reasoning, it is simply the object of men's desire.

But whatsoever is the object of any man's appetite or desire, that is it which he for his part calleth *good*: and the object of his hate and aversion, *evil*; and of his contempt, *vile* and *inconsiderable*. For these words of good, evil and contemptible, are ever used with relation to the person that useth them: there being nothing simply and absolutely so; nor any common rule of good and evil, to be taken from the nature of the objects themselves. (I, vi)

If reason is to perform its task efficiently, it must employ language which is as concise, clear and unambiguous as possible. The first stage in the process of reasoning is accurate definition, for 'in the right definition of names lies the first use of speech; which is the acquisition of science' (I, iv). But even this preliminary is difficult, for our use of words is biased by self-interest and emotion.

. . . in reasoning a man must take heed of words; which besides the signification of what we imagine of their nature, have a signification also of the nature, disposition, and interest of the speaker. . . . And therefore such names can never be true grounds of any ratiocination. Nor more can metaphors and tropes of speech: but these are less dangerous, because they profess their inconstancy; which the other do not. (I, iv)

Given exact definitions, we can proceed 'to assertions made by connexion of one of them to another', and then to 'the connexions of one assertion to another, till we come to a knowledge of all the consequences of names appertaining to the subject in hand' (I, v). The opposite of this is to employ 'metaphors, and senseless and ambiguous words, [which] are like *ignes fatui*; and reasoning upon them is wandering amongst innumerable absurdities' (I, v).

But Hobbes believes that language is more than simply an instrument of reason. We have seen that he distinguishes logical discourse from persuasion and teaching, and from language as a means of aesthetic pleasure. Logic is one thing, rhetoric and poetry are quite different.

Hobbes's interest in literature lasted all his life. His earliest published work was a translation of *The Peloponnesian War* of Thucydides (1629) and amongst his last publications were his verse-translations of Homer's *Iliad* and *Odyssey* (1673–6). Writing of the latter in his preface to the *Fables*, Dryden said that Hobbes had turned to poetry 'as he did mathematics, when it was too late', but nevertheless Hobbes's work was remarkable for some one approaching ninety. As a young man he had counted among his friends Ben Jonson, Lord Herbert of Cherbury, and the Scottish poet, Robert Aytoun. Of this period John Aubrey tells us that 'Before Thucydides, he spent two yeares in reading romances and playes, which he haz often repented and sayd that these two yeares were lost of him.'[1] But Hobbes's love of literature never left him. His friends in later life included Waller, Cowley and Davenant, and his writings show not only a speculative interest in literary questions, but a mastery of style, a brilliant concision, and a deft use of the telling phrase.

While he was tutor to William Cavendish, son of the Duke of Devonshire, Hobbes dictated to his young pupil an abstract of Aristotle's *Rhetoric*. It was published as *A Briefe of the Art of Rhetorique* and was entered in the Stationers' Register in 1636. This rather free and condensed version of Aristotle's treatise is an early work and partly a translation, and it does not neces-

---

[1] Aubrey, *Brief Lives*, ed. Andrew Clark (Oxford, 1898), I, 361.

sarily represent Hobbes's mature views, but it still has a certain interest. In the second chapter of the *Briefe*, where he defines rhetoric, he writes: 'Proofs are, in *Rhetorick*, either *Examples*, or *Enthymemes*, as in *Logick*, *Inductions*, or *Syllogismes*. For an *Example* is a short *Induction*, and an *Enthymeme* a short *Syllogisme*; out of which are left as superfluous, that which is supposed to be necessarily understood by the hearer; to avoid prolixity.'[1] When he came to elaborate his own system of logic he left no place for induction, and 'Examples', being all particular, were held to prove nothing. But 'Examples' could still provide practical wisdom and graphic illustrations of truths which had been arrived at by other means, and this is one of the functions Hobbes assigns to literature. So also it is possible for literary discourse to condense long chains of logical argument and to relieve the monotony of syllogistic reasoning by rhetorical devices. His own prose gives a vivid demonstration of how to write philosophy with style, of how to achieve persuasiveness without sacrificing logical consistency.

There is nothing in this contrary to the traditional theory of the period. On the first of these points Hobbes is echoing Sidney, who wrote of the poet in his *Apologie for Poetrie*: 'whatsoever the Philosopher sayth shoulde be doone, hee [i.e. the poet] giveth a perfect picture of it in some one, by whom hee presupposeth it was doone. So as hee coupleth the generall notion with the particuler example.'[2] The second point reaffirms Bacon's definition of 'the office of Rhetoric' in the *Advancement of Learning*, which is '. . . to apply and recommend the dictates of reason to imagination in order to excite the appetite and will.'[3] The development of Hobbes's philosophy, however, brought some changes in his literary theory. These occur in his later writings, and it is in the *Answer to D'Avenant* that their nature and extent are most evident. In this he leans heavily on Aristotle's *Poetics*. For instance, '. . . the subject of

[1] *A Briefe of the Art of Rhetorique* (1681 edition), ch. ii. Father W. J. Ong, S.J., in his 'Hobbes and Talon's Ramist Rhetoric in English', *Trans. Cambridge Bibliographical Society*, i (1951), argues that Hobbes's definition of an enthymeme derives not from Aristotle but Ramus. There may be some truth in this, but his contention that Hobbes was a Ramist in logic is unlikely. On a point of central importance they are divided; Hobbes was a nominalist whereas Ramus was a realist.
[2] *Apologie*, ed. J. Churton Collins (Oxford, 1907), p. 17.
[3] *The Philosophical Works of Bacon*, ed. J. M. Robertson (London, 1905), p. 535.

a Poem,' he writes, 'is the manners of men, not natural causes; manners presented, not dictated; and manners feigned, as the name of Poesy imports, not found.'[1] But when he relates poetry to his own theory of knowledge he is more original and controversial. In a famous passage in which he presents his theory of the poetic imagination he writes:

Time and Education begets experience; Experience begets memory; Memory begets Judgement and Fancy; Judgement begets the strength and structure, and Fancy begets the Ornaments of a Poem. The Ancients therefore fabled not absurdly in making memory the Mother of the Muses. For memory is the World (though not really, yet so as in a looking glass) in which the Judgement, the severer Sister, busieth her self in a grave and rigid examination of all the parts of Nature, and in registring by Letters their order, causes, uses, differences, and resemblances; Whereby the Fancy, when any work of Art is to be performed findes her materials at hand and prepared for use.[2]

Here Hobbes's empiricist psychology is brought into use to explain the literary imagination. The outside world, by impinging on our sense-organs, produces images in our minds; when the objects themselves are no longer present these images are stored in the memory, which Hobbes describes as no other than 'decaying sense'.[3] This store of sensory images gives rise to judgement and fancy (or imagination). Fancy is the ability to discern likenesses between things, whereas judgement is the power of distinguishing differences; together they make up wit, which is the facility for linking one idea to another. 'The former, that is, fancy, without the help of judgment, is not commended as a virtue: but the latter which is judgment, and discretion, is commended for itself, without the help of fancy' (I, viii). We can understand why Hobbes makes judgement responsible for 'the strength and structure' of a poem, for he continues,

. . . without steadiness, and direction to some end, a great fancy is one kind of madness; such as they have, that entering into any discourse, are snatched from their purpose, by every thing that

---

[1] *The Answer to D'Avenant*, in *Critical Essays of the Seventeenth Century*, ed. J. E. Spingarn (Oxford, 1908), vol. II, p. 56.
[2] *Op. cit.*, vol. II, p. 59.
[3] *Leviathan*, I, ii.

comes in their thought, into so many, and so long digressions, and parentheses, that they utterly lose themselves. (I, viii)

Nor does he contradict what he says in his *Answer to D'Avenant*, when he maintains in *Leviathan* that 'In a good poem, whether it be *epic*, or *dramatic*; as also in *sonnets*, *epigrams*, and other pieces, both judgment and fancy are required: but the fancy must be more eminent; because they please for the extravagancy; but ought not to displease by indiscretion' (I, viii). But poetry is one thing, logical discourse another. When truth is our concern there is scarcely a place for fancy.

In demonstration, in counsel, and all rigorous search of truth, judgment does all, except sometimes the understanding have need to be opened by some apt similitude; and then there is so much use of fancy. But for metaphors, they are in this case utterly excluded. For seeing they openly profess deceit; to admit them into counsel, or reasoning, were manifest folly. (I, viii)

Fancy, then, according to Hobbes, is not only the younger sister: she must put herself in tutelage to the elder if she is to be useful as well as beautiful. When indeed she becomes the handmaid of philosophy, her accomplishments are almost as great as civilization itself.

But so far forth as the Fancy of man has traced the ways of true Philosophy, so far it hath produced very marvellous effects to the benefit of mankinde. All that is beautiful or defensible in building, or marvellous in Engines and Instruments of motion, whatsoever commodity men receive from the observations of the Heavens, from the description of the Earth, from the account of Time, from walking on the Seas, and whatsoever distinguisheth the civility of Europe from the Barbarity of the American savages, is the workmanship of Fancy but guided by the Precepts of true Philosophy. But where these precepts fail, as they have hitherto failed in the doctrine of Moral vertue, there the Architect, Fancy, must take the Philosophers part upon her self.[1]

The word 'doctrine' in the last sentence of this passage has led some commentators[2] to suggest that Hobbes considers moral philosophy bankrupt and thinks poetry can take its place. But the word is used here in its older sense of 'teaching', and he is

---

[1] *The Answer to D'Avenant*, ed. cit., vol. II, pp. 59–60.
[2] Cf. D. G. James, *The Life of Reason* (London, 1949).

making the traditional point that poetry can be a better moral teacher than philosophy because it provides example as well as precept. Great and genuine as his admiration for the power of the imagination undoubtedly is, it never leads him to the belief that poetry allows us to dispense with philosophy.

There is a good deal in Hobbes's account that is unoriginal. The conception of poetry as a more persuasive way of teaching morality than philosophy can achieve is almost a commonplace in Renaissance rhetoric and poetic. What gives his account novelty is his empiricist psychology and theory of knowledge. No one before Hobbes had paid much attention to the mental processes involved in writing literature, and his description of the writer's mind at work proved so convincing that it became generally accepted by his contemporaries. There were strong objections to his philosophy, especially from the Cambridge Platonists, but it was left to a later generation to realize that if the philosophy were at fault, it was likely that the theory of literature derived from it would also be unsatisfactory.

The central weaknesses of Hobbes's philosophy when looked at from the standpoint of literature—and indeed from any standpoint—are his restriction of reason to the process of reasoning and his belief that the mind can arrive at truth only by logical demonstration. This leaves literature with only two roles; it can propagate truths arrived at by reasoning, and it can entertain. Truth for Hobbes was a property of propositions; the notion that truth can be adumbrated in myth, symbol and image, was simply the chimera of a distempered mind. A theory of imagination of the kind advanced by Coleridge, which sees the imagination as an 'agent' of the reason, or, as Wordsworth put it in *The Prelude*, 'reason in her most exalted mood', would have been quite alien to the positivist temper of his thought. For him there is no interplay of reason and imagination by which the mind is given greater insight, no reciprocity between symbol and concept which will extend the boundaries of man's knowledge.[1] The relation between reason and imagination is that of master and servant; judgement controls the

---

[1] The failure to realize this detracts from the value of C. D. Thorpe's account of Hobbes's theory of imagination in *The Aesthetic Theory of Thomas Hobbes* (Ann Arbor, 1940).

excesses of fancy, which must always have a subordinate position.

The difference between these two conceptions of the imagination is shown by the analogies Hobbes and Coleridge use to describe the imagination. With Hobbes the process of imagination is little more than a review of the images stored in the memory. For him imagination and memory are almost identical.

This *decaying sense*, when we would express the thing itself, I mean *fancy* itself, we call *imagination*, as I said before: but when we would express the decay, and signify that the sense is fading, old, and past, it is called *memory*. So that imagination and memory are but one thing, which for divers considerations hath divers names.[1]

The images he uses to describe the imaginative process are humble and even pedestrian; it operates '. . . as one would sweep a room, to find a jewel; or as a spaniel ranges the field, till he find a scent; or as a man should run over the alphabet, to start a rhyme' (I, iii).[2] How different from Coleridge's 'divine analogy'[3] which sees the imagination '. . . as a repetition in the finite mind of the eternal act of creation in the infinite I AM.'[4] In some respects then, Hobbes is a traditionalist who repeats the Renaissance orthodoxy that poetry combines pleasure and instruction. In other and important respects he is an innovator, bringing to criticism a new and more sophisticated awareness of the mental processes involved in literary composition. His empiricist psychology and his scep-

---

[1] *Leviathan*, I, ii.

[2] That this account influenced literary critics is seen in both Dryden and Dennis. In the preface to *Annus Mirabilis* (London, 1667), Dryden writes: 'The faculty of imagination in the writer . . . like a nimble spaniel, beats over and ranges through the field of memory, till it springs the quarry it hunted after'; *Essays*, ed. W. P. Ker (Oxford, 1900), I, 14. And the dog turns up again with canine fidelity in Dennis's *Remarks on the Dunciad*: 'For Memory may be justly compar'd to the Dog that beats the Field, or the Wood, and that starts the Game; Imagination to the Falcon that clips it upon its Pinions after it; and Judgment to the Falconer who directs the Flight and who governs the whole'; *Critical Works of Dennis*, ed. E. N. Hooker (Baltimore, 1939–43), vol. II, p. 363.

[3] Cf. letter to Richard Sharp (15 January 1804), in which Coleridge calls the imagination 'a dim Analogue of Creation'; *Collected Letters of Coleridge*, ed. E. L. Griggs, vol. II (Oxford, 1956), p. 1034.

[4] *Biographia Literaria*, ch. xiii.

tical philosophy were to have a decisive influence upon critical theory and literary discourse in the period that followed.

One of the chief effects of Hobbes's philosophy on contemporary poetry lay in its 'demythologizing' tendency. Professor Willey, in his *Seventeenth Century Background*, was one of the first to draw attention to the fate of the heroic poem in an age of science, and to show how the status of the epic declined in the rarified atmosphere of the Royal Society. But it was not only science that put the future of the epic in jeopardy. Hobbes, for all his interest in epic, was equally influential in bringing about a change of attitude towards it. Indeed, his interest was partly responsible, for it led him to express his views with a cogency that his contemporaries found difficult to rebut.

A turning point in the fortunes of epic poetry was the appearance in 1651 of Davenant's unfinished epic *Gondibert* which, as well as the author's own preface, was preceded by Hobbes's *Answer to D'Avenant* and prefatory poems by Waller and Cowley. These men had given much thought to the role of the epic in the new climate of intellectual opinion created in the mid-seventeenth century. Davenant's preface and Hobbes's *Answer* were both written in Paris, where all these writers were in exile, and their authors no doubt took part in the discussions which were starting there on this subject. Davenant begins his preface by calling in question the authority of Homer and Virgil. He censures both for what he considers an unwarrantable intrusion of the supernatural in their poems. Homer

. . . doth too frequently intermixe such Fables as are objects lifted above the Eyes of Nature; and as he often interrogates his Muse, not as his rational Spirit, but as a *Familiar*, separated from his body, so her replys bring him where he spends time in immortal conversation, whilest supernaturally he doth often advance his men to the quality of Gods, and depose his Gods to the condition of men.

Virgil, too, is equally to blame; since '. . . He hath so often led him [the reader] into Heaven and Hell, till by conversation with Gods and Ghosts he sometimes deprives us of those natural probabilities in Story which are instructive to humane life.'[1]

_____
[1] *Critical Essays of the Seventeenth Century*, ed. Spingarn, vol. II, p. 2.

It is not that Davenant wishes to remove religion from the epic; he chooses a Christian subject for his poem and believes that poetry can be the handmaid of religion. But his theme is Christian virtue rather than dogma, and he dispenses with any mythological framework, even of the kind which received Scriptural sanction. Similarly, when Cowley's *Davideis* appeared in 1656, it emphasized the historicity of the Biblical narrative and tried to accommodate the traditional Christian cosmology to contemporary scientific discovery. Religious imagery there certainly is in *Davideis*, but as Thomas Sprat observed in his *Life and Writings of Cowley* (1668)—and it is significant that he uses Hobbes's terminology to make his point —'His Fancy flow'd with great speed, and therefore it was very fortunate to him that his Judgment was equal to manage it. He never runs his Reader nor his Argument out of Breath.'[1]

Hobbes himself, in his *Answer to D'Avenant*, quite explicitly repudiates the supernatural in epic poetry. He approves Davenant's departure from the customary invocation to God and the poet's claim to heavenly inspiration.

In that you make so small account of the example of almost all the approved Poets, ancient and modern, who thought fit in the beginning, and sometimes also in the progress of their Poems, to invoke a Muse or some other Deity that should dictate to them or assist them in their writings, they that take not the laws of Art from any reason of their own but from the fashion of precedent times will perhaps accuse your singularity. . . . But why a Christian should think it an ornament to his Poem, either to profane the true God or invoke a false one, I can imagin no cause but a reasonless imitation of Custom, of a foolish custome, by which a man, enabled to speak wisely from the principles of nature and his own meditation, loves rather to be thought to speak by inspiration, like a Bagpipe.[2]

Nature, he maintains, is the final criterion, and we are left in little doubt that the concept is to be interpreted in terms of matter and motion in accordance with his own philosophy.

For as truth is the bound of Historical, so the Resemblance of truth is the utmost limit of Poeticall Liberty. In old time amongst the Heathen such strange fictions and Metamorphoses were not so remote from the Articles of their Faith as they are now from ours,

---

[1] *Critical Essays of the Seventeenth Century*, vol. II, p. 130.   [2] *Ibid.* vol. II, pp. 58–9.

and therefore were not so unpleasant. Beyond the actual works of nature a Poet may now go; but beyond the conceived possibility of nature, never.[1]

The test of probability derives of course from Aristotle, but with him it had meant internal consistency rather than correspondence to the natural order, and embraced even a 'probable impossibility'. With Hobbes, probability means simply what is likely to be verified by experience, and for him the empirically verifiable has nothing to do with knowledge in the philosophical sense. All that the epic poet can do is to present characters and events, whether true or false, which by example might point the way to virtue. This is made manifest in his much later 'Preface concerning the Vertues of an Heroique Poem' (1675), prefixed to his translation of Homer's *Odyssey*, where he tells us that '. . . the Designe [of an epic poem] is not only to profit, but also to delight the Reader. By Profit, I intend not here any accession of Wealth, either to the Poet, or to the Reader; but accession of Prudence, Justice, Fortitude, by the example of such Great and Noble Persons as he introduceth speaking, or describeth acting.'[2]

The epic will present the reader with feigned experience and like experience itself this will provide no more than a knowledge of particulars. Poetry is *poiema*, that is, a making or fiction; it is not *logos*, or rational knowledge. We may agree with Hobbes that poetry is *poiema* and not *logos*, but the trouble is that his philosophy leaves no possibility of any living relation between the two. Poetic images are merely the reflexion of sensory objects in the mirror of our minds and can never become symbols which stimulate the reason to frame new concepts. Even the power of poetry to foster virtue may be ineffective, 'For', as he admits, 'all men love to behold, though not to practise, Vertue.' But with this gone all that epic can do is to entertain; its high religious purpose and supernatural reference have vanished. Hobbes is not afraid to admit this consequence. 'So that at last the work of an Heroique Poet is no more but to furnish an ingenuous Reader (when his leisure abounds) with the diversion of an honest and delightful Story, whether true or feigned.'[3]

[1] *Ibid.* vol. II, p. 62.   [2] *Ibid.* vol. II, p. 68.   [3] *Ibid.* vol. II, p. 68.

Not only is knowledge divorced from experience in Hobbes's system, but it is separated from faith. This separation of faith and knowledge was not peculiar to Hobbes of course, for many of his contemporaries, especially those who looked to the Royal Society for guidance, were inclined to agree that knowledge is a matter of secondary causes. So impressive were the achievements of scientific method that it was easy to assume that what was real was a world of atoms in motion, explicable in mathematical terms, whose only relation to God was that of a machine that has been set going by a divine clockmaker. As Cudworth, the Cambridge Platonist, pointed out, such a view made '. . . . God to be nothing else in the world, but an idle spectator of the various results of the fortuitous and necessary motions of bodies . . . and made a kind of dead and wooden world, as it were a carved statue, that hath nothing neither vital nor magical at all in it.'[1]

It was a view difficult to reconcile with traditional Christian belief, and one that changed the character of poetry. For the writer of epic, who had traditionally been regarded as someone between a priest and prophet, it could only provide a diminished status. It is true that the Royal Society included in its ranks poets as well as scientists, and that Cowley, one of its earliest and most enthusiastic members, was himself an epic poet. But it is significant that the *Davideis* was never finished, and few have thought it a successful poem. Johnson in his *Life of Cowley* put his finger on its chief defect when he wrote, 'Cowley gives inferences instead of images', for it rarely rises above literal discourse to the level of symbol and myth. Yet in spite of all this, we have to remember that this was the age which achieved the greatest epic in English literature, *Paradise Lost*, and the question arises of how Milton succeeded in such an accomplishment. Professor Willey and others have given convincing answers, and all that is required here is to bring out a few salient points which relate the discussion to Hobbes.

On nearly every important issue of religion, philosophy and poetry, Hobbes and Milton are absolutely divided. In writing of Milton, John Aubrey tells us that 'His widowe assures me

[1] *The True Intellectual System of the Universe* (London, 1678), ed. J. Harrison (London, 1845), vol. I, pp. 220–1.

that Mr T. Hobbs was not one of his acquaintance, that her husband did not like him at all, but he would acknowledge him to be a man of great parts, and a learned man. Their interests and tenets did run counter to each other.'[1] Hobbes believed that we can know nothing of God, that all the qualities we attribute to him have no significance in reality; for, he writes: '. . . in the attributes which we give to God, we are not to consider the signification of philosophical truth; but the signification of pious intention, to do him the greatest honour we are able.'[2] But for the Christian, who believes that God was revealed in Christ, there is real meaning in attributing goodness and mercy and other qualities to the godhead. God, the Christian believes, was revealed in history; the Incarnation, indeed, is the central point which gives the historical process pattern and meaning. Hobbes on the other hand, saw history as a series of meaningless particulars from which, at best, we can derive only the virtue of prudence. It is this conviction of history, and especially Biblical history, as having meaning, which is the mainspring of Milton's poem.

The main theme of *Paradise Lost* is not, as is so often supposed, Man's Fall but his Redemption. Milton's poem is concerned not only with original sin but with the intervention in history of the second Adam and with the reconciliation he brings. Nevertheless a good deal of the action lies outside history and beyond the bounds of human experience, and he sees the historical events themselves as a divine drama. The Biblical story is both history and myth. Milton is even prepared to accept pagan myth as a prefiguration of the truth revealed in Scripture, and as a Christian poet is ready to believe that fiction can embody truth. In Raphael's speech to Adam, which describes Satan's rebellion, he is also perhaps indicating the difficulties of his own task:

> High matter thou enjoin'st me, O prime of Men,
> Sad task and hard; for how shall I relate
> To human sense th'invisible exploits

---

[1] Aubrey, *Brief Lives*, ed. A. Clark, vol. II, p. 72. For an excellent discussion of the philosophical and religious differences between the two men, cf. M. H. Nicolson, 'Milton and Hobbes', *Studies in Philology*, XXIII (1926), pp. 405–33.

[2] *Leviathan*, II, xxxi.

> Of warring Spirits ? . . .
> . . . how, last, unfold
> The secrets of another world, perhaps
> Not lawful to reveal ? Yet for thy good
> This is dispensed; and what surmounts the reach
> Of human sense I shall delineate so,
> By likening spiritual to corporal forms,
> As may express them best.[1]

Milton was sustained in his writing, he believed, by the heavenly Muse who visited him in sleep and inspired his imagination; unlike Hobbes he did not consider that his divine assistance turned him into a 'bagpipe', but rather that it made his poetry an instrument of the truth.[2] Hobbes was contemptuous of such a suggestion.

> For if a man pretend to me, that God hath spoken to him supernaturally and immediately, and I make doubt of it, I cannot easily perceive what argument he can produce, to oblige me to believe it. . . . To say he hath spoken to him in a dream, is no more than to say he dreamed that God spake to him.[3]

For Milton, not only the Bible, but the whole of experience is a means of knowing God; the world of nature is not simply particular concrete objects which by pressure on our senses bring about images in the mind. It is rather a secondary revelation of its Creator. Raphael, in addressing Adam, does not commit himself to any precise description, but suggests something of the relation between the natural and the supernatural, when he says,

> . . . what if Earth
> Be but the shadow of Heaven, and things therein
> Each to other like, more than on Earth is thought ? (v, 574–6)

This was a difficult doctrine for Milton to hold, for it was a matter of Puritan conviction that the world of Grace and the world of Nature had been rent asunder by the Fall, and in some

---

[1] *Paradise Lost*, v, 563–74.

[2] In his *Reason of Church Government* (1642) Milton had written that the great epic on which he was embarking would be guided by help not 'to be obtained by the invocation of Dame Memory and her Siren daughters, but by devout prayer to that eternal Spirit who can enrich with all utterance and knowledge'. This is in direct contradiction to Hobbes's theory of the imagination.

[3] *Leviathan*, III, xxxii.

respects the new scientific rationalism was easier to combine with Puritanism than was Renaissance humanism. Milton's achievement in *Paradise Lost* was, then, a precarious one,[1] and in *Paradise Regained* and *Samson Agonistes* he turned to a literal presentation of the historical and Biblical narrative and a style largely devoid of rhetorical figures. But if his Puritanism left him disposed to accept a dualism between the natural and supernatural, it did not lead him to accept Hobbes's division of reason and faith.

Reason and faith in Hobbes are not merely separate but almost antithetical, and we should not think there is any conscious irony when he tells us that '. . . it is with the mysteries of our religion as with wholesome pills for the sick; which swallowed whole, have the virtue to cure; but chewed, are for the most part cast up again without effect.'[2] In Milton reason and faith are almost synonymous. Reason is that part of man which approximates to the divine nature, and his treatment of the Fall suggests that he regarded it as the overthrow of reason by the passions. Hobbes, on the other hand, affirmed that reason is the servant of the passions. 'For the thoughts are to the desires, as scouts, and spies, to range abroad, and find the way to the things desired' (i, viii). With Milton reason is divine illumination, an active principle in man which is more than the faculty of intellection; it makes judgements of value and conduces to virtue. The best known passage in which Milton advances this Platonic conception is in Book v of *Paradise Lost*, where Raphael describes for Adam's benefit the great chain of being which reaches from grossest matter to the life of the spirit. Coleridge chose this passage as a heading for the famous chapter in *Biographia Literaria* in which he defines the poetic imagination. For Milton, as for Coleridge (at any rate if we interpret the passage as Coleridge does), the reason

[1] Marvell realized something of this when he wrote in 'On Mr Milton's Paradise Lost',

> . . . the Argument
> Held me a while misdoubting his Intent,
> That he would ruine (for I saw him strong)
> The sacred Truths to Fable and Old Song.

That Milton recognized this difficulty I have tried to show in my *Reason and Imagination* (Oxford, 1960), ch. II.

[2] *Leviathan*, III, xxxii.

is a product of both the imagination and the understanding. It works both discursively and intuitively; with man the truth will most often be reached through logical discourse, but at times he will reach the angelic heights of direct apprehension. Matter, Raphael tells Adam, will

> . . . by gradual scale sublim'd
> To vital spirits aspire, to animal,
> To intellectual, give both life and sense,
> Fansie and understanding, whence the Soule
> Reason receives, and reason is her being,
> Discursive, or intuitive; discourse
> Is oftest yours, the latter most is ours,
> Differing but in degree, of kind the same. (v, 483–90)

Reason and freedom are identical for Milton; man is perfectly free when he obeys reason and is enslaved only when governed by his passions. Unlike Hobbes, who argued that the will is simply the last link in a chain of determined mental processes, he believed man to be free to choose between his reason and his passions. God made man a rational being and man is free when he acts in accordance with his own nature.

> But God left free the Will; for what obeys
> Reason is free; and Reason he made right. (IX, 351–2)

This difference between their conceptions of the reason lies at the basis of their different political philosophies. Hobbes's system of thought envisaged a time when men lived in a state of nature, before society had become organized. The life of natural man, in his most famous phrase, was 'solitary, poor, nasty, brutish, and short', for every man lived in a chaos of competition with his fellows. It was to deliver themselves out of this miserable condition that men contracted to vest supreme authority in a sovereign who should exercise power over them. Their motives in doing this were fear of each other and the desire for peace. This account, which is as mythological as anything in the book of Genesis, is very different from Milton's view of how society came into being. For Milton, unfallen man was in no need of government; Adam and Eve before the Fall lived in a state of concord which was founded upon the rule of reason. Obedience to reason meant individual freedom and an identity of interest between them. Except for the Fall their progeny could have continued living in a community of free wills all recognizing the sway of reason, which is no other than the law of God. If men were rational they would realize that their interests are all identical, and there would be hardly any need for government in the authoritarian sense. But because men are fallen and have allowed their passions to usurp the place of reason, government becomes necessary, and men's sinfulness will lead, on occasion, to the emergence of tyranny. Milton puts this theory into the mouth of the archangel Michael, who tells Adam,

> . . . yet know withall,
> Since thy original lapse, true Libertie
> Is lost, which alwayes with right Reason dwells
> Twinnd, and from her hath no dividual being:
> Reason in man obscur'd, or not obeyed,
> Immediately inordinate desires
> And upstart Passions catch the Government
> From Reason, and to servitude reduce
> Man till then free . . .
> . . . Tyrannie must be,
> Though to the Tyrant thereby no excuse.
> Yet sometimes Nations will decline so low
> From Vertue, which is Reason, that no wrong,
> But Justice, and some fatal curse annext
> Deprives them of their outward Libertie,
> Their inward lost. (XII, 82–101)

Both men regard authoritarian government as a result of man's sinful nature, but Hobbes believes it to be the best that can be achieved, whereas Milton thinks that if man would obey the dictates of reason he could establish democratic rule. Good government, according to Milton, depends upon self-government; for Hobbes it must always be imposed from outside.

If Milton wrote in conscious opposition to Hobbes, in Dryden we meet someone who was in many respects his professed disciple. Aubrey describes Dryden as Hobbes's 'great admirer' and says that he 'oftentimes makes use of his doctrine in his plays—from Mr Dryden himself'.[1] A good deal has been

---

[1] Aubrey, *Brief Lives*, ed. A. Clark, vol. I, p. 372.

written already of Hobbes's influence on Dryden. Professor Bredvold[1] has indicated the extent of Dryden's debt to Hobbes in the plays, and it has long been recognized that the various accounts of poetic composition in Dryden's work, especially that in the preface to *Annus Mirabilis*, owe a great deal to Davenant and Hobbes. But we can also perceive the effect of Hobbes on Dryden's own poetry.

Dryden, although firstly an Anglican and then a Roman Catholic, was, as he himself tells us, sceptical by temperament, and this natural disposition was strengthened by the intellectual pressures of his times. It is perfectly possible to combine philosophical scepticism with religious faith, as we see in the anti-metaphysical character of so much theology today. But such a combination was more difficult for an Anglican in the second half of the seventeenth century, since Anglican theology from the time of Hooker had insisted on the reasonableness of the Christian religion. It was because he felt the Latitudinarian tendency of the Church of England to be the beginning of a slippery slope that Dryden retreated to the safer position of rendering unto faith the things that are faith's and to reason the things that are reason's. Such a circumscription of reason does not necessarily derive from one source, of course, but the kind of separation of reason and faith to be found in Hobbes's writings was undoubtedly congenial to Dryden's mind. The fear that rational theology was likely to end in deism led Dryden to embrace the Roman Catholic faith, but its presence is already manifest in *Religio Laici* (1682), written to defend the Anglican position. The magnificent opening lines of this poem express the Hobbesian view that reason is not a speculative but a practical faculty; reason does not show us the ultimate truth but enables us to live ordered and decent lives.

> Dim as the borrow'd beams of Moon and Stars
> To lonely, weary, wandring Travellers
> Is Reason to the Soul: And as on high
> Those rowling Fires discover but the Sky
> Not light us here; So Reason's glimmering Ray
> Was lent, not to assure our doubtful way,
> But guide us upward to a better Day.

---

[1] *The Intellectual Milieu of John Dryden* (Ann Arbor, 1934).

The ending of *Religio Laici* is even more in the manner of
Hobbes, for here reason is frankly subordinated to a political
end; public order is the great good and if reason runs counter
to this, it is better to disregard it.

> 'Tis some Relief, that points not clearly known,
> Without much hazard may be let alone:
> And after hearing what our Church can say,
> If still our Reason runs another way,
> That private Reason 'tis more Just to curb,
> Than by Disputes the publick Peace disturb.
> For points obscure are of small use to learn.

The acceptance of this dualism between reason and faith,
together with an admiration for the poetry of Davenant and
Cowley, might well have led to a coolness towards Milton on
Dryden's part. But Dryden was too good a critic not to
recognize the greatness of *Paradise Lost*. His writings in many
places express his admiration for the epic and his own unful-
filled aspiration to write in this form. 'Heroic Poetry . . . has
ever been esteemed, and ever will be, the greatest work of human
nature.'[1] Nor is he ready to join those who wish to 'de-
mythologize' the epic. Horace, he writes, '. . . taxed not
Homer, nor the divine Virgil, for interesting their gods in the
wars of Troy and Italy; neither, had he now lived, would he
have taxed Milton, as our false critics have presumed to do,
for his choice of a supernatural argument.'[2] And yet we cannot
be unaware of the great gulf between Milton and Dryden.
The above quotations come from 'The Author's Apology for
Heroic Poetry', which Dryden prefixed to *The State of Innocence
and Fall of Man* (1677), an opera based upon *Paradise Lost*. To
move from Milton's epic to Dryden's opera is more than to
exchange the splendour of Milton's blank verse for the rather
trite quality of Dryden's rhymed couplets. We have changed
our entire world. Such is Milton's genius that we feel in reading
Paradise Lost that we are being presented with eternal truths
of a cosmic significance; in Dryden the same 'great argument'
has been trimmed to meet the needs of a stage entertainment.

Such a comparison is unfair, of course, for Milton's poem
was the fruit of years of preparation and composition, while

[1] *Essays of Dryden*, ed. W. P. Ker, vol. i, p. 181.   [2] *Ibid.* vol. i, pp. 189–90.

Dryden's opera, according to Johnson, was written in a month. But this fact in itself establishes the point we are making. For all Dryden's admiration for the epic, his genius flowered in other forms; forms which he often had to devise or adapt to suit his own talents and the material available. The work which best illustrates how he matched his individual genius to the situation in which he found himself is *Absalom and Achitophel* (1681–2). This poem is written in the heroic manner, and like *Paradise Lost* its central scene is the temptation and fall of the hero. Although it is in the strict sense an occasional poem, Dryden raises the theme of rebellion to a universal significance, on a political if not a cosmic level. It is not difficult, indeed, to catch echoes of Milton, but its total effect owes more to Hobbes. If Absalom's fall is the overthrow of reason by the passions, we are left in little doubt that reason's chief end should be to secure settled government and that Dryden considers this best achieved by the absolute sovereignty of the monarch.

> Yet, if the Crowd be Judge of fit and Just,
> And Kings are onely Officers in trust,
> Then this resuming Cov'nant was declar'd
> When Kings were made, or is for ever bar'd . . .
>
> For who can be secure of private Right,
> If Sovereign sway may be dissolv'd by might?
> Nor is the Peoples Judgment always true:
> The most may err as grossly as the few. (ll. 765–82)

If the style is heroic, so is much of the characterization. And yet the poem lacks not only epic dimensions but a purely epic purpose. In chapter IX of the *Leviathan*, Hobbes had categorized the objects of poetry as 'magnifying' and 'vilifying', and that of rhetoric as 'persuading'. Dryden's poem combines all three. Dryden was not the first, of course, to bring poetry and rhetoric together, but he does so in a very individual manner, one which probably owes something to Hobbes. Hobbes, it will be remembered, had followed Aristotle in suggesting that rhetorical discourse depends upon example and enthymeme. Earlier poets had employed both of these, but never to such an extent as Dryden. In *Religio Laici*, *The Hind and the Panther* and *Absalom and Achitophel* they became the chief features of his style. No one before him had brought poetry so close to logical discourse; he was, as Johnson observed, 'the first who joined argument with poetry', and 'sentences were readier at his call than images'. There were other forces, such as the work of the Royal Society, which helped to bring about the *rapprochement* between poetry and prose at this time, but one can hardly doubt, considering Dryden's debt to Hobbes in so many other ways, that here too Hobbes was a decisive influence. His insistence on clear and distinct ideas and his distrust of metaphor are reflected in the simplicity and concision of Dryden's style. But more than this, his belief that truth is reached by propositions linked together in consecutive argument finds its most appropriate poetic form in the rhymed couplet.

Hobbes's philosophy was one of the most powerful influences that brought about the approximation of poetry to rhetoric in the Augustan period. But there were other forces counterbalancing this which were to draw poetry and poetics away from rhetoric towards aesthetics. In many ways the history of eighteenth-century poetic theory can be recounted in terms of the gradual ascendancy of aesthetic concepts over rhetorical ones. Hobbes himself in the *Answer to D'Avenant* had echoed the Horatian maxim *ut pictura poesis* when he wrote, 'Poets are Painters',[1] and Dryden developed this theme in an essay on 'The Parallel betwixt Painting and Poetry', which he prefixed to a translation of Du Fresnoy's *De arte graphica* (1695). With the turn of the century poetry was seen once more not only as verbal discourse but as analogous to the plastic arts. The growing regard for landscape which derived from painting, and the new interest in the nature of aesthetic experience which revealed itself in discussions of the beautiful and the sublime, were accompanied by a re-birth of imagery. But imagery now had a somewhat different function; it came increasingly to be used for description and the symbolization of feeling, and less as a vehicle for meaning. The eighteenth century started as an age of sense but it ended as one of sensibility.

It might be thought that Hobbes's philosophy would have been inimical to this development, but this is not wholly true. The influence of a great thinker is often self-contradictory, and

[1] *Critical Essays of the Seventeenth Century*, ed. Spingarn, vol. II, p. 61.

must be seen in the opposition he provokes as much as in the assent he commands. If the immediate effect of Hobbes's thought was to bring poetry closer to rhetoric, we must remember that he stands at the beginning of English aesthetics. In particular, his discussion of literature in psychological terms was an innovation, and had repercussions which have lasted to the present day. Psychological criticism turned attention from the work of art itself to its effectiveness and, for good or ill, hastened the dissolution of fixed literary 'kinds'. It gave a new importance to questions both of artistic creation and aesthetic experience; concepts such as genius and the sublime may have been difficult to account for in terms of his psychology, but it is doubtful if eighteenth-century critics would have formulated them but for Hobbes.

We often forget that Hobbes believed man to be a creature of the passions. Good, according to him, lies in the satisfaction of the appetites: a doctrine which manifested itself, in critical theory, in the concept of taste and the decline of rational standards, and which led in literature to a more plangent expression of the feelings. Such a doctrine could accord with a liberal and optimistic notion of human nature, but in Hobbes it is accompanied by a fundamental pessimism. This is reflected in his view of society as something achieved almost in opposition to human nature and without any foundation in natural law, and in a deep scepticism concerning man's knowledge. Both the optimism and the pessimism are present in Augustan literature and are brought together in Pope's famous paradox about man as 'the glory, jest, and riddle of the world!'

Hobbes, though he was disliked and feared by more people than admired him, was one of those thinkers whose influence is too great and pervasive to trace in detail. Whether in opposition or allegiance, those who followed him were obliged in no small measure to think in the categories which he had framed and to write in a language he had helped to form. His contemporary, Leibniz, could rightly say that Hobbes was 'among the deepest minds of the century'. Leibniz could not foresee the future but, if he had been able to do so, he might have added that Hobbes was also one of the founding fathers of the century to come.

3

JOHN LOCKE AND THE RHETORIC OF THE SECOND TREATISE

BY THEODORE REDPATH

The *Two Treatises of Government* of John Locke (1632–1704) appeared anonymously in the autumn of 1689, a few months before the great *Essay*. The Second Treatise, or 'An Essay Concerning the True Original, Extent and End of Civil Government', is known to have had a most persuasive influence in shaping democracy in Great Britain and the United States; and there is good reason to believe that it has influenced the evolution of democracy in some other countries also. It may be of interest to scrutinize in some detail the logical status of the ways in which Locke endeavours to support his main positions in this influential work. This will involve considering how far and when he appeals to generalizations from experience; how far and when he relies on deductive logic; how far and when he invokes propositions which he claims to be self-evident; and how far and when he employs (whether deliberately or spontaneously) some form of rhetoric, such as evocative language or imagery, persuasive definitions, appeals to reverenced authority, or tendentious equivocation.

Let us first look at one of the most fundamental positions of the Second Treatise, the doctrine of the natural equality of men. This position is stated very near the outset, at the beginning of chapter II:

To understand political power aright, and derive it from its original, we must consider what state all men are naturally in, and that is a state of perfect freedom to order their actions and dispose of their possessions and persons as they think fit, within the bounds of the law of nature, without asking leave, or depending upon the will of any other man.

A state also of equality, wherein all the power and jurisdiction is reciprocal, no one having more than another; there being nothing more evident than that creatures of the same species and rank, promiscuously born to all the same advantages of nature, and the use of the same faculties, should also be equal one amongst another without subordination or subjection, unless the Lord and Master of them all should by any manifest declaration of his will set one above another, and confer on him by an evident and clear appointment an undoubted right to dominion and sovereignty. (II, 4)[1]

What does this argument for the natural equality of men come to? It has the semblance of a deduction. Locke considers it to be in the highest degree evident that 'creatures of the same species and rank, promiscuously born to all the same advantages of nature, and the use of the same faculties, should also be equal one amongst another without subordination or subjection'. The argument, more fully set out, is that men are creatures of the same rank . . .; that creatures of the same rank . . . should also be equal one amongst another without subordination or subjection; and that therefore men should be equal one amongst another without subordination or subjection. Now Locke gives this argument a curious speciousness by the use of certain particular words, namely 'rank', 'all' and 'same' (especially in the expressions 'same advantages' and 'same faculties'—the expression 'same species' carries less weight). The word 'rank' really guarantees the validity of the argument. It does so, however, at the cost of making it circular. Nothing could be more certain than that creatures of the same 'rank' should be 'equal one amongst another without subordination or subjection'—that is the very significance of *rank*. Again, if creatures really did have 'all the same advantages of nature', it would not seem at all unreasonable that they should be considered as 'naturally equal'. Unfortunately for the status of his position, however, Locke nowhere establishes that all human beings do naturally have the same 'rank', nor does he demonstrate that they have naturally 'all the same advantages of nature'. It might indeed have been hard for him to show that there were no natural morons or natural geniuses.

---

[1] *The Second Treatise of Civil Government*, ed. J. W. Gough (Oxford, 1946, revised 1956); cf. *Two Treatises of Government*, ed. Peter Laslett (Cambridge, 1960). Quotations are from Gough's text, and references to chapter and paragraph apply to both.

In point of fact, later in the Treatise, at a stage where the admission (based on some very fair empirical generalizations) might no longer seem damaging to his fundamental doctrine, Locke makes some concessions, admissions of natural human *inequality*. The highly interesting passage where he does so reads as follows:

Though I have said above (chapter II) that all men by nature are equal, I cannot be supposed to understand all sorts of equality. Age or virtue may give men a just precedency. Excellency of parts and merit may place others above the common level. Birth may subject some, and alliance and benefits others, to pay an observance to those to whom nature, gratitude, or other respects may have made it due. And yet all this consists with the equality which all men are in, in respect of jurisdiction or dominion, one over another; which was the equality I there spoke of as proper to the business in hand, being that equal right that every man hath to his natural freedom, without being subjected to the will or authority of any other man. (VI, 54)

'I cannot be supposed to understand all sorts of equality.' Who, indeed, could possibly believe that a respectable philosopher like Locke could have meant anything so absurd? For no intelligent person would really be inclined, on reflection, to accept the view that nobody was even 'naturally' superior to anybody else in any way. Yet Locke had, as we have seen, used very wide language, and when he spoke of all human beings as having the same 'rank', and being 'born to all the same advantages of nature, and the use of the same faculties', it would hardly have been unforgivable in a reader to imagine that Locke *was* to 'be supposed to understand all sorts of equality'. Indeed, if all that he was meaning was that the 'creatures' were all of the same species, then his argument for natural equality would have had very little persuasiveness; while if, on the other hand, he simply meant by saying that they had the same 'rank' that they had the same status with respect to the issue of subordination or subjection, his argument would have been nothing but a lame tautology. However, let us suppose him not to have meant that men were naturally equal in all respects. Let us suppose that he really meant to admit frankly, all the time, that 'age or virtue may give men a just precedency', that 'excellency of parts and merit may place others above the common level', that 'birth may subject some, and alliance or benefits others, to pay an observance to those to whom nature, gratitude, or other respects may have made it due'. Suppose he had written these things in so many words in chapter II, would not a reader naturally have raised such questions as: 'Should not elders and betters, or the more intelligent, or the more benevolent, individuals, be regarded as having some claim to rule those less favoured by nature in these respects?' Locke is now, indeed, allowing some practical rewards to such people. His words, however, appear to be cautiously chosen. Such people may be 'given a just precedency', 'placed above the common level', have an 'observance' 'paid' to them. The rewards are all circumspectly tame. There is never a hint that such people might have any claim whatever *to rule over others*. But it is Locke's continuation that deserves the prize. If one did not know what an honest and good man he was, one would be tempted very seriously to believe him guilty of gross deceitfulness: 'And yet all this consists with the equality which all men are in, in respect of jurisdiction or dominion, one over another.' '*All this* consists', writes Locke, employing a usefully vague phrase. Naturally, *the tame rewards* 'consist' admirably with that equality. They were cut down to size precisely in order that they should do so. But if the expression 'all this' be taken to refer also to the claims that 'age', 'virtue', 'excellency of parts and merit', 'birth', and so on, might well be considered to have (and might well have been supposed by a reader to have, had not the passage worked on him by conceding the tame rewards), then it is by no means clear that 'all this' 'consists with the equality which all men are in, in respect of jurisdiction or dominion, one over another'. Indeed, on the contrary, 'all this' and the 'equality' would be wholly inconsistent. The true situation then, is that in chapter II, where Locke was concerned to establish firmly the natural equality of men, he made no mention at all of those inconvenient natural inequalities, while in chapter VI, where, after a convenient interval, he may well have felt safer, he mentions the natural inequalities but, disregarding their political claims, allows them only some social sops which might decoy all but really alert readers, and prevent them from discerning the possibility of the disregarded political claims.

Before leaving Locke's invalid attempt to establish the doctrine of the natural equality of men, let us return to chapter II, and cast a glance at what follows the passage already quoted. Locke does not continue the argument. He simply makes an appeal to authority, which also involves a repetition of his claim that the doctrine is self-evident:

This equality of men by nature the judicious Hooker looks upon as so evident in itself and beyond all question, that he makes it the foundation of that obligation to mutual love amongst men on which he builds the duties they owe one another, and from whence he derives the great maxims of justice and charity. (II, 5)

The appeal to the reverenced authority of 'the judicious Hooker' ('judicious' being, of course, a potent rhetorical epithet) would have had considerable persuasive force for many readers at the time, but to us who are perhaps less impressed by such appeals to authority, it reveals itself fairly readily as mere rhetoric.

All the support, then, that Locke offers for his fundamental doctrine of the natural equality of men is a bare assertion of self-evidence, bolstered by some hollow pseudo-deduction, and buttressed by a mere appeal to authority. The position rests on professed intuition and on rhetorical devices. What logic is offered is shaky or tautologous. And of the empiricism usually associated with Locke's name, the only trace appears in some concessions which could be fatal to his position.

Let us pass now to a position much further up the tree of Locke's political thought: his condemnation of absolute monarchy. Locke's most explicit condemnation of absolute monarchy occurs in a passage fairly far on in chapter VII of the Treatise, which expresses the conclusion of some argumentation:

Hence it is evident that absolute monarchy, which by some men is counted the only government in the world, is indeed inconsistent with civil society, and so can be no form of civil government at all (VII, 90).

This is certainly a very severe condemnation. Locke does not even allow that absolute monarchy is an inferior kind of civil government. He does not admit that it is any kind of civil government at all. When, however, we look into the process by which Locke arrives at this startling conclusion, we find that he does so by simple deduction from his definition of 'civil society'. That definition occurs earlier in the same chapter: 'Those who are united into one body, and have a common established law and judicature to appeal to, with authority to decide controversies between them and punish offenders, are in civil society one with another' (vii, 87). Now that definition looks eminently reasonable, and it is even, curiously enough, not far removed from the definition propounded by Hobbes, the champion of that very absolutism which Locke rejects. Both Hobbes and Locke would place the difference between the state of nature and a civil society in the absence in the former, and the presence in the latter, of a legislative, executive, and judicial authority. From the words of Locke's definition, indeed—and therein lies its rhetorical power—it would be impossible to predict the use he was to make of it, in which, of course, he deviated so utterly from Hobbes. Locke was going on to say that, since an absolute monarch is not necessarily subject to the 'common established law and judicature', absolute monarchy does not fall within the scope of civil society:

For the end of civil society being to avoid and remedy those inconveniences of the state of nature which necessarily follow from every man's being judge in his own case, by setting up a known authority to which every one of that society may appeal upon any injury received or controversy that may arise, and which every one of the society ought to obey; wherever any persons are who have not such an authority to appeal to and decide any difference between them, these persons are still in the state of nature. And so is every absolute prince, in respect of those who are under his dominion. (vii, 90)

Now whether the definition of civil society included absolute monarchy or not really depended on how the apparently innocent word 'common' was to be interpreted. If it was to be interpreted as applying to all citizens, though not to the sovereign himself, then Hobbesian absolutism would fall within its scope. If, on the other hand, it was to be interpreted as asserting that the sovereign himself was to be subject to the law, then Locke's conclusion was guaranteed. We can therefore say that in trying to establish this capital point in his system Locke has, indeed, made use of deductive logic. His conclusion follows perfectly from the definition he had propounded, provided one ambiguous word in it be suitably interpreted. There was, however, that ambiguous term, and Locke's interpretation of it could well be challenged. Moreover, quite apart from the ambiguity, it would be easy to question the definition even as Locke himself understood it. In point of fact, it would only have been necessary, at the time Locke wrote the Second Treatise, to travel the twenty-odd miles across the English Channel to come upon a great and flourishing kingdom which would not have accorded with the definition of a civil society as Locke understood it, but which was nevertheless the most civilized state in Europe, and one of the most civilized states in the whole world. An unbiased empiricist might well have been dissuaded by this fact from formulating or accepting a definition of civil society such as that propounded by Locke and bearing the sense he intended. By the sense he attaches to the terms of his definition, however, and particularly by the sense he attaches to the word 'common', Locke reveals himself as no unbiased empiricist, but a tendentious idealist, making conscious or unconscious use of a rhetorical ambiguity. His definition of 'civil society' is a persuasive definition. It is a definition of what *he believes to deserve* the name of 'civil society', not of what would have been generally admitted by untendentious users of language to fall within the scope of the term to be defined. Locke wishes to persuade readers with a different conception of civil society from his own to adopt his conception instead of theirs. In order to achieve this object he uses language in his definition (whether deliberately or spontaneously) which could be perfectly acceptable to many, at least, of those readers; but which could also be interpreted, and would actually come to be interpreted later in the Treatise, in such a way as to guarantee the condemnation of absolute monarchy as beyond the pale of civil society.

Apart from this appeal to his definition of civil society, however, Locke does offer other considerations to support his

condemnation of absolute monarchy. He cites the recent history of Ceylon as an instance of 'what the protection of
absolute monarchy is, what kind of fathers of their countries
it makes princes, and to what a degree of happiness and
security it carries civil society, where this sort of government
is grown to perfection' (VII, 92).

This might at first sight seem to be at last a simple empirical
appeal to fact; but although there is certainly an empirical
element in the appeal, there are other features of a different
kind in the passage that deserve close attention. First, there
is the bitterly ironical tone of each of the clauses, cumulative
in effect and a powerful persuasive force. This tone by itself
might, to one familiar with Locke's ways of writing, be considered a symptom of some weakness in the argument. Indeed,
logically, the argument *is* weak, though the passage has a
certain rhetorical strength. If, however, one were to try to
impugn the argument on the simple ground that it is an
argument from a single case of absolute monarchy to the condemnation of all cases, one would not be doing justice to
Locke's subtlety or showing sufficient awareness of the working
of the passage. The focal point is in fact the expression 'grown
to perfection', which is ambiguous. It might seem at first sight
that Locke is impeccably arguing from the most favourable
case of absolute monarchy, so that *a fortiori* all other cases of
absolute monarchy would be in a worse position. The reader
who is on his guard, however, can see that what Locke is really
referring to is a conspicuously *bad* example of absolute government. Whether deliberately or not, Locke has thus once again
employed sleight-of-language. If by 'grown to perfection' he
meant 'the most absolute', he would be arguing about an
extreme case, and the argument would therefore carry no
weight against absolute government in general. But this is,
in fact, all his words could properly mean if he is not arguing
from the most favourable case, and we have already seen that
he is not doing that. What Locke *is* doing is worse than all
this; for he is, in point of fact, arguing from a very bad case,
offering it as representative of a whole class which might (and
indeed *would*) contain far more favourable examples, and, to
crown all, making it appear by the use of the term 'grown to

perfection' as if the case he was citing was not a very bad case but the most favourable that could be thought of. In view of the shady character of Locke's argument, all and more of that irony was needed for the passage to have a good chance of convincing a reader of even average perceptiveness, by putting him off his guard.

But it is time to leave this topic, and to pass on to consider certain features of Locke's account of the institution of what he calls 'lawful governments'.

As is well known, Locke's account of the institution of lawful governments presupposes a 'state of nature' in which all men are equal, and no one subordinate socially or politically to anyone else. An interesting question is whether Locke believed that such a state had ever really existed or whether he regarded it as a mythical construction, so that lawful governments were to be considered to be *as if* they had arisen from a state of nature, even if they had not actually done so. It is proper to raise such a question; but the answer to it is in fact quite easy. It is perfectly clear that Locke believed that states of nature had actually existed, and indeed that they had everywhere preceded the institution of all lawful governments.

Now the proposition that states of nature had actually existed, and everywhere preceded the institution of all lawful governments, at least *seems* to be in large measure—if not indeed completely—an empirical proposition. We might therefore reasonably demand that Locke should offer empirical evidence for it. Let us see what he in fact provides.

The first time in the Treatise that Locke raises the question is towards the end of chapter II, where he writes:

'Tis often asked as a mighty objection, Where are, or ever were there, any men in such a state of nature? To which it may suffice as an answer at present: That since all princes and rulers of independent governments all through the world are in a state of nature, 'tis plain the world never was, nor ever will be, without numbers of men in that state. (II, 14)

Hobbes had already urged that the state in which sovereign princes existed in relation to one another was a state of nature. But such a view is not really very satisfactory. It was true enough *ex hypothesi* that the sovereign princes had not agreed to accept a common legislative and judicial authority. But was it really true also that any two sovereigns were 'naturally equal' to each other, either as individuals or considered together with the states they ruled? Moreover, did they all really have the power to punish any other sovereign that warred against them, as Locke maintained that any individual in the state of nature did have? The differences between the cases of sovereign princes or states on the one hand, and individuals on the other, are too great for the former to be considered even as *examples* of the state of nature as described by Locke, let alone as evidence for the existence, past or present, of a state of nature among individuals; and *a fortiori*, of the invariable temporal precedence of lawful government by states of nature.

Locke next appeals once more to 'the judicious Hooker', who certainly believed in the real existence of states of nature before the founding of political societies. But Locke goes further than his master: 'I moreover affirm that all men are naturally in that state, and remain so, till by their own consents they make themselves members of some politic society; and I doubt not, in the sequel of this discourse, to make it very clear' (II, 15).

Before we look to 'the sequel' (i.e. to passages later in the Treatise) it is worth pausing a moment to observe exactly what Locke is claiming here. He is claiming that everybody was free and equal until they *agreed* to join in a political society.

Let us, however, now consider what further support for his affirmation Locke offers later in the Treatise. The most relevant passages occur in the first part of chapter VIII (99–110). The matter is introduced by a passage in which Locke recapitulates his conclusions concerning the process of the institution of 'lawful governments':

Whosoever therefore out of a state of nature unite into a community must be understood to give up all the power necessary to the ends for which they unite into society, to the majority of the community, unless they expressly agreed in any number greater than the majority. And this is done by barely agreeing to unite into one political society, which is all the compact that is, or needs be, between the individuals that enter into or make up a commonwealth. And thus that which begins and actually constitutes any political society is nothing but the consent of any number of freemen capable of a majority to unite and incorporate into such a society. And this is that, and that only, which did or could give beginning to any lawful government in the world. (VIII, 99)

Locke continues: 'To this I find two objections made. First: That there are no instances to be found in story of a company of men, independent and equal one amongst another, that met together and in this way began and set up a government' (VIII, 100).

Locke spends some time on his answer to this objection. He first counters that it is not surprising that history says very little of men in a state of nature, since they would not be likely to stay in it for long. Also, historical records are only made after a civil society has been in existence for a long time. These considerations, however, clearly do not afford, and Locke does not intend them to afford, any objection even to the view that men may never have been in a state of nature. But he does go on to make the substantial claim that the records we do have of the beginnings of civil societies ('excepting that of the Jews, where God himself immediately interposed') do either indicate 'plain instances' of a beginning such as he had described, 'or at least have manifest footsteps of it'. He cites the beginnings of Rome and Venice, and draws on Josephus Acosta's account of the foundation of Peru, which referred to similar cases at the time in Florida and Brazil, 'and many other nations', which had no certain kings but, as occasion was offered in peace or war, chose their captains as they pleased. Now it is surely clear that all these references are very vague. The references to Rome and Venice are of the barest kind; and the passage from Acosta does not say whether all the people were naturally free and equal, and had equal rights in choosing their captains. The only other historical reference Locke cites is from Justin Martyr, about a body of men who left Sparta with Palantus, and, writes Locke, 'set up a government over themselves, by their own consent'. He goes on to announce, with entirely misplaced satisfaction, that he has 'given several examples out of history of people free and in the state of nature that, being met together, incorporated and became a commonwealth'.

5

Here then, though he has made some attempt at empirical justification, it has been a very feeble one.

It may well be that Locke himself realized that his empirical evidence was not too substantial, for in the very next paragraph he writes as follows:

> But to conclude, reason being plain on our side that men are naturally free, and the examples of history showing that the governments of the world, that were begun in peace, had their beginning laid on that foundation, and were made by consent of the people, there can be little room for doubt, either where the right is, or what has been the opinion and practice of mankind, about the first erecting of governments. (VIII, 104)

The passage certainly strongly suggests that however much Locke was relying on 'the examples of history' as evidence for the institution of government by consent, it was on 'reason' that he was relying for the doctrine of natural equality, and therefore for the doctrine of the state of nature.

Locke, indeed, does candidly admit that if we look back as far as possible in history we shall generally find commonwealths ruled by single persons (VIII, 105), but he regards this as quite consistent with his view that political societies were actually formed by the consent of naturally free and equal individuals. He is quite right; but his point only rebuts a possible objection to his view. It provides no positive evidence for it. He goes on to try to explain why in early ages men would naturally choose patriarchs or monarchs to rule them, but he does not establish that such elections were actually made, and he is still further from showing that, *if they were*, they were made by naturally free and equal men, all of whom then became members of that political society.

Let us now scrutinize more closely Locke's account of how political societies were formed, and of the immediate implications of that formation. As we have seen, he states early in chapter VIII that this always takes place by the agreement of any number of free and equal men to enter into or make up a commonwealth. The reader may have noticed, however, that in the passage last quoted Locke added a qualification: 'the governments of the world, *that were begun in peace*, had their beginning laid on that foundation' (my italics) (VIII, 104).

Typically, Locke does not immediately indicate the full purport of the qualification. He only does this some pages later, when he writes:

And thus much may suffice to show that, as far as we have any light from history, we have reason to conclude that all peaceful beginnings of government have been laid in consent of the people. I say peaceful, because I shall have occasion in another place to speak of conquest, which some esteem a way of beginning of governments. (VIII, 112)

I shall give special consideration to Locke's treatment of conquest. Meanwhile, suffice it to suggest that Locke will need to give very strong reasons for denying that political societies can be instituted by conquest. For the present, however, let us consider what support Locke provides for his view that in all other cases political societies come into being by the consent of free and equal men.

Some of the flimsy evidence Locke offers has already been discussed, but it is worth spending a little time on considering the attempts he makes to square with his theory of consent the many cases, whose existence he could not deny, of patriarchal rule and of absolute monarchy. With regard to patriarchal rule, Locke concedes that where a family was numerous enough to subsist by itself, and stayed together as a whole without mixing with other people, as often happened where there was a good deal of land and few inhabitants, the government commonly began in the father:

For the father having, by the law of nature, the same power with every man else to punish as he thought fit any offences against that law, might thereby punish his transgressing children, even when they were men, and out of their pupilage; and they were very likely to submit to his punishment, and all join with him against the offender, in their turns, giving him thereby power to execute his sentence against any transgression, and so in effect make him the lawmaker and governor over all that remained in conjunction with his family. He was fittest to be trusted; paternal affection secured their property and interest under his care; and the custom of obeying him in their childhood made it easier to submit to him rather than to any other. If therefore they must have one to rule them, as government is hardly to be avoided amongst men that live together, who so likely to be the man as he that was their common father;

unless negligence, cruelty, or any other defect of mind or body, made him unfit for it ? (VIII, 105)

Many things could be said about this passage: we must confine our attention to the most important point. It should be urged that, though the picture Locke has painted is a very engaging one, and may even have corresponded to reality in a number of cases, its rhetorical force should not mislead us into believing that every single case of patriarchal rule arose and continued in that way. Locke leaves entirely out of account the operation of fear of the father or of other members of the family in leading individuals to allow the inauguration or continuation of patriarchal rule; and he also neglects the possibility of intrigues and cabals within the family; and of recognized but irksome subordination. The 'consent' to patriarchal rule may surely, in many a case, have only been 'consent' in some highly Pickwickian sense of the term.

As to the setting up of non-hereditary rulers, Locke writes in continuation:

But when either the father died, and left his next heir, for want of age, wisdom, courage, or any other qualities, less fit for rule, or where several families met and consented to continue together, there is not to be doubted but they used their natural freedom to set up him whom they judged the ablest and most likely to rule well over them. (VIII, 105)

Now there may well have been a considerable number of cases where new rulers were set up in such circumstances, but if by the vague and trapping word 'they' in the last clause Locke means (as he must for his theory) all the individuals in the one or in the several families, he gives us no good reason to accept his account as a universal one; and indeed, a little imagination may well lead us to suspect that there were a large number of cases in which things happened very differently.

Locke's tendency to assimilate unjustifiably all cases to one paradigm is exemplified again in his statement a little later in chapter VIII that 'it is plain that the reason that continued the form of government in a single person was not any regard or respect to paternal authority, since all petty monarchies, that is, almost all monarchies, near their original, have been commonly—at least upon occasion—elective' (VIII, 106).

Just because a family sometimes elected a non-hereditary ruler for the reason that he seemed fitter to rule, it would not at all follow that there were not other cases in which *hereditary* rulers, for one reason or another, were allowed to continue to rule, even though they were not the fittest persons to do so. Locke's logic is again at fault; and he certainly offers his readers nothing like a fair empirical survey of the cases.

A host of other observations could be made on Locke's account of the institution of 'lawful governments'; but there is only space to mention one more point in the account: Locke's doctrine that the institution implies majority rule. The passage in which Locke draws the implication is a very curious one:

When any number of men have so consented to make one community or government, they are thereby presently incorporated, and make one body politic, wherein the majority have a right to act and conclude the rest.

For when any number of men have, by the consent of every individual, made a community, they have thereby made that community one body, which is only by the will and determination of the majority. For that which acts any community being only the consent of the individuals of it, and it being necessary to that which is one body to move one way, it is necessary the body should move that way whither the greater force carries it, which is the consent of the majority; or else it is impossible it should act or continue one body, one community, which the consent of every individual that united into it agreed that it should; and so every one is bound by that consent to be concluded by the majority. (VIII, 95–6)

It is evident that Locke is here appealing to his readers by the use of a compelling *image*—the image of a body which cannot move except in the direction in which 'the greater force' carries it. The image is clearly drawn from dynamics, and would have had a special appeal in the age of Newton. Indeed, it might well have blinded readers to the very dubious character of the analogy between the consent of a majority and the dominant force which consists in the resolution of all forces acting on the parts of a body. The analogy is certainly dubious, to say the least; first, though not of primary importance, because in the case of a body in Newtonian dynamics forces act on it from outside, whereas the individual men each have their own desires and impulses; and secondly, and of capital importance, because, though every part of a uniform body (and it seems to be a uniform body that Locke is assuming) might be thought to count for as much as any other part, it is only by assuming that the desires and impulses of all the individual men are of equal power (let alone of equal merit) that the analogy could be made really plausible. Locke may indeed be making this assumption about individual men, but as we have seen, he has offered his readers no good reasons for accepting such an assumption. Here, then, Locke's rhetoric, not for the first time, reveals itself as a good deal stronger than his logic.

I must pass now, however, to Locke's treatment of conquest.

Locke was especially concerned to repudiate the idea that a political society could be founded on conquest. His general position is clearly stated at the start of chapter XVI:

Though governments can originally have no other rise than that before-mentioned, nor polities be founded on anything but the consent of the people, yet such has [*sic*] been the disorders ambition has filled the world with, that, in the noise of war, which makes so great a part of the history of mankind, this consent is little taken notice of; and therefore many have mistaken the force of arms for the consent of the people, and reckon conquest as one of the originals of government. But conquest is as far from setting up any government as demolishing a house is from building a new one in the place. (XVI, 175)

It is noteworthy that Locke not only repudiates the idea that conquest could found a political society without the consent of the conquered, but also implicitly rejects the view of Hobbes that conquest may result in the acquisition of sovereignty through the express or implied consent of the conquered to obey the victor in exchange for their life and liberty. Noteworthy also, however, is the rhetorical texture of the passage. Locke makes out as if in the bluster and noise and disorder of wars the still small voice of the people, expressing consent or dissent, had wrongfully remained unheard. The emotive force of the suggestion is considerable, but it affords no substantial argument against the harsh reality—that many states have in fact been founded on conquest. Again, the image of the demolition of a house is telling, but it provides no good reason for believing that a political society could not arise from conquest *followed by the decrees of the conqueror.* Locke equates conquest with demolition, and the image makes it seem as if the matter ended there; but it leaves out of account what the conqueror might subsequently decide without regard to the wishes of the conquered, or by forcing his will on them.

Locke's general position on conquest is as stated in the passage quoted; but he does go on to make a number of distinctions, some of which are worth brief consideration here. His main distinction is between cases of *just* wars and *unjust* wars. The conqueror in an *unjust* war could never, in his view, acquire any rights over the conquered. He compares such a conqueror to a robber or pirate, maintaining that 'the injury and the crime is equal, whether committed by the wearer of a crown or some petty villain' (xvi, 176). The injustice of an unjust war Locke defines in terms of 'unjustly invading another man's right' (xvi, 176). In the state of nature this would no doubt refer to forcible invasion of another man's liberty and right to reasonable consumption of the produce of the earth. In a civil society it would mean unlawful aggression or invasion of established rights by any other member or members of the society, or by any outside power. Locke no doubt assumes that his readers will know which cases would be unjust. But surely there are cases where it is far from clear? And even were we to assume that the cases were quite clear, would it really be plausible on careful scrutiny to suggest, for instance, that none of the conquests of the Romans, save those where the conquered freely consented to the new order, really founded political societies? Locke is clearly assuming that no political society worthy of the name could ever be founded unjustly; and no doubt he regarded this as self-evident: but many of us would regard it as far from self-evident. Moreover, whether self-evident or not, it is not an empirical generalization, and in making the assumption Locke therefore again shows himself to be a very different kind of thinker from the pure empiricist he is so often taken to be.

In any case, Locke's whole repudiation of conquest as a foundation for a political society is logically based on his conception of the rights of men first in the state of nature, and second, in an already existing political society. For without those rights a conquest could clearly never be *unjust*. Moreover, Locke's conception of the rights of men in a political society is ultimately based on his conception of the rights of men in the state of nature. If they had no rights in the state of nature they could, in his system, have no rights in a political society. The result is that Locke's repudiation of conquest as a foundation for a political society has no greater validity than his doctrine of the rights of men in the state of nature. Furthermore, since it is logically dependent upon it, and adds no further empirical element to it, all we have said about the empirical status of that doctrine applies to the repudiation of conquest also.

Typically, the reputedly mild Locke tries to push his case by the use of some fairly strong language. He compares an individual who uses force unjustly, i.e. to infringe the rights of others or of the community, not only to a robber or pirate but also to a 'savage ravenous beast' (xvi, 181), to a 'noxious creature' (xvi, 182), to 'the imperious wolf' and to 'Polyphemus' (xix, 228), and he also calls such a person 'the common enemy and pest of mankind' (xix, 230). Moreover, to counter the contention that in some cases of unjust conquest the conquered *consent* to the rule of the conqueror, Locke compares the conquered in such a case to a man who delivers his purse to a thief who demands it pointing a pistol at his victim's breast. These are vigorous expressions of Locke's indignation, but they should be recognized for what they are—mere rhetoric. They may have strengthened the actual effect of his book on readers then and since, but they were and are no valid substitute for solid argument or empirical generalization.

With regard to *lawful* or *just* wars, Locke's view is that a conqueror only obtains any rights over those who 'have actually assisted, concurred, or consented to that unjust force that is used against' the conqueror. Moreover, his rights only extend to their persons, not to their possessions, since, according to Locke, that would involve a loss to their innocent children, for, since 'nature willeth the preservation of all mankind as much as possible', the possessions in such a case belong to the children (xvi, 182). Here, then, once again, we find at the root of Locke's reasoning a far from empirical generalization, 'nature willeth the preservation of all mankind as much as is possible'. One wonders how Locke managed to discover that momentous proposition! But Locke's limitation of the conqueror's rights over the conquered to those who 'have actually assisted, concurred, or consented' to the unjust force, is also worth probing. The reason he gives in support is that the people *could not* have given their governors power to do anything unjust, since they never had such a power themselves. This is another instance of an illegitimate use of words, and it almost certainly springs from a confusion of concepts. The concepts in question are those of 'power' and 'right'. Locke states categorically that the people in the kind of case under consideration did not give their governors power to do an unjust thing. He does not, however, cite any examples. He says they did not give their governors that 'power', because they never had the 'power' themselves to give—that is, we might say, they *did not* give the power because they *could not* give it—never having had it. Locke has taken 'the high *priori* road'. But, to push the matter further: what does 'power' here mean? The term is evidently being used in a curious sense. No one could ever, in that sense, have the 'power' to do anything unjust. How fortunate everyone might be if this were the case! In the most normal sense of the term, 'power' can 'corrupt', but in this sense of Locke's such corruption would be impossible. Locke is simply using the term to mean 'right'. Why, then, it may be asked, did he not simply use the term 'right' instead? The answer, I believe, is that it would not have served his turn. Locke wished to argue that among the conquered all those innocent of injustice owed no allegiance to the conqueror. Now, to say that people gave no 'right' to their governors to be unjust, because they had no 'right' to be unjust themselves, would, indeed, not be saying anything about their innocence at all. To say that they gave no 'power' to their governors to be unjust, on the other hand, might well be a substantial assertion of their innocence, and would certainly have that appearance to readers understanding language in a normal way. As we have seen, however, Locke, in order to guarantee the truth of the statement, actually takes away its substance. For 'innocence', where guilt was logically impossible, was at best an illusory kind of innocence, and could hardly have earned any privileges for the individuals who possessed it.

Locke's discussion of the dissolution of governments, which occupies the last chapter of the Treatise (xix), is of vital importance in his general political theory. His primary concern is to show that a government can in certain circumstances, rightly be dissolved from within a political society. He distinguishes between two classes of case: (1) 'When the legislative is altered'; (2) 'When the legislative or the prince, either of them, act contrary to their trust.'

Let us pass in review Locke's position on each of these two classes of case.

Locke specifies four kinds of case within class (1): (a) When a single person or prince sets up his own will against the declarations of the legislative (by so doing he sets up a new legislative); (b) When the prince hinders the legislative from assembling when it ought or from acting freely for the purposes for which it was constituted; (c) When he alters the electors or methods of election without the consent and contrary to the common interest of the people; (d) When the prince or the legislative delivers the people into the subjection of a foreign power. Locke also adds another case, which he evidently considers to be closely connected with the other four, though possibly not to be actually an *example* of the legislative itself being altered; (e) When the executive abandons its function. In all these cases Locke maintains that the people have the right to set up a new legislative, and he also maintains that they have the right to try to *prevent* any of these occurrences from happening. Locke considers the 'essence and union' of a society to lie in its having one will, and holds that this is declared by the legislative. This is the basic principle. In all cases Locke presupposes that the legislative consists of a hereditary person with supreme executive power, an assembly of hereditary nobility, and an assembly of representatives chosen *pro tempore* by the people. Now what support does Locke offer for his evident preference for the will of the representative assembly in cases of conflict between it and the will of the prince or of the nobles? It seems clear that the only support he has to offer is that the representative assembly represents the will of the people more fully than do the other two elements in the legislative. But it is possible to raise the question whether a more fully representative body is always more likely than a prince or hereditary nobility to make laws which are for the real benefit of the society as a whole, considered not only in the widest but also in the deepest significance. This question Locke never squarely faces. He evidently assumes, possibly unconsciously, that superior intelligence, ability and benevolence would not characterize the prince or the nobles; and there seems no good reason to assent to such an assumption. Once again, in any case, Locke does not write as an empiricist.

As to the right of the people in these cases to set up a new legislative or even to try to prevent any of the specified events from taking place, Locke would support this by his principle that the will of the people can only be declared by a legislative appointed by them; and he would maintain that in all these cases the legislative is not really the same as that which they did appoint. This is the explanation of his using the rather strange word 'altered' which applies to some of the cases (e.g. to (b)) only in a very strained sense, if at all. Apart from the fishiness of subsuming all these cases under the idea of 'alteration', however, the fiction of the 'will of the people', which Locke took to be expressed in majority rule, is unsatisfactory. The term cannot connote the will of all the people, nor that which is concerned for the good of the people as a whole, including the prince and the nobles; for majority rule does not *necessarily*, or even always *actually*, correspond to either of these concepts. The majority of an assembly, as we know from experience, may not even represent the majority of the people. Locke's concept of the 'will of the people' is a metaphysical fiction which, whatever its advantages, is not the creation or tool of an empiricist.

Let us now consider Locke's discussion of the second class of cases: (2) 'When the legislative or the prince, either of them, act contrary to their trust.' Locke says that this happens whenever the legislative try to 'invade the property of the subject, and to make themselves or any part of the community masters or arbitrary disposers of the lives, liberties, or fortunes of the people'. It is made quite clear that Locke bases his conception of breach of trust in such cases on his doctrine of the formation of political societies; and it is therefore quite certain that, if that doctrine is shaky, then his conception of breach of trust is at least equally so. Locke's introduction of the notion of a trust was, however, quite an ingenious move. It circumvented the Hobbesian point, in favour of absolutism, that the sovereign was not bound by contractual obligations, since he was not a party to the social contract. Moreover, the term 'trust' itself has a powerful emotive force—a 'trust' sounds more sacred than a 'contract'. Again, though constructive trusts might have been a somewhat suspicious class of entity, quasi-contracts were probably more suspicious still. In any case an individual could, in a number of circumstances, readily be supposed to occupy a fiduciary position in respect of another individual, where it would be hard to establish the existence of even *quasi*-contractual obligations.

Among the most interesting parts of Locke's treatment of dissolution of government, however, is his attempt to show that his 'hypothesis' was not likely to result in frequent changes of government or to encourage rebellion (XIX, 223 f.). He argues that people are too conservative to want to change their governments frequently. This is, indeed, an empirical generalization, but it is of very doubtful validity. Locke only refers specifically to England, and he has to admit that in England there had been 'many revolutions'. He tries to attenuate the admission, however, by pointing out that, in the end, the constitution had always been kept as, or reverted to, that of King, Lords, and Commons; and also that even when a sovereign had been deprived of his crown, it had always remained in the same dynasty. Actually, of course, 'reversion' to the same constitution was not inconsistent with frequent rebellion, and though the general pattern of the constitution might have persisted, the relative power of its constituent elements had radically changed, and was to change still further. Moreover, in any case, England was far from being a fair sample on which to base sweeping generalizations.

As to the danger of frequent rebellion, Locke argues curiously.

His 'hypothesis' would not, he says, encourage it more than any other:

> For when the people are made miserable, and find themselves exposed to the ill-usage of arbitrary power, cry up their governors as much as you will for sons of Jupiter, let them be sacred and divine, descended, or authorized from heaven, give them out for whom or what you please, the same will happen. The people generally ill-treated, and contrary to right, will be ready upon any occasion to ease themselves of a burden that sits heavy upon them. (XIX, 224)

Was Locke disingenuous, or was he deceiving himself, when he wrote that passage? Did he really believe that his propaganda against absolute monarchy, and his advocacy of the right of revolution, would not make people any less likely to put up with serious monarchical abuses, or any more likely to cut off the heads of kings and hereditary nobles? It is hard to imagine that he was being as naïve as that. On the other hand, if he was not being naïve he was being something at least as bad.

Locke goes further, however, and tries to turn the tables on the absolutists by a linguistic trick. He maintains that the right of revolution (or, as he blandly puts it, 'this power in the people of providing for their safety anew by a new legislative') 'is the best force against rebellion' (XIX, 226). It is a startling and clever stroke and, within his system, Locke provides support for it. 'Rebellion', according to him, is opposition 'not to persons, but authority'. Authority derives from law, which was introduced by the people for the preservation of property, peace and unity. Those who do not keep the laws, therefore, 'do *rebellare*—that is, bring back again the state of war—and are properly rebels'; and, he adds, those most likely to do this are those who are in power. It is a masterpiece of rhetorical ingenuity; and it has a full meaning and justification within Locke's system. But the system itself is, as I hope I have shown, too shaky to stand; and therefore, except as art, the rhetoric must fall with it.

Those parts of the political system of the Second Treatise which we have examined contain very little empirical substance. Their deductive logic is sometimes sound, but in several instances close analysis reveals tautology or circularity. The rhetoric is often efficient and sometimes ingenious, but it cannot carry the conclusions which Locke wished to establish. Locke's value-judgements are another matter. They have not been the subject of the present essay. Whatever wisdom they may have had, however, the system in which they are embedded is too quaint and insubstantial to deserve the admiration it has received.

4

SHAFTESBURY'S HORSES OF INSTRUCTION

BY J. B. BROADBENT

The tigers of wrath are wiser than the horses of instruction. Blake.

Dryden accused Achitophel of being over-intellectual, devitalized and guilt-ridden, yet selfish too:

> Punish a body which he could not please,
> Bankrupt of life, yet prodigal of ease.

This is what the Romantics were to accuse the Augustans of at large: and their objection can be studied in Achitophel's grandson, Anthony Ashley Cooper, third earl of Shaftesbury (1671–1713). I add this note to Professor Willey's chapter in *The Eighteenth Century Background* (1940)[1] because, while Shaftesbury stands so obviously for what the Romantics were against, in some ways he approaches their position.

Shaftesbury qualifies as a type because his philosophy—though he was tutored by Locke—is amateur and his method literary. His *Characteristics of Men and Manners* (1711) is a sociable work. It comprises *A Letter Concerning Enthusiasm* (1708), *An Essay on Wit and Humour* (1709), *An Inquiry Concerning Virtue* (1699) and *The Moralists: a Philosophical Rhapsody, being a Recital of Certain Conversations on Natural and Moral Subjects*. Ethical, aesthetic and social opinions are mingled here; and Shaftesbury hardly distinguished them in his system of philosophy.

The *Inquiry* is conversational because conversation is sociable and fair. So is virtue. Shaftesbury refutes the self-interest that Hobbes imputed to man, on the ground that not even Hobbesian philosophers are really as selfish as their theory requires—

---

[1] See also R. L. Brett, *The Third Earl of Shaftesbury* (London, 1951); and Ernest L. Tuveson, 'The Importance of Shaftesbury', *Journal of English Literary History*, xx (1953). My references are to the *Characteristics*, ed. John M. Robertson, 2 vols. (London, 1900).

people are, in fact, nice to one. Far from being naturally
aggressive and selfish, men are inherently affectionate—if well-
bred. Good breeding produces social affection automatically,
in the same way as it produces good taste; social affection is
virtue; and virtue is a kind of good taste in behaviour.

Shaftesbury is a typical Augustan in recommending a wide
generality of kindly sentiment, a diffused affection similar to
the sense of beauty, or good taste. But in practice it will work
only within his own class, 'the Club' of 'gentlemen and
friends who know one another perfectly well . . . those to whom
a natural good genius, or the force of good education, has given
a sense of what is naturally graceful and becoming' (*Wit and
Humour*, I, 53, 89). Shaftesbury's morality, then, is the aesthetic
of an aristocracy. So it is for James Thomson, arranging the
philosophic moment:

> See on the hallowed hour that none intrude
> Save a few chosen friends, who sometimes deign
> To bless my humble roof, with sense refined,
> Learning digested well, exalted faith,
> Unstudied wit, and humour ever gay.
> Or from the Muses' hill will Pope descend,
> To raise the sacred hour, to bid it smile,
> And with the social spirit warm the heart.
>
> > (*Winter*, ll. 545–52)

Thomson is imitating the invocation at the start of Book III of
Paradise Lost. Milton had claimed the company of Homer and
Aeschylus, but he wrote as one alone. Wordsworth similarly
was to acknowledge the influence of men, and of The Friend
in particular, but still wrote alone. But Thomson and Shaftesbury need company. Shaftesbury's ethics aim at making a man
comfortable in the Club. Augustan poetry aims at much the
same: 'the very passion which inspires them [poets] is itself
the love of numbers, decency and proportion; and this too, not
in a narrow sense, or after a selfish way (for who of them composes for himself?), but in a friendly social view' (*Wit and
Humour*, I, 90).

The positives in the *Inquiry* are 'social affection' and 'natural
temper'. As in the *Essay on Man* (1734), they are assumed to
inhere in men living in an orderly creation. They are confirmed

by education if it be gentlemanly: "'Tis well for you, my friend, that in your education you have had little to do with the philosophy or philosophers of our days. A good poet and an honest historian may afford learning enough for a gentleman' (*Wit and Humour*, I, 81). Virtue may also be confirmed by looking at art, whether made by God or man:

This too is certain, that the admiration and love of order, harmony, and proportion, in whatever kind, is naturally improving to the temper, advantageous to social affection, and highly assistant to virtue, which is itself no other than the love of order and beauty in society. In the meanest subjects of the world, the appearance of order gains upon the mind and draws the affection towards it. But if the order of the world itself appears just and beautiful, the admiration and esteem of order must run higher, and the elegant passion or love of beauty, which is so advantageous to virtue, must be the more improved by its exercise in so ample and magnificent a subject. For 'tis impossible that such a divine order should be contemplated without ecstasy and rapture. . . . (*Inquiry*, I, 279)

When virtue is 'the love of order and beauty *in society*', it is easy to see how satire can be an art-form; and our current way of judging satire turns out to be historically right. We judge not so much what is described as the attitude with which it is described, the manner in which the satirist contemplates society. We find his poetic virtue in the 'love of order and beauty' implicit in his style and in his hatred of chaos and ugliness—which is just where Shaftesbury would find a man's moral virtue.

Shaftesbury's social affection, like Pope's, is prudential: we are nice to one another because it gives us pleasure, both directly (a warm feeling) and by reflexion (do as you would be done by). But for Blake, 'Prudence is a rich ugly old maid, courted by Incapacity'. That is to say, he saw the connexion between religion and the rise of capitalism; and he believed the restraint was due to impotence rather than to strength. Reading Shaftesbury, you feel Blake must be right. Shaftesbury presumes so easily to social affection that you cannot believe he ever really loved an individual at all.

It was not until the Romantic period, though, that people began to worry about emotional incapacity. Some of Pope's women are heartless, but that is a solecism, at worst a vice; for

6

Mill it is a tragic disease. He found 'analytic habits . . . favourable to prudence and clear-sightedness, but a perpetual worm at the root both of the passions and of the virtues; and, above all, [they] fearfully undermine all desires, and all pleasures' other than the merely physical.[1] Mill there puts prudence and virtue on opposite sides. Virtue and happiness depend (as they do for Shaftesbury) on 'sympathy with human beings, and the feelings which made the good of others, and especially of mankind on a large scale, the object of existence'. But, unlike Shaftesbury, Mill is not assured of feeling that way: 'to know that a feeling would make me happy if I had it, did not give me the feeling'. For practical purposes we can say that the essential difference between Augustans and Romantics is that Augustans are afraid of feeling too much and Romantics of feeling too little.

Shaftesbury arranges pleasures in a hierarchy; and from it we can see why Augustan poetry is relatively weak in particularity and strong in social sense:

the variety of Nature is such, as to distinguish everything she forms, by a peculiar original character. . . . But this effect the good poet and painter seek industriously to prevent. They hate minuteness, and are afraid of singularity; which would make their images, or characters, appear capricious and fantastical . . . the best artists are said to have been indefatigable in studying the best statues: as esteeming them a better rule than the perfectest human bodies could afford. (*Wit and Humour*, I, 95–6)

We can also see why Augustan poetry seems cut off from the body. For Shaftesbury, the pleasures of the body are inferior to those of the mind because mental pleasures are more constant and serene, less dependent on accident, than the physical. The highest pleasure of all is social, because the sense of being a member of the Club is 'more intense, clear, and undisturbed' than 'the satisfaction of thirst, hunger, and other ardent appetites' (*Virtue*, I, 295). Shaftesbury is most pleased by what produces 'a constant flowing series or train of mental enjoyments' (I, 294)—that is, by the Augustans' version of the Thames, calm, and full, but not to overflowing: 'Oh, could I flow like thee!'

---

[1] John Stuart Mill, *Autobiography* (London, 1873), ch. v.

Blake was to see that river as 'the chartered Thames', and
this part of Shaftesbury's philosophy shows us very clearly what
it was that Blake abhorred in the eighteenth-century tradition—
the dualism (mind superior to body); the diffused (social) but
selfish (prudential) benevolence; the aristocratic impassivity
('elegant passion', 'clear and undisturbed'); and the serene
inactive hedonistic mental virtuousness ('constant flowing . . .
train . . . of mental enjoyments').

> If moral virtue was Christianity,
> Christ's pretensions were all vanity . . .
> The vision of Christ that thou dost see
> Is my vision's greatest enemy:
> Thine has a great hook nose like thine [the clubman],
> Mine has a snub nose like to mine;
> Thine is the Friend of all Mankind;
> Mine speaks in parables to the blind.
>
> (*The Everlasting Gospel, c.* 1818)

Shaftesbury's other positive, 'natural temper' is halfway
between asceticism and Blake's exuberance. It is a good-
tempered temperance, a better-bred Aristotle. Here is the
theory behind the Augustans' satirizing of 'ruling passions'. It
also justifies the careful balance of their art, even the balance
of actual couplets and architraves:

Whoever is the least versed in this moral kind of architecture [*sc.*
natural social affection], will find the inward fabric so adjusted, and
the whole so nicely built, that the barely extending of a single
passion a little too far, or the continuance of it too long, is able to
bring irrecoverable ruin and misery. He will find this experienced
in the ordinary case of frenzy and distraction, when the mind,
dwelling too long upon one subject (whether prosperous or calamit-
ous) sinks under the weight of it, and proves what the necessity is
of a due balance and counterpoise in the affections. He will find
that in every different creature and distinct sex there is a different
and distinct order, set, or suit of passions, proportionable to the
different order of life, the different functions and capacities assigned
to each. . . . The inside work is fitted to the outward action and
performance. So that where habits or affections are dislodged, misplaced, or changed, where those belonging to one species are inter-
mixed with those belonging to another, there must of necessity be
confusion and disturbance within. (*Inquiry*, I, 314–15)

The soul is seen as a building, morality as architecture. Here is the moral and aesthetic engineering that Coleridge's organic form displaced. Shaftesbury warns that 'the barely extending of a single passion a little too far', like a misplaced girder, will bring ruin and misery; Blake says, 'The road of excess leads to the palace of wisdom'. Shaftesbury sees virtue and happiness in 'a due balance and counterpoise in the affections'; Blake sees famine—'Bring out number, weight and measure in a year of dearth.' Shaftesbury fears 'dwelling too long upon one subject', and the mixing of one species of affection with another; the Romantics specialize in spondaic emphasis, hungover lines, particularity, and synaesthesia:

> Some snow-light cadences
> Melting to silence. . . .
>
> On gold sand impearl'd
> With lily shells, and pebbles milky-white . . .
>
> Old rusted anchors, helmets, breast-plates large
> Of gone sea-warriors . . .
> . . . gold vase emboss'd. . . .
>
> (Keats, *Endymion*)

The Romantics were to see the passions in terms of nature or myth, unified under one supernal energy such as Love or Imagination; Shaftesbury sees them as a pack of cards, each with 'a different and distinct order, set or suit'.

This passage also reveals the Augustan terror of 'confusion and disturbance within'. One of the reasons why virtue is social is that only social affection can alleviate the horror of Hobbesian loneliness:

How thorough and deep must be that melancholy which, being once moved, has nothing soft or pleasing from the side of friendship to allay or divert it? Wherever such a creature turns himself, whichever way he cast his eye, everything around must appear ghastly and horrid; everything hostile and, as it were, bent against a private and single being, who is thus divided from everything, and at defiance and war with the rest of Nature.

'Tis thus, at last, that a mind becomes a wilderness, where all is laid waste, everything fair and goodly removed, and nothing extant beside what is savage and deformed. Now if banishment from one's country, removal to a foreign place, or anything which looks like solitude or desertion, be so heavy to endure, what must it be to feel this inward banishment, this real estrangement from human commerce, and to be after this manner in a desert, and in the horridest of solitudes even when in the midst of society ? What must it be to live in this disagreement with everything, this irreconcilableness and opposition to the order and government of the universe ? (*Inquiry*, I, 335–6)

One can list the characteristic Augustanisms. Friendship is 'soft and pleasing', like Thomson's women in 'Summer', not like the stormy *femmes fatales* of Fuseli, *Lamia* and *Alastor*. Loneliness is defined in terms which at that date clustered round the very word 'romantic'—'ghastly and horrid . . . wilderness . . . desert . . . horridest'.

It was Shaftesbury's fear of 'unaccommodated man', of feeling himself 'a private and single being', which made it impossible for the Augustans to write tragedy. To be in society, on the other hand, is to engage in 'commerce'. It is a usual turn of phrase, but it is a sign of the relationship between mercantilist economics and prudential ethics. Thomson's poetry is full of commerce; Dryden likens trade to the circulation of the blood; and Shaftesbury, in the *Essay on Wit*, demands free trade in conversation. This is the economics of the periodical and the comedy of manners.

In the same essay, Shaftesbury refers to the secret idols of the mind, and recommends that they be exposed to raillery: 'They may perhaps be monsters, and not divinities . . . which are kept thus choicely in some dark corner of our minds' (I, 44). He was afraid of the monsters. To be alone is to be in the midst of what is 'savage and deformed'—that is, to be the nasty brutish man of Hobbes's state of nature. But the monsters were there, under the tempered surface. So Shaftesbury allowed them controlled exercise. In the *Inquiry*, the contemplation of order produces virtue; in *The Moralists* the contemplation of sublimity discharges dangerous enthusiasm. The enthusiast, Theocles, is not of course alone: his ironic friend Philocles looks after him:

. . . I am resolved not to go on till you have promised to pull me by the sleeve when I grow extravagant.
Be it so, said I; you have my promise.

But how if instead of rising in my transports I should grow flat and tiresome; what lyre or instrument would you employ to raise me?

The danger, I told him, could hardly be supposed to lie on this hand. His vein was a plentiful one, and his enthusiasm in no likelihood of failing him. His subject, too, as well as his numbers, would bear him out. And with the advantage of the rural scene around us, his numbered prose, I thought, supplied the room of the best pastoral song. (II, 115)

Indeed, Theocles' raptures go straight into the blank verse of *The Seasons*:

How oblique and faintly looks the sun on yonder climates, far removed from him! How tedious are the winters there! How deep the horrors of the night, and how uncomfortable even the light of day! The freezing winds employ their fiercest breath, yet are not spent with blowing. The sea, which elsewhere is scarce confined within its limits, lies here immured in walls of crystal. The snow covers the hills, and almost fills the lowest valleys. How wide and deep it lies, incumbent over the plains, hiding the sluggish rivers, the shrubs and trees, the dens of beasts and mansions of distressed and feeble men! (*Moralists*, II, 119)

> Obliquely looks the sun on yonder climes,
> How far removed from his sustaining beam!
> Where tedious the half-year winter runs,
> How deep the horrors of the endless night,
> And e'en the light of day how faint and chill!
> The freezing winds employ their fiercest breath,
> The sea immured in walls of crystal lies.
> Incumbent on the plains the snow lies deep,
> Hiding the sluggish rivers, shrubs, and trees,
> The dens of beasts and man's distressful lodge.

At length, the patient recovers—and it is his recovery, not the scenery or the pastoral prose, that Philocles is concerned with:

Here he paused a while and began to cast about his eyes, which before seemed fixed. He looked more calmly, with an open countenance and free air, by which, and other tokens, I could easily find we were come to an end of our descriptions, and that whether I would or no, Theocles was now resolved to take his leave of the sublime, the morning being spent and the forenoon by this time well advanced. (II, 124)

There are faint reminiscences of *Lear* and *The Tempest* in this passage; they show that the more enthusiastic and moralizing kinds of natural description in the eighteenth century were an alternative to the tragedy they could not write.

Shaftesbury's view of romanticism was still 'horrid' and 'Gothick': 'all those who are deep in this romantic way are looked upon, you know, as a people either plainly out of their wits, or overrun with melancholy and enthusiasm. We always endeavour to recall them from these solitary places' (*Moralists*, II, 125–6). But Shaftesbury was already thinking of romanticism as a kind of mad Platonic wisdom, superior to the apparently rational.

Theocles is *in love with* 'the rude rocks, the mossy caverns, the irregular unwrought grottoes and broken falls of waters, with all the horrid graces of the wilderness itself'. It is a Platonic love, an aspiration towards the Form of Beauty.

Shaftesbury is careful about enthusiasm, though. Theocles has 'nothing of that savage air of the vulgar enthusiastic kind' (*Moralists*, II, 24): 'All was serene, soft, and harmonious.' When that is the case, enthusiasm may be genuinely religious— Theocles is deliberately named. Shaftesbury says that it is possible for natural beauty to produce virtuous action only when one believes that the beauty is of God; and then '"tis impossible that such a divine order should be contemplated without ecstasy and rapture', as well as virtue (*Inquiry*, I, 279). It would be unhelpful to distinguish such a view too carefully from Wordsworth's, and it is certainly Thomson's. But the response to nature must be 'serene, soft, and harmonious'. As Hume says, beauties 'dispose to tranquillity; and produce an agreeable melancholy, which, of all dispositions of the mind, is the best suited to love and friendship'.[1] Similarly Thomson:

> He comes! he comes! in every breeze the Power
> Of Philosophic Melancholy comes!
> His near approach the sudden-starting tear,
> The glowing cheek, the mild dejected air,
> The softened feature, and the beating heart,
> Pierced deep with many a virtuous pang, declare.
> O'er all the soul his sacred influence breathes;

[1] 'Of the Delicacy of Taste and Passion' in *Essays* (Edinburgh, 1742).

Inflames imagination; through the breast
Infuses every tenderness; and far
Beyond dim earth exalts the swelling thought.

(*Autumn*, ll. 1004 f.)

It is in such a lugubrious enthusiasm, here brought on by con-
templating autumn, that social love expands into world-wide
benevolence:

devotion raised
To rapture, and divine astonishment;
The love of nature unconfined, and, chief,
Of human race. . . .
The sympathies of love and friendship dear;
With all the social offspring of the heart.

This is a recollection of Milton—

Relations dear, and all the Charities
Of Father, Son, and Brother.[1]

Yet it is not the influence of Milton's verse that counts in the
eighteenth century, but the pervasion of Shaftesburian philosophy. However sympathetic and benevolent the Romantics
were, they cut themselves off from the eighteenth century by
insisting on particularity of sentiment. This meant giving up
the calm of Shaftesbury and Thomson: for individuated affection must be as packed and rugged as, compared with Augustan
couplets, Romantic verse is; and it will be tragic.

Crabbe saw the nemesis of Shaftesbury's calm social affection
in his clergyman:

Though mild benevolence our priest possessed,
'Twas but by wishes or by words expressed:
Circles in water, as they wider flow,
The less conspicuous in their progress grow;
And when at last they touch upon the shore,
Distinction ceases, and they're viewed no more.
His love, like that last circle, all embraced,
But with effect that never could be traced.[2]

Crabbe could not see the way out. Blake saw it in a reversal
of Shaftesbury. Shaftesbury is *tame*. Defining natural temper,

[1] *Paradise Lost*, IV, 756–7.
[2] *The Borough* (London, 1810), Letter III.

he says that if a domestic animal becomes, 'contrary to his natural constitution, fierce and savage, we instantly remark the breach of temper, and own the creature to be unnatural and corrupt'; but if it later becomes tame again we say it is now 'good and natural' (I, 249). That is, man is analogous to a tame animal. It is against this that Blake's tiger snarls—not to destroy, but to admit ferocity as an element in human nature; without it, language and sympathy are like circles in water.

5

BERKELEY AND THE STYLE OF DIALOGUE

BY DONALD DAVIE

Soon after *The Principles of Human Knowledge* (1710) had appeared, the still youthful Berkeley (1685–1753) wrote to his friend Percival expressing his disappointment that Samuel Clarke had refused to be drawn into discussion of that work:

> That an ingenious and candid person (as I take him to be) should declare I am in an error, and at the same time, out of modesty, refuse to shew me where it lies, is something unaccountable. . . . I never expected that a gentleman otherwise so well employed should think it worth his while to enter into a dispute with me concerning any notions of mine. But being it was so clear to him that I went on false principles, I hoped he would vouchsafe in a line or two to point them out to me that so I may more closely review and examine them.[1]

We do not always understand what a writer of Berkeley's period meant when he says of some one, as Berkeley says here of Clarke, that he is a candid person. For 'candid' and 'candour' are words of much narrower meaning now than in the eighteenth century. The idea of candour was then relevant in fields of experience where the modern reader, used only to the attenuated notion current today, is not at home with it. And this breadth of meaning seems a characteristic of terms which are crucial to the thinking of man in any given time. It is an interesting question whether the breadth of meaning attached to a word is a consequence of that word's standing for something important, or whether it is not the cause of that importance.

At any rate there is little doubt that an understanding of what 'candour' meant for the Augustans is a key to much that seems odd or elusive in their thought; and this is as true of

---

[1] Benjamin Rand, *Berkeley and Percival* (Cambridge, 1914), p. 94.

Berkeley as of the rest. To understand Berkeley's idea of candour leads, by way of profitable surmise, into that part of his thought to which he never gave systematic expression—it leads us to his ethics.

No one claimed more for candour than Blifil in *Tom Jones* (1749), when he was arguing that nowhere in Scripture did 'charity' mean giving things away:

'The Christian religion', he said, 'was instituted for much nobler purposes than to enforce a lesson which many heathen philosophers had taught us long before, and which, though it might perhaps be called a moral virtue, savoured but little of that sublime, Christianlike disposition—that vast elevation of thought, in purity approaching to angelic perfection—to be attained, expressed, and felt only by grace. Those,' he said, 'came nearer to the Scripture meaning who understood by it candour, or the forming of a benevolent opinion of our brethren, and passing a favourable judgment on their actions; a virtue much higher and more extensive in its nature than a pitiful distribution of alms, which, though we would never so much prejudice or even ruin our families, could never reach many; whereas charity, in the other and truer sense, might be extended to all mankind.' (II, v)

Berkeley never makes candour mean as much as this. Nor indeed does Fielding; for Blifil of course is a scoundrel, and here he is damning himself out of his own mouth—the passage is heavily ironical. Yet there would be no point to the irony if claims as large as this were not indeed made for candour in the society which Fielding wrote for. And sure enough, the biblical scholar Edward Harwood, reading in the First Epistle to the Corinthians how charity (which he called 'benevolence') 'beareth all things, believeth all things, hopeth all things, endureth all things', translated this by: 'It throws a vail of candour over all things. . . .'[1] When Berkeley gave Clarke the credit of thinking him a candid person, he was expecting him to do more than just speak his mind. And similarly Dryden was asking a great deal of the speakers in his conversationpiece *Of Dramatick Poesie* (1668), when, in his prefatory epistle

---

[1] *A Liberal Translation of the New Testament*, 2 vols. (London, 1768); quoted by James Sutherland, 'Some Aspects of Eighteenth-Century Prose', in *Essays on the Eighteenth Century Presented to David Nichol Smith* (Oxford, 1945), p. 109.

to Buckhurst, he promised that they would dispute 'like gentle-men, with candour and civility', and not 'like pedants, with violence of words'.

When Berkeley calls Clarke 'candid' he does not mean only what we should mean, that Clarke speaks his mind without fear or favour. He means that and he means more—that Clarke is so concerned to arrive at the truth that he lets nothing stand in the way of helping others to do so. He means even (in the manner of Captain Blifil) that Clarke is prepared to give any man the benefit of the doubt and think him an earnest seeker after truth rather than a whipper-snapper eager to make his mark by dint of outrageous novelty. For I do not think there is anything ironical in Berkeley's letter. If it raises a smile, it is at Berkeley's simplicity, in thinking Clarke could set him right without entering into a dispute with him. And yet perhaps this is not simplicity at all. It takes two to make a quarrel, and perhaps Berkeley was confident of restraining himself even if he found Clarke's objections of no weight. That would be candid; and Berkeley took candour seriously.

Candour, in any sense, is a virtue that shows itself most plainly in intelligent conversation. And unless we realize the presence of candour in the background, we are at a loss to explain the importance that the Augustans gave to 'polite con-versation'. Herbert Davis has pointed out how important this was to Swift.[1] How can we explain that the value of good con-versation is one of the few positive values to be found in the writings of that supremely negative and destructive mind? It seems to argue in Swift a disastrous lack of proportion—unless we remember that for the Augustans conversation was the chief opportunity for the exercise of candour, and that candour was to them a virtue sometimes hard to distinguish from charity itself.

Herbert Davis appropriately ends his essay with a tribute to Berkeley for introducing 'qualities of good conversation' into philosophical writing, as Addison had introduced them into the *Spectator*'s 'Saturday sermons'. This is nothing new, of

---

[1] Herbert Davis, 'The Conversation of the Augustans', in *The Seventeenth Century: Studies in the History of English Thought and Literature from Bacon to Pope, by Richard Foster Jones and Others Writing in his Honor* (Palo Alto, 1951).

course; it is a tribute often paid to Berkeley in particular as to the Augustans in general. But if we take 'candour' into account, then the tribute has an added force. Besides, the qualities of good conversation have an obvious and immediate relevance to a literary form that Berkeley made his own—the dialogue or the conversation-piece. Professor Davis makes his point about Berkeley by quoting from his preface to *Three Dialogues between Hylas and Philonous* (1713). It would have been more elaborate, but also more telling, to illustrate 'qualities of good conversation' from the dialogues themselves, from something that is, however trimmed and elevated, at bottom conversation exemplified.

Berkeley, as a writer of dialogues, has been compared with Plato and Leopardi, and contrasted with Landor, because 'his dialogues embody ideas instead of exhibiting characters'[1]; and the same biographers have endorsed Sir Herbert Read's judgement that in Berkeley's hands, as in Plato's, 'the dialogue has been purged of its dramatic nature. . . .' But this turns out to rest upon a quibble, for 'if the essential of drama is the portrayal of action, then the essential of dialogue is the creative activity of ideas—ideas in action, one might say'. Indeed one might; and if one did, then, on Sir Herbert's definition of drama, the dialogues of Berkeley would be as dramatic as Landor's.

Berkeley's later dialogues in *Alciphron* (1732) are very different from the *Three Dialogues*, and part of the difference is that there is more 'character' in *Alciphron*. But this does not mean that *Alciphron* is more dramatic. The essential difference between the two works is stated conclusively by Hone and Rossi: 'In the *Dialogues between Hylas and Philonous*, both interlocutors are well disposed persons and lovers of truth; and if there is conflict, it is the conflict of the slow intelligence and the lively one.'[2] In other words, Hylas is as wrong as Alciphron is; but he is candid, where Alciphron is not. It is in the *Three Dialogues* that we see candour, as it were, in action.

Before showing this by example, it will be as well to recall what a large undertaking it was. There is a famous work of

[1] J. M. Hone and M. M. Rossi, *Bishop Berkeley* (London, 1931), pp. 79–80.
[2] Hone and Rossi, *loc. cit.*

literature where the same thing is attempted without much success—and this is Dryden's *Of Dramatick Poesie*. E. M. W. Tillyard once made the point: 'Dryden did not reach perfection of tone at once. There is something rather set and formal about the way he treats Ancients, French, and English in the *Essay of Dramatic Poesy*, as if he were arguing for freedom and impartiality, not taking them serenely for granted.'[1] And Tillyard goes on to show that in later critical writings Dryden deals freely and impartially, with less fuss than in the Essay. But it is surely necessary to take into account, in this connexion, the form of the Essay. By throwing it into the form of a conversation-piece Dryden is trying to fulfil the promise he makes in his prefatory Epistle, to show that controversial subjects can be handled 'with candour and civility' in the society for which he writes. As I have argued elsewhere,[2] and as Tillyard obliquely confirms, Dryden was unsuccessful in this. Who or what is to blame for this, whether Dryden in particular or Restoration society at large, is something we cannot determine; if the society failed its poet, the poet too was at fault in mistaking the temper of his society, and looking to it for models which it could not provide. And if we think that Berkeley in the *Three Dialogues* succeeded where Dryden failed, we should be chary of taking the credit for this from Berkeley himself so as to argue that society under Queen Anne was more civilized than it had been under Charles II.

Oddly enough (yet is it so strange?) the words 'candour' and 'candid' do not appear in the *Three Dialogues*. At times 'ingenuous' is used where it seems that 'candid' is meant:

Phil. . . . But, can you think it no more than a philosophical paradox, to say that *real sounds are never heard*, and that the idea of them is obtained by some other sense? And is there nothing in this contrary to nature and the truth of things?

Hyl. To deal ingenuously, I do not like it. And, after the concessions already made, I had as well grant that sounds too have no real being without the mind.

---

[1] E. M. W. Tillyard, 'A Note on Dryden's Criticism', in *The Seventeenth Century*, *op. cit.*, pp. 334–5.

[2] 'Dramatic Poetry: Dryden's Conversation Piece', *Cambridge Journal*, v (1952), pp. 553–61.

Phil. And I hope you will make no difficulty to acknowledge the same of *colours.*

Hyl. Pardon me: the case of colours is very different. . . .[1]

There is a sense in which this is thoroughly theatrical dialogue. As we read we put ourselves into the posture of the speakers, of Hylas in particular; what Hylas says is said in a certain, though always changing tone, which is conveyed to us. 'To deal ingenuously . . .' which is rueful; 'I had as well grant . . .' (reluctant, without being grudging); 'Pardon me: . . .' (suddenly alert and assured). We even supply appropriate gestures, an unwilling rub of the nose or the jaw, the biting of a lip. Hylas is by far the more engaging and attractive of the speakers; and this is because of his candour. Repeatedly embarrassed, always pressed hard, he admits the points made against him and is never near to losing his temper, or to escaping through a deliberate quibble. And Philonous too, though he is less sympathetic because always on the winning side, is fair, and more than fair, to his opponent, letting him take his time, letting the argument circle and eddy and return upon itself.

In short, the dialogues are, among other things, an example of good manners and disinterested behaviour. Yet (this is the real achievement) the effect is not obtained by emasculating controversy. In Dryden the speakers are so careful, each of the other's *amour propre*, that they dare not push their disagreements to a point. Not so Hylas and Philonous; neither of them need pull his punches:

Hyl. You may draw as many absurd consequences as you please, and endeavour to perplex the plainest things; but you shall never persuade me out of my senses. I clearly understand my own meaning.

Phil. I wish you would make me understand it too. . . . (p. 393)

Hyl. I know not how to maintain it; and yet I am loath to give up *extension*, I see so many odd consequences following upon such a concession.

Phil. Odd, say you? After the concessions already made, I hope you will stick at nothing for its oddness. (p. 400)

[1] 'The First Dialogue between Hylas and Philonous'; *Works*, ed. A. C. Fraser, vol. 1 (Oxford, 1901), p. 392. Future references to Berkeley are to this edition.

Phil. How many shapes is your Matter to take ? Or, how often must it be proved not to exist, before you are content to part with it ? (p. 433)

There is excellent comedy here, not only the drama of a slow mind and a quick one, but the chastening comedy of how the human mind will twist and turn (unconsciously) to evade unpalatable conclusions, to cling to what is familiar. The candour comes with the realization by both speakers that the game has rules which the mind (however unwillingly) must observe. Hence the frequent excursions into logic:

Hyl. You have indeed clearly satisfied me—either that there is no difficulty at bottom in this point; or, if there be, that it makes equally against both opinions.

Phil. But that which makes equally against two contradictory opinions can be a proof against neither.

Hyl. I acknowledge it. (pp. 468–9)

Hyl. I own myself entirely satisfied for the present in all respects. But, what security can I have that I shall still continue the same full assent to your opinion, and that no unthought-of objection or difficulty will occur hereafter ?

Phil. Pray, Hylas, do you in other cases, when a point is once evidently proved, withhold your consent on account of objections or difficulties it may be liable to ? . . . (p. 481)

Disputation observes a discipline, an order that the shifty mind continually seeks to evade. To admit the discipline and bring one's own mind into line—this is one aspect of candour.

The sharpest sarcasm is permissible; and at least once the sarcasm becomes something more elaborate, a Swiftian irony:

Phil. But is it not strange the whole world should be thus imposed on, and so foolish as to believe their senses ? And yet I know not how it is, but men eat, and drink, and sleep, and perform all the offices of life, as comfortably and conveniently as if they really knew the things they are conversant about.

Hyl. They do so : but you know ordinary practice does not require a nicety of speculative knowledge. Hence the vulgar retain their mistakes, and for all that make a shift to bustle through the affairs of life. But philosophers know better things.

Phil. You mean, they *know* that they *know nothing*.

Hyl. That is the very top and perfection of human knowledge. (p. 443)

On the other hand, a plain admission of confusion deserves a helping hand:

> *Phil.* ... This point I thought had been already determined.
> *Hyl.* I own it was; but you will pardon me if I seem a little embarrassed: I know not how to quit my old notions.
> *Phil.* To help you out, do but consider. ... (p. 401)

Undoubtedly the disputants, and Hylas in particular, are idealized. We can hardly believe that such self-control and compliance was to be found in the conversations of Augustan London, even in the conclave of the Scriblerus Club. On the other hand, we cannot think that the dialogue had no basis in reality; apart from anything else, the vivid movement of authentic speech is there to prove the contrary—'But the novelty, Philonous, the novelty ! . . .', '. . . That is not fair, Philonous . . .'. 'Things ! You may pretend what you please; . . .' In other words, if the conversation is idealized, it is the most useful kind of idealization, near enough to reality to incite men to realise it. And to that extent, the *Three Dialogues* can be thought of as implicitly a treatise in ethics, an exemplification of the virtue of candour.

Ellen Douglass Leyburn, in a valuable essay, has found a striking similarity between what we take to be the ethical views of Berkeley and what we know to be the views of Dr Johnson: 'It is impossible to read *Alciphron* with Johnson in mind without finding there sentiments that almost make us forget relations of time and space and think them echoes of *Rasselas* and *The Rambler*.'[1] However it may displease the Irish admirers of Berkeley, for whom his Irishness is his greatest virtue, I think this comparison is valid and striking. There *is* a similarity between Berkeley's outlook on human conduct and Johnson's. And it seems plain, when we consider Johnson's mostly disparaging comments on Berkeley, that he had probably read none of Berkeley's works, and almost certainly not *Alciphron*. On the other hand, there is one matter on which they plainly part company. There can be little doubt that Berkeley enjoyed disputation, but hardly in the sense in which it was 'Johnson's

---

[1] 'Bishop Berkeley, Metaphysician as Moralist', in *The Age of Johnson: Essays Presented to Chauncey Brewster Tinker* (New Haven, 1949), p. 328.

7

favourite sport'.[1] And he would surely have disapproved of a
conversationalist who disputed to gain the victory at any cost.
Berkeley, I fear, would have found Johnson a not wholly candid
man.

Berkeley's achievement in the *Three Dialogues* can be valued at
the rate it deserves if that work is compared with Shaftesbury's
The Moralists: a Philosophical Rhapsody. Despite the ominous
sound of 'rhapsody' in the title, *The Moralists* is in fact one of
the best things in the *Characteristics* (1711). And—what is more
surprising—it is, at its best, genuinely expansive and enlivening,
precisely in its rhapsodical passages, where Shaftesbury's
optimism builds on a Spinozistic basis with most enthusiasm.
Though on scrutiny seldom genuinely eloquent, yet these
passages are placed in the economy of the whole—and so,
to some extent, 'placed' in another sense, so as to quell our
disquiets about them—by rising out of dialogue. For this is
Shaftesbury's own experiment in the manner of dialogue which
elsewhere in the *Characteristics* he has recommended as a philosophical and literary form, a recommendation which he here
repeats. As the sub-title indicates ('a Recital of Certain Conversations on Natural and Moral Subjects'), *The Moralists* is
itself a dialogue, though one in which the conversations are
for the most part reported instead of being *oratio recta*. As such,
it is by no means unattractive. Particularly interesting is the
presence of two shadowy figures, named only as an old gentleman and his younger companion, who—though they say very
little—considerably enliven the scene for as long as they are
present. There is for instance an admirably contrived situation
in which Philocles, one of the principal speakers, explicitly
speaks as *advocatus diaboli*, on the side of irreligion. This is a
convention which Philocles' antagonist, Theocles, can agree to
for the sake of discussion, whereas the old gentleman, continually blurring convention into reality, supposes that Philocles
must be truly an infidel. This is a far subtler effect than any
contrived by Dryden or, to take another instance, by Mandeville; it looks forward to the use of false-naïveté by one of the

---

[1] 'Bishop Berkeley, Metaphysician as Moralist', in *The Age of Johnson: Essays
Presented to Chauncey Brewster Tinker* (New Haven, 1949), p. 321.

speakers in Berkeley's second set of conversation-pieces, his *Alciphron* of 1732. Yet as a whole *The Moralists* is best compared with *Three Dialogues*, Berkeley's earlier attempt at the dialogue form. For Shaftesbury had made it very plain that in his view the Dialogue could give only an idealized image of the common pursuit of truth, since in actuality candour and civility were so wholly lacking in the society of his and Berkeley's time. In *The Moralists* he wrote:

You know too, that in this academic philosophy I am to present you with, there is a certain way of questioning and doubting, which no way suits the genius of our age. Men love to take party instantly. They cannot bear being kept in suspense. The examination torments them. They want to be rid of it upon the easiest terms. 'Tis as if men fancied themselves drowning whenever they dare trust to the current of reason. They seem hurrying away they know not whither, and are ready to catch the first twig. There they choose afterwards to hang, though ever so insecurely, rather than trust their strength to bear them above water. He who has got hold of an hypothesis, how slight soever, is satisfied. He can presently answer every objection, and, with a few terms of art, give an account of everything without trouble.[1]

The image of the current of reason and the twigs of hypothesis is as good as anything Shaftesbury ever achieved. Hardly less admirable is his comparison of these modish thinkers with geometers ('They are all Archimedeses in their way, and can make a world upon easier terms than he offered to move one'). And the same assurance informs his next paragraph:

In short, there are good reasons for our being thus superficial, and consequently thus dogmatical in philosophy. We are too lazy and effeminate, and withal a little too cowardly, to dare doubt. The decisive way best becomes our manners. It suits as well with our vices as with our superstition. Whichever we are fond of is secured by it. If in favour of religion we have espoused an hypothesis on which our faith, we think, depends, we are superstitiously careful not to be loosened in it. If, by means of our ill morals, we are broken with religion, 'tis the same case still: we are as much afraid of doubting. We must be sure to say, 'It cannot be', and ''tis demonstrable. For otherwise who knows? And not to know is to yield!'

[1] Shaftesbury, *Characteristics*, ed. John M. Robertson, vol. II (London, 1900), pp. 7–8. Future references to Shaftesbury are to this edition.

The attack is rounded off with a backward glance at earlier periods 'when not only horsemanship and military arts had their public places of exercise, but philosophy too had its wrestlers in repute' (we may think, justly enough, of the first page of Sidney's *Apologie*), and the point is made that in such an age as Shaftesbury's the philosophical dialogue could be written only by swimming against the current, by taking few hints from the actual conduct of conversations and disputations and many more from the sense of how they should have been conducted. Accordingly, Shaftesbury's Theocles and Philocles are idealized further than Berkeley's Hylas and Philonous— further, and also less skilfully, less persuasively, for Theocles is pompous and priggish.

Shaftesbury in these passages argues that the difficulty of writing the philosophical dialogue in the early eighteenth century derived from a deep-seated intellectual insecurity in English society of that time—not the sort of thing we are invited to think about the English Augustan Age. Elsewhere, however, and chiefly in the *Advice to an Author*, Shaftesbury finds not psychological but social and historical reasons. *Advice to an Author* is conducted so diffusely, and contains so much of the affected writing which Shaftesbury called 'rhapsody', that it is hard and inconvenient to recognize that what Shaftesbury says about the dialogue is interesting good sense. Though Berkeley was right in *Alciphron* to ridicule the affectation with which Shaftesbury elaborated his idea to begin with, yet his ideal of 'mirror-writing', of the author in dialogue with himself, could be said to contain all Romanticism in embryo. Moreover, Shaftesbury quite justly extends the idea of dialogue to comprehend, as the true end of the noblest literature, the dramatic and the objective. It is thus that he can link together Plato and Homer. And however strangely it may consort with his proto-Romanticism, and still more with the self-regarding affectation of his own style, Shaftesbury's preference for this objective and dramatic manner to the direct wooing of the reader by the writer is a lesson worth learning in an age like the present, when 'tone' in the writer counts perhaps for too much.

As Shaftesbury develops his theme, the dialogue of a writer

with himself becomes the dialogue of a writer with his subject, with 'Nature'. It is still opposed to the dialogue of writer with reader:

An author who writes in his own person has the advantage of being who or what he pleases. He is no certain man, nor has any certain or genuine character; but suits himself on every occasion to the fancy of his reader, whom, as the fashion is nowadays, he constantly caresses and cajoles. All turns upon their two persons. And as in an amour or commerce of love-letters, so here the author has the privilege of talking eternally of himself, dressing and sprucing himself up, whilst he is making diligent court, and working upon the humour of the party to whom he addresses. This is the coquetry of a modern author, whose epistles dedicatory, prefaces, and addresses to the reader are so many affected graces, designed to draw the attention from the subject towards himself, and make it be generally observed, not so much what he says, as what he appears, or is, and what figure he already makes, or hopes to make, in the fashionable world. (I, 131)

Shaftesbury's conspicuous refusal to write dedications and prefaces suggests that his other affectations, like his wayward-ness, his launchings into rhapsody and jerkings out of it, are clumsily devised to make the effect dramatic and objective—as a soliloquy overheard, not a speech addressed to the reader, who on the contrary by these means is continually wrong-footed. The dialogue, Shaftesbury goes on to say, excludes all this 'pretty amour and intercourse of caresses between the author and reader':

. . . here the author is annihilated, and the reader, being no way applied to, stands for nobody. The self-interesting parties both vanish at once. The scene presents itself as by chance and un-designed. You are not only left to judge coolly and with indifference of the sense delivered, but of the character, genius, elocution, and manner of the persons who deliver it. . . . (I, 132)

Then, after copying the abruptness and lack of ceremony with which at the start of a Platonic dialogue the poor philosopher accosts a powerful dignitary, Shaftesbury observes:

Whilst I am copying this . . . I see a thousand ridicules arising from the manner, the circumstances and action itself, compared with modern breeding and civility.—Let us therefore mend the matter if possible, and introduce the same philosopher, addressing himself in a more obsequious manner, to *his Grace, his Excellency,* or *his Honour,* without failing in the least tittle of the ceremonial. . . . Consider how many bows and simpering faces! how many preludes, excuses, compliments!—Now put compliments, put ceremony into a dialogue, and see what will be the effect!

This is the plain dilemma against that ancient manner of writing which we can neither well imitate nor translate, whatever pleasure or profit we may find in reading those originals. (1, 133–4)

Though Shaftesbury here seems to mistake the symptoms for the disease, he puts his finger on that feature of his society which had distorted Dryden's conversation-piece. And his conclusion—'Our commerce and manner of conversation, which we think the politest imaginable, is such, it seems, as we ourselves cannot endure to see represented to the life'—brings it home to us why Dryden had to fail, and why Berkeley, in order to succeed with *Three Dialogues,* had to depart from verisimilitude.

If Shaftesbury had lived to read *Alciphron,* he would hardly have admitted that these were dialogues in which 'the self-interesting parties both vanish at once'. For no one will contradict R. L. Brett when he protests that in *Alciphron* Berkeley is unfair to Shaftesbury.[1] He is unfair to Shaftesbury, and to Mandeville too, chiefly because he uses the *argumentum ad hominem.* These arguments are not philosophical; but then, *Alciphron,* though it contains much philosophy, is a work of Christian apologetics, to which the precept which Berkeley observes, 'By their fruits shall ye know them', is appropriate though 'unfair'. And of course there is nothing unfair about his procedures if they are seen as procedures of literature. Berkeley plays the game according to the rules not of the philosopher but the dramatist; and his arguments are no less telling for being embodied in character and situation. For *Alciphron* is an altogether different affair from the *Three Dialogues.* True, the free-thinkers' arguments are rebutted time and again with strict logic; and if this is philosophical, it is also (as

[1] R. L. Brett, *The Third Earl of Shaftesbury: a Study in Eighteenth-Century Literary Theory* (London, 1951), p. 170.

Berkeley does it) intensely dramatic. But over and above this there is the point, made by drama in a less abstracted sense, that both the free-thinkers, Lysicles and Alciphron, are un- candid. Berkeley says, in effect, 'These arguments can be demolished, as I show; but, in any case, what sort of person uses them ?' And he shows that too. Lysicles is a young puppy; but Alciphron is a more formidable disputant, and a subtler portrait. In many ways he is a model of good breeding; and yet there is something wrong about him. It is hard to define this, except in the way that Berkeley hints at. Briefly, he lacks candour. He is more concerned to score a point than to get at the truth; that is one way of putting it. In any situation he prefers to think the worst; that is another.

Probably a score of readers will enjoy *Alciphron* for every one who will enjoy *Three Dialogues*. For we like in prose what we would not approve in conversation, hard-hitting vigour and vividness, sarcasm, bitterness, eloquence, the full battery of rhetorical resources. What we respond to most immediately in Dryden, for instance, are the places where he is fighting hard and remorselessly, arguing with his back to the wall or else in complete confidence about the rightness of his case, and using all the tricks of argument, candid or uncandid, to make his point. In his preface to *The State of Innocence* (1677), for example, Dryden's apology for poetic licence, however right and timely, is conducted by way of blank assertions, ridicule, sarcasm, all the tricks of the rhetorical trade. We would not tolerate it in conversation; it is *not* candid, it is *not* civil—and if it were we should like it much less. Very often, when candour and civility are achieved in literature, they bore us. To the perfect good manners of Addison, or of Berkeley in the *Three Dialogues*, we prefer the relatively uncandid Swift, or Johnson as Boswell reports him, or the Berkeley of *Alciphron*. It is tempt- ing to say that we are right to feel thus; that what we look for in literature, and rightly, is to have our emotions played upon by the rhetorician, not our reasons satisfied by fair and scrupulous argument. But of course, even if literature is a province of rhetoric, not essentially of logic or dialectic, there is abundant ancient precedent for not absolving the rhetorician, however brilliant and resourceful he may be, from responsibility for the truth of what he is saying as well as for the effect of it upon his readers. And when we read works which are eloquent and candid as well, such as the *Three Dialogues* or Johnson's review of Soame Jenyns,[1] it is hard not to think that the literary pleasure these afford, to just the degree that it is less immediate and vivid, is more elevated, more substantial, and more refined.

If it is true, as Aubrey Williams has argued in his book on *The Dunciad*,[2] that Pope's lifetime saw a crisis in the status and understanding of the traditional discipline of rhetoric, and in particular a general agreement not to require of the orator truth in his matter as well as winningness in his manner, then the development of the dialogue in this period might seem a particular instance of this crisis. After the relative failure of Dryden's conversation-piece had shown that English society did not after all provide models for candour and civility, two courses were open—to use the dialogue as an image of what should be, or of what was. Berkeley followed the first course in *Three Dialogues*; the second in *Alciphron*.

The second course was perhaps easier than the first. But it required great capacities. If *Three Dialogues* should be compared with Shaftesbury, *Alciphron* earns our respect when it is set beside Mandeville's dialogues in Part 2 (1729) of *The Fable of the Bees*. Mandeville there grumbles:

When partial Men have a mind to demolish an Adversary, and triumph over him with little Expence, it has long been a frequent Practice to attack him with Dialogues, in which the Champion, who is to lose the Battel, appears at the very beginning of the Engagement, to be the Victim, that is to be sacrifised, and seldom makes a better Figure, than Cocks on Shrove-Tuesday, that receive Blows, but return none, and are visibly set up on purpose to be knock'd down.[3]

This is what Mandeville accuses Berkeley of in *A Letter to Dion* (1732), where he maintains that Lysicles and Alciphron are mere men of straw. Mandeville has a very skilful and amusing parody of Berkeley's style in *Alciphron*. But the very fact that

[1] *The Literary Magazine*, XIII–XV (1757), reprinted in *Johnson: Prose and Poetry*, ed. Mona Wilson (London, 1950), pp. 351–74.

[2] Aubrey L. Williams, *Pope's Dunciad: a Study of its Meaning* (London, 1955).

[3] Bernard Mandeville, *The Fable of the Bees*, ed. F. B. Kaye, vol. II (Oxford, 1924), p. 8.

he misses or ignores the sharp distinction between Berkeley's
Alciphron and his Lysicles is enough to make Mandeville's
criticism wide of the mark. And in Mandeville's own dialogues
his Antonio is far more of a man of straw, far less credible, than
either Lysicles and Alciphron. Mandeville seems to have
grown tired of the dialogue form as he proceeded with it, for
the character of Antonio as sketched in the preface, together
with some rather clumsy attempts at verisimilitude in the first
two dialogues, suggest that Mandeville meant to make of him
what Berkeley made of Alciphron, a study in lack of candour;
but if that was his original intention he soon wearied of it.
Moreover, the colloquialism which the dialogue demands of
Mandeville in the second part of *The Fable of the Bees* precludes
the eloquence and fanciful imagery which quite often in Part 1
(1714) dignify his rough and hearty style. Mandeville's
Antonio, after a little perfunctory huffing and puffing in the
first two dialogues, takes the instructions of Cleomenes even
more meekly than Hylas in his dealings with Philonous; and
yet, at the same time, at the beginning of each dialogue there
is an attempt at tedious and irrelevant verisimilitude which is
no more than stage-business. Mandeville's dialogues fall between the two stools of the consciously idealized candour of
Hylas and Philonous, and the far more lifelike behaviour of the
four speakers in *Alciphron.*

The point of comparing Berkeley with distinguished contemporaries like Mandeville and Shaftesbury is to make it clear
that Berkeley, when he wrote his conversation-piece, did not
share in a general bounty vouchsafed to all cultivated and
energetic men. It was not Augustan society nor 'the spirit of
the age' which wrote *Three Dialogues* and *Alciphron.* James
Sutherland, in an essay to which all students of eighteenth-
century prose are indebted,[1] quotes an admirable passage from
Colley Cibber's autobiography, and then observes:

Nobody taught Cibber to write like this; he learnt to write this
admirable prose by having first learnt to write dialogue for his
comedies, and he learnt to write that partly by imitating Congreve,

---

[1] James Sutherland, 'Some Aspects of Eighteenth-Century Prose', *op. cit.*, p. 101.

and partly by listening to the conversation of gentlemen, and so in time acquiring it, or something like it, himself.

As a verdict on Cibber this may well be just. Yet the principle is a dangerous one. The Augustans themselves did not have such a high opinion of the conversation of the gentlemen of their day, as Swift's *Tatler* essay 'On Corruptions of Style' may remind us. In the Augustan age as in any other, to deal candidly with oneself, still more to give a lively and edifying image of candour in others—these achievements were won by the lonely and exacting labour of distinguished individuals who were not carried by the current of their times but strove against it.

6

JOSEPH BUTLER

BY GEORGE WATSON

A mass of mistaken history stands between our age and the achievement of Bishop Butler (1692–1752), though even the errors of the handbooks cannot disguise its scale and its depth. We have been taught to think of the reigns of George I and George II, in which he wrote and preached, as the age of the popular divine, and mistake 'popular' for 'popularizing', as if all the great preachers of the age were doing for the sermon what Addison and Steele had done for periodical literature. Some of them were; but Butler's prose, in its own way, is at least as complex as Carlyle's or Ruskin's, and yet his sermons at the Rolls Chapel in London, first published in 1726, seem to have been celebrated. The absurd legend that the early eighteenth century was an 'Age of Reason', too, an illusion recorded even in the titles of some modern textbooks, is still far from dead, even though no major writer of the period—neither Swift, nor Addison, nor Pope—can convincingly be quoted in support of it; so that when we read in Butler that reason is 'the only faculty we have wherewith to judge concerning any thing, even Revelation itself',[1] we are inclined to think he is uttering a commonplace of his times rather than what emerges, in its context, as a deliberate and radical paradox. And lastly, he is still chiefly famous for having destroyed the vogue for natural religion in favour of a reaction to the religion of Revelation; whereas, in fact, Butler believed in natural religion—though he also believed that Revelation was historically necessary, the heathen world being what it was. Nature and Revelation, in his view, complement each other; both being from God, they 'coincide with each other, and together make up one scheme of Providence' (II, iii, 5).

---

[1] *The Analogy of Religion* (London, 1736), II, iii, 3.

These are historical illusions. They are blatant, and because they are blatant they are easily exposed. What is far more difficult is to reveal the subtle web of literary precedent which animates the prose of a writer as seemingly 'unliterary' as Butler—a writer who rarely quotes, who fails even to name his adversaries in debate, who seems indifferent or hostile to the usual demands of literary elegance, and who cannot be shown to have had literary acquaintances or to belong to a school. He poses a special difficulty to the critic; but even if his case were ordinary, we might not be much better off, for our ignorance of English philosophical prose during the Enlighten-ment is nearly total, and a strange neglect on the part of literary critics for the Empiricist achievement leaves almost everything to be done. So much we may venture for a start: the eighteenth century lacked an assured literary form for philosophical prose, and felt the lack: the careers of Shaftesbury, Berkeley, and Hume, in their different ways, all illustrate the fact. The Platonic dialogue did not, as a form, give the universal assurance it had once seemed to promise, though Shaftesbury tried it on one occasion, and though Berkeley triumphed in it more than once. Hume is the last great imitator of the form in English. The independent philosophical paper of the length we should now expect of an article was little practised before the nineteenth century. The treatise, such as Hobbes's *Leviathan* (1651) or Locke's *Essay* (1690), was in decay: it bulked all too much like a leviathan for the Augustan reader, who had been pampered by works designed to be read at a sitting, and the indifference with which Hume's first work, the *Treatise* of 1739–40, was greeted probably reflects the impatience of Georgian England for works of such scale, just as Hume's decision to re-shape it into the more manageable *Enquiries* represents a considered attempt to placate the taste of his age. The record, in fact, is a chaotic one; a chaos challenging, perhaps, to a philosopher as accomplished in his literary interests as Berkeley, but confusing for most English philosophers in its absence of any certain model.

And yet, throughout this chaos, the sermon survived, and the place of a preacher like Butler was in this sense uniquely advantageous. He possessed in the sermon a form already evolved by two generations of Restoration preachers. No one,

indeed, could accuse Butler's early prose of a lack of organization and formality. Inheriting an established literary form, he
successfully invested it with all the dignity and seriousness of
pure logical inquiry. And in his treatise *The Analogy of Religion*
(1736) which appeared ten years after his collection of *Fifteen
Sermons Preached at the Rolls Chapel*, he showed how coherently
he could organize an argument over a wider area. 'The proper
force of the following Treatise', he announced proudly in his
introductory Advertisement to the *Analogy*, 'lies in the whole
general analogy considered together'; but even in the *Fifteen
Sermons*, delivered during his tenure of the Rolls Chapel in
London (1719–26), it is already clear that Butler possesses a
larger intelligence than the composition of a half-hour sermon
requires. The individual sermons are themselves often like
little treatises, or parts of treatises; for in some cases the inter-
connexions are clearly pre-designed and fully conscious. The
first three sermons of the fifteen, for example, all entitled 'Upon
Human Nature', form a continuous argument in support of
'the supremacy of conscience' over human behaviour, and, at
the end of the third sermon, the argument of all three is
summarized:

Reasonable self-love and conscience are the chief or superior principles in the nature of man: because an action may be suitable to
this nature, though all other principles be violated; but becomes
unsuitable, *if either of those are*. Conscience and self-love, if we
understand our true happiness, always lead us in the same way.
Duty and interest are perfectly coincident. . . .[1] [my italics]

Nearly everything that matters in Butler's prose is represented
in this passage from his third sermon: a coolness of tone, utterly
without a hint of triumph, in which a conclusion at once
momentous and paradoxical is unfolded; an honest sobriety, a
sheer determination to get a right answer; and an utter lack of
fastidiousness, for all the care for the truth he is ready to take—
a lack which defeats charm, grammar, and even, at times,
lucidity itself. The expression 'if either of those are', considered
as an abbreviation for 'if either self-love or conscience is
violated', is evidence of a disregard for his congregation in the

[1] *Fifteen Sermons*, ed. W. R. Matthews (London, 1949), p. 68. Future references
to the sermons are to this edition.

Rolls Chapel which could be paralleled again and again. The Establishment that promoted him to the bishopric of Bristol in 1738 (shortly after the *Analogy* appeared), to the deanship of St Paul's two years later, and finally, in 1750, to the rich see of Durham itself, was rewarding a devoted apologist for Christianity in an age of fashionable scepticism; but it deserves credit, too, for honouring one who held himself so unfashionably aloof from the usual self-indulgences of the great, and from the easy success of a pungent style.

Difficulty, indeed, is the first mark of Butler's English, and there have been plenty of readers since to complain about the difficulty of reading him. It is the theme-song of Butler criticism. Walter Bagehot, in one of his earliest essays, complained of the sheer hard tack in the sermons and the *Analogy*. 'No one', he objected with memorable irrelevance, 'could tell from his writings that the universe was beautiful.' There are, he complained, no literary allusions, and no literary interest either: 'Butler, so far from having the pleasures of eloquence, had not even the comfort of perspicuity. . . . In some places the mode of statement is even stupid; it seems selected to occasion a difficulty.'[1] This poses a question that needs to be raised and answered too: is Butler difficult, when he is so, out of stylistic ineptness, out of perversity, out of necessity, or out of a considered theory of language ? The battery of complaint, even from his admirers, is too loud to be ignored; even Gladstone, who admiringly edited the entire works of Butler in the last two years of his life, found his prose positively Greek in its concentration: 'Who is there among them', he asked rhetorically of the ancient philosophers, 'unless perhaps Aristotle, the tissue of whose thought is closer?' (I, x). And a modern admirer has renewed the charge of obscurity in a more damaging form: 'His method is piecemeal and untidy—he omits, he repeats himself, he contradicts himself.'[2]

To understand the language of Butler's sermons, and the startling novelty of their 'difficulty', we must first inquire into origins. Butler inherited a Restoration tradition of simplicity

[1] Bagehot, *Prospective Review* (October 1854), reprinted in his *Literary Studies*, ed. R. H. Hutton (London, 1879–95), vol. III, pp. 115, 125–6.
[2] D. M. MacKinnon, *A Study in Ethical Theory* (London, 1957), p. 180.

in the style of preaching, a tradition which associated enthusiasm, richness of syntax and imagery, and ingenious theology, with Puritanism and regicide—though, of course, before the Civil War such impeccable royalists as Jeremy Taylor had used the rich old style as well. Scott hits off the contrast with great accuracy in *Old Mortality* (1816), a novel describing the defeat of the Scottish Covenanters in the sixteen-seventies, where Henry Morton, the moderate hero, confronts the Presbyterian enthusiast Balfour of Burley:

'And can you doubt of our principles,' answered Burley, 'since we have stated them to be the reformation both of church and state, the rebuilding of the decayed sanctuary, the gathering of the dispersed saints, and the destruction of the man of sin?'

'I will own frankly, Mr Balfour,' replied Morton, 'much of this sort of language which, I observe, is so powerful with others, is entirely lost on me. . . . I revere the Scriptures as deeply as you or any Christian can do. I look into them with humble hope of extracting a rule of conduct and a law of salvation. But I expect to find this by an examination of their general tenor, and of the spirit which they uniformly breathe, and not by wresting particular passages from their context, or by the application of Scriptural phrases to circumstances and events with which they have often very slender relation.' (ch. xxi)

Morton the moderate speaks for the world that Butler inherited. In 1670 the extreme Royalist Samuel Parker, later Bishop of Oxford, had demanded an Act of Parliament 'to abridge preachers the use of fulsome and lushious metaphors', which he evidently associated with Puritanism and enthusiasm: 'For were men obliged to speak sense as well as truth, all the swelling mysteries of fanaticism would immediately sink into flat and empty nonsense.'[1] This is Sprat's prescription for science carried over into the world of theology. The demand was supported and widely practised, the *Directions Concerning the Matter and Stile of Sermons* (1671) by James Arderne, later Dean of Chester, being one practical handbook of great influence. Arderne opposes 'nice speculations' of theology in favour of a simple three-part structure for a sermon. He recommends a

---

[1] *A Discourse of Ecclesiastical Politie* (London, 1670); cf. R. F. Jones, 'The Attack on Pulpit Eloquence in the Restoration', *Journal of English and Germanic Philology*, xxx (1931), reprinted in Jones *et al.*, *The Seventeenth Century* (Palo Alto, 1951).

proposition, conveniently defined by a text from Scripture; a confirmation; and an inference. Metaphors, in his view, should be admitted only cautiously, provided always that 'they stand not too thick together', and he utterly condemns extended analogies or 'larger allegories'. In one large matter, indeed, he condemns all imagery: 'you must never compare God to any thing.' It is no wonder that Herbert's *Temple* remained out of print throughout the eighteenth century, except in the adaptations of the enthusiast John Wesley.

By Butler's time, as he himself makes clear, this exercise in simplification was already complete, and sermons were generally expected to be simple both in structure and in language. 'The title of *Sermons* gives some right to expect what is plain and of easy comprehension', he wrote in the 1729 preface, in apology for the obscurity of his own; and his purpose, a radical one in the pulpit of the seventeen-twenties, was to sacrifice simplicity, where necessary, in favour of the complexity of large debate. His literary achievement is to invest the popular sermon with the dignity of a firm logical structure. His *forte* is argument, and especially the development of argument over a wide area—a cause in which he is ready to sacrifice 'easy comprehension' in favour of amplitude. In the *Durham Charge*, years later, he complained of the difficulty of refuting fashionable Deism by mere talk: 'how impossible it must be, in a cursory conversation, to unite all this into one argument, and represent it as it ought.' In him the three-part recipe of the Restoration sermons is only cursorily observed, an initial scriptural quotation being used as a point of entry into a complex argument rather than a point of reference, and it is rarely a point of return. What Arderne, half a century before, had called 'inference' occupies almost the whole of a Butler sermon. And yet the complexity is uniquely that of argumentation, never of diction; the style, with almost total consistency, retains the stamp of that aversion to imagery, and especially to massed or extended imagery, that is characteristic of neoclassical prose. The famous analogy between our moral nature and a watch, in the 1729 preface to the *Sermons*, is not (as I shall try to show), an exception but rather a confirmation of Butler's Augustan bareness of style. Hobbes's vast analogy between the State and a human, or monstrous, body called a 'leviathan' he roundly condemns in the first sermon, and for the reason, pregnant enough for one who was to enhance his fame by an *Analogy* of his own, that such 'likenesses' are only worth what, at first sight, they seem to be worth, and cannot be pushed anywhere: 'as there is scarce any ground for a comparison between society and the mere material body, this without the mind being a dead inactive thing; much less can the comparison be carried to any length' (p. 32). So much for playing games with metaphors—games which, in Hobbes's hands, must have seemed to Butler cynical and even sinister. From now on the language will not be trusted an inch. 'Language is, in its very nature, inadequate, ambiguous, liable to infinite abuse', he warns us austerely in the *Analogy* (II, iii, 15). There are good reasons, in fact, for supposing that the right answer to Bagehot's challenge that his language 'seems selected to occasion a difficulty' would be Butler's own answer: moral philosophy is difficult enough anyhow; and language makes it more difficult still. Difficulty, in this view, is inevitable, in the nature of the task attempted, even a warrant of truth.

Of course Butler's claim to interest easily survives his difficulty, however charmlessly, by weight of the sheer significance of what he has to say about the complexity of human motives. He is the most analytical student of humanity in an age which accepted Man, in Pope's words, as 'the proper study of mankind', and his refutation of Hobbes's cynical theory of human motives has the finality of great logical demonstration. Butler's moral philosophy is not at the centre of my subject here, but a summary will serve at this point to bring my analysis of Butler's language to bear more fully upon the language itself.[1] Man,

---

[1] For a detailed analysis involving a distinction between the *Sermons* and the *Analogy*, see Thomas H. McPherson, 'The Development of Bishop Butler's Ethics', *Philosophy*, xxiii–xxiv (1948–9), with replies by D. D. Raphael and A. R. White, xxiv (1949) and xxvii (1952): 'In the earlier work', McPherson argues, 'Butler held that we come to know right as a result of a process of careful reasoning; in the later [i.e. in the *Analogy*], he holds that we know right immediately, by "intuitions".' The change, which can easily be overstated, was perhaps caused by Butler's advancing consciousness of man's ignorance, and it is certainly true that the *Analogy* is more theological than the earlier *Sermons*; paradoxically, they contain little that is specifically religious.

for Butler, is not a simple essence of selfish instincts, either actively at war with his fellows or bent upon getting the best possible contract out of them in the interest of his own survival. He is a complex of properties which Butler marshals into a hierarchy of four. First, there are the instincts which Hobbes had mistakenly placed at the centre of his system, such 'particular passions or affections' as hunger, anger, or sexual desire. Second, there is self-love, the faculty by which we coolly seek our own happiness. Thirdly, there is that faculty celebrated by Shaftesbury as benevolence—one which, like self-love, is calculating. And finally there is conscience, which is supreme over the others, as benevolence and self-love are supreme over our raw passions. This supremacy is not, for Butler, an aspiration or an injunction. It is simply a matter of fact, of the very constitution of man, as he insists in the preface he added to the second edition (1729) of the sermons. Conscience, he argues there,

seems in great measure overlooked by many, who are by no means the worst sort of men. It is thought sufficient to abstain from gross wickedness, and to be humane and kind to such as happen to come in their way. Whereas in reality the very constitution of our nature requires that we bring our whole conduct before this superior faculty; wait its determination; enforce upon ourselves its authority. . . . (pp. 14–15)

Here lies the basic fault, he goes on, of Shaftesbury's *Inquiry Concerning Virtue* (1699). It is not that Shaftesbury was wrong in calling virtue the happiness of man; but that such benevolism omits particular cases (such as the sceptic who does not admit it), whereas Butler's does not. Not all men are Shaftesburian benevolists: but all, whether they know it or not, have a conscience.

It is in terms of such a hierarchy of human propensities that Butler conducts his quiet, remorseless overthrow of Hobbesian ethics. To argue that men behave, in all circumstances, according to 'self-love', or their own estimate of their own interest, as Hobbes had assumed, is for Butler simply false. 'Men daily, hourly sacrifice the greatest known interest to fancy, inquisitiveness, love or hatred, any vagrant inclination.' If only men *did* coolly calculate their own interests: 'The thing to be lamented is, not that men have so great regard to their own good or interest in the present world, for they have not enough' (p. 24). The silly notion, still accepted by Socialists, Fascists and many Christians, that human actions are to be condemned to the extent that they are selfish, was exploded by Butler more than two centuries ago. His frank assertion that selfishness may be a virtue, utterly convincing as it is in these terms, still comes oddly from a Christian apologist; and certainly Butler adds a new dimension to Christian ethics at this point, without quite shattering the structure of the whole. It is a dimension that enlarges Christianity, beneficently, in the direction that it took in the following century towards utilitarianism, self-help, and Benjamin Jowett. And so does Butler's insistence that happiness is more like an escalator than a pedestal: 'Whoever will in the least attend to the thing', he tells us in his last sermon, 'will see that it is the gaining, not the having of it, which is the entertainment of the mind.'

All this deliberately tends to schematize Butler's case to a point which falsifies, if not his meaning, at least the tone and atmosphere in which he writes. The last charge to be made against him would be over-simplification, and his hierarchy of moral faculties is offered with a full realization of the difficulties of their interrelations. Matthew Arnold was badly off the track when, in one of the first and worst of his sonnets, 'Written in Butler's Sermons', he objected:

> Affections, Instincts, Principles, and Powers,
> Impulse and Reason, Freedom and Control—
> So men, unravelling God's harmonious whole,
> Rend in a thousand shreds this life of ours. . . .

Butler is not denying that man is a harmonious whole which is God-given. He is simply concerned, in order to explain what the whole is, to study its parts; and, in his analogy of the watch in the 1729 preface, he is clear that the parts in isolation would not merit study at all, but only in 'the respects and relations which they have to each other'. He is, in fact, quite unusually aware—and far more aware than Hobbes, or Locke, or Shaftesbury—of the essential complexity of our moral life. The very obscurity of his language, against which Bagehot and Gladstone protested, is open to the defence he makes for it in the preface to the *Sermons*—the complexity of the subject itself:

> It must be acknowledged that some of the following discourses are very abstruse and difficult; or, if you please, obscure; but I must take leave to add, that those alone are judges *whether or no, and how far*, this is a fault, who are judges *whether or no, and how far*, it might have been avoided. . . . (p. 5. My italics.)

This is the solution to the problem of Butler's obscurity which we owe it to him, at least tentatively, to accept. And yet the lumbering ineptness of the syntax of this sentence illustrates another and more banal kind of difficulty: the double conjunction 'whether or no, and how far', heavily repeated, has a certain painstaking precision, but it is the laborious precision of a twentieth-century Government White Paper rather than of Butler's own world of Augustan Oxford and London; and it is far from being the worst he has to offer. Consider for example, this sentence from the first sermon:

> It may be added, that as persons without any conviction from reason of the desirableness of life, would yet of course preserve it merely from the appetite of hunger; so by acting merely from regard (suppose) to reputation, without any consideration of the good of others, men often contribute to public good. (pp. 37–8)

Can anyone doubt that this kind of obscurity in Butler is avoidable? It surely calls for nothing more nor less than simple sub-editing, like this:

> Just as some people, without any reason to desire life, eat simply because they are hungry; so do those who seek only reputation often contribute to the public good

—a version half as long as the original, and twice as lucid.

The notion of difficulty-as-a-warrant-of-truth, then, which Butler is inclined to fall back on as a defence of his own obscurity, is not applicable at every point: sometimes he is just long-winded and careless. It is odd to watch Butler's consciousness of language, which is always a consciousness of the difficulties of language, perverting itself into a lame excuse for avoidable obscurity. But this is a small matter compared with his intuitions about language itself, which are pre-eminent, in that age, for their sophistication and force.

Butler openly rejects the Baconian doctrine, largely accepted by the Royal Society in the Restoration and for years after, that words are mere 'counters', each word ideally representing a single object, notion or relationship. Locke's notion of language is at bottom no better than this: he is forever talking as if lucidity is the same thing as simplicity; he cannot see that the truth might be so complex, or so approximate, that only a complex or approximate statement might be accurate. One of his favourite tactics in a debate with an adversary is to impute obscurity: 'Matters of such consequence as this is should be in plain words', he objures Filmer in the *Two Treatises of Government* (1690) (I, 108). The general consciousness of language in the age of Pope was surely less hamfisted than this, or Pope's poetry could not have had the vogue that it had, and that poetry must surely have helped to make it so; but it would still be difficult to parallel, as early as the seventeen-twenties, an account of language as subtle as Butler's insistence that words define themselves contextually, if at all: they are multiples of meaning, so to say, rather than single counters.[1] His three-fold account of the word 'nature', for example, in the second sermon, begins by recognizing that usage allows more than one sense: there is one sense in which to act well is to act according to our nature; another in which *all* our actions are according to nature. 'Did ever any one act otherwise than as he pleased ?' (p. 51). Butler's insistence here is arrestingly modern. It is not to seek one, or even several, definitions of 'nature', but to explain what men actually mean when they use such a word in the varying circumstances of moral discussion, and how these variations are the key to such discussion:

the real question of this discourse is not concerning the meaning of words, any otherwise than as the explanation of them may be needful to make out and explain the assertion *that every man is naturally a law to himself*, that *every one may find within himself the rule of right, and obligations to follow it;* . . . nature is considered in different views, and the word used in different senses. . . . (p. 51)

---

[1] Butler's view is well in advance of Dr Johnson's, thirty years later, for Johnson in the *Dictionary* (London, 1755) was content to follow Locke, and does not seem to have noticed Butler at all. Cf. Rackstraw Downes, 'Johnson's Theory of Language', *Review of English Literature*, III (1962).

The plain fact of the inequality of words according to the varying purposes to which they are put is simply accepted here, uncomplainingly, and the absence of complaint and the respect for existing usage is striking after the reformist zeal of seventeenth-century philosophers. Butler sceptically takes English as it was left to him, bare, serviceable, but still full of knotty ambiguities; and then uses it, ambiguities and all, to reveal the errors to which it has regrettably but unavoidably given rise. The teasing out of the word 'nature' in the second sermon is not a unique example of Butler's novel acceptance of the essential complexity of language. In the eleventh sermon, for instance, 'Upon the Love of our Neighbour', Butler claims that in one significant sense the passions of man are as 'disinterested' as benevolence itself, since 'they both equally desire of and delight in the esteem of another'. Another moralist might have gone on to demand a new definition of 'interested' and 'disinterested', but Butler's concern is quite different:

The most intelligible way of speaking of it seems to be this: that self-love, and the actions done in consequence of it . . . are interested; that particular affections towards external objects, and the actions done in consequence of those affections, are not so. But every one is at liberty to use words as he pleases. All that is here insisted upon is, that ambition, revenge, benevolence, all particular passions whatever, and the actions they produce, are equally interested or disinterested. (p. 174)

And yet, for all his wise acceptance of English as it was, and his subtlety in disentangling its confusions, Butler is not concerned with a total theory of language. 'Every one is at liberty to use words as he pleases'—this might be the most sensible place in the world for a student of language to start. But it is not, for Butler, the start of a linguistic inquiry at all: it is a point of entry into certain confusions which concern him as a Christian moralist. He is occasionally playful with a dead or dying metaphor, but it is only play, and he surely does not ascribe to traditional language any particular profundity. Our possession of the faculty to perceive causality, he observes in the *Analogy*, and so to predict for ourselves joy or suffering, might by the sceptic be ascribed to the general course of nature. True. This is the very thing which I am observing. It is to be ascribed to the general course of nature: i.e. not surely to the words or ideas, *course of nature*; but to him who appointed it, and put things into it: or to a course of operation, from its uniformity or constancy, called natural; and which necessarily implies an operating agent. (I, ii, 4)

This is culpably sophisticated, and unfortunately characteristic of a good deal of the *Analogy*, a work of partisan apologetics so inferior to the *Sermons* as to make one wonder at its celebrity. And that celebrity is truly staggering. It seems to have been accepted in its own age as an unanswerable refutation of scepticism, was never in fact answered except by one or two insignificant pamphlets, preserved the young James Mill (according to his son) from unbelief 'for some considerable time',[1] and as late as the eighteen-twenties marked for the young John Henry Newman 'an era' in his religious opinions.[2] Leslie Stephen exposed the book with finality when he protested that 'the whole appearance of plausibility is obtained by [Butler's] stating facts in his own language, and then assuming that, because they can be so stated, the theory embodied in the language is confirmed'. The attempt to reanimate a half-forgotten sense of the word 'course' as being necessarily uniform or constant, and therefore subject to a divine agent, is quite unlike the cool, hard argumentative line of the best of the sermons. It is slightly cheap. It is also unsustained. Butler, in spite of his title, is not interested in analogy as a rhetorical device. The term simply means for him what it had meant to Locke, the 'grounds of probability' we derive from matters 'not within the scrutiny of the human sense',[3] such as the faculty of the magnet to draw iron; and the 'analogy of religion' is the body of argument by which Christian doctrines, too, can be shown to be probable. Locke, in the same passage from his fourth book, had hinted at the use to which his theory of analogy or probability could be put in Christian apologetics by reference to the old doctrine of a Great Chain of Being, and it is this hint and this doctrine that Butler enlarges:

[1] John Stuart Mill, *Autobiography* (London, 1873), ch. ii.
[2] *Apologia pro vita sua*, ch. i; *Newman: Prose and Poetry*, ed. Geoffrey Tillotson (London, 1957), p. 586.
[3] Locke, *Essay* (London, 1690), IV, xvi.

Observing . . . such gradual and gentle descents downwards in those parts of the creation that are beneath men, the rule of analogy makes it probable that it is so also in things above us and our observation; and that there are several ranks of intelligent beings, excelling us in several degrees of perfection, ascending upwards towards the infinite perfection of the Creator. . . .

That is all analogy means to Butler—'the proof of the uncertain by the certain', as he quotes from Quintilian (i, vi, 4) on the title-page of the *Analogy*. It constitutes the shape of his argument, not a rhetorical form. The language of the *Sermons* and of the *Analogy* is, indeed, so effortlessly bare of analogical forms—whether metaphor, or simile, or conceit—as to suggest that for Butler rhetorical analogy was not even a temptation. Metaphor, especially, is scarcely even a possibility in his language. It is exceptional for him to use any rhetorical form of analogy except open illustration ('suppose that . . .'); and illustration is the form of analogy that sits most lightly to language, being the image (if it deserves to be rated as an image at all) that can most easily be lifted clear of the argument, and the one most conscious of its own limitations. This is just the way in which the illustration of the watch works in the 1729 preface to the *Sermons*. Everything in nature and art, Butler argues there, including man's moral nature, is a system. And our nature is systematic in a familiar sense:

Let us instance in a watch—Suppose the several parts of it taken to pieces, and placed apart from each other: let a man have ever so exact a notion of these several parts, unless he considers the respects and relations which they have to each other, he will not have anything like the idea of a watch. . . . Thus it is with regard to the inward frame of man. (p. 10)

Butler is fully aware how inessential and inorganic his illustration is, how little his argument depends upon it, and how soon the limits of the analogy are reached:

. . . This is merely by way of explanation, what an economy, system, or constitution is. And thus far the cases are perfectly parallel. If we go further, there is indeed a difference, nothing to the present purpose, but too important an one ever to be omitted. A machine is inanimate and passive: but we are agents. . . . (p. 11)

This is the safest form of analogy, and he employs it in the *Analogy* too:

Thus suppose a prince to govern his dominions in the wisest manner possible, by common known laws. . . . (ii, iii, 6)

But now, on the contrary, suppose two men competitors for any thing whatever, which would be of equal advantage to each of them . . . (*Of the Nature of Virtue*, § 12)

Butler always knows exactly where he is at such moments, and is rarely so easy to follow: the argument, in a manner that seems to predict Hume's peculiar kind of clarity, moves easily from proposition to illustration to triumphant confirmation. It is the central rhetorical form of eighteenth-century philosophy, a form still familiar in philosophical argument and one which depends on the distrust of imagery and love of literalness characteristic of his age. For its excellence lies in being controlled within a bare and formal language; and the moment that control ceases, or is wilfully abandoned, as in much of the *Analogy of Religion*, conviction gives place to a mere admiration of the philosopher's ingenuity in spinning out a plausible argument. Butler's case for the immortality of the soul is like this. It exploits illustration unscrupulously: it allows it to take control and guide the argument itself. All creatures, he argues, at various times enjoy various 'degrees of life and perception',

the change of worms into flies, and the vast enlargement of their locomotive powers by such change; and birds and insects bursting the shell their habitation, and by this means entring into a new world, furnished with new accommodations for them. . . .

But the states of life in which we ourselves existed formerly, in the womb and in our infancy, are almost as different from our present in mature age as it is possible to conceive any two states or degrees of life can be. *Therefore*, that we are to exist hereafter in a state as different (*suppose*) from our present, as this is from our former, is but according to the analogy of nature. . . . (i, i, 2–3. My italics.)

Butler's 'suppose' is a vestige of his old self-control: his 'therefore' a mark of his new corruption. The art of reading him well lies beyond the notorious obscurity of his language, even beyond the modern sophistry that pretends to see the highest merit only in the prose of the good old days before Charles II. It lies in distinguishing between his honest use of illustration and his specious use of analogy, while confessing him a master of both.

7

DAVID HUME:
REASONING AND EXPERIENCE

BY RAYMOND WILLIAMS

In the republic of letters a man can live as himself, but in the bureaucracy of letters he must continually declare his style and department, and submit to an examination of his purpose and credentials at the frontier of every field. The influence of bureaucracy even extends to his readers, nervous under the stare of critics who are conducting what looks like a census of occupations. Is David Hume (1711–1776) moralist, logician, historian, essayist? Under which of these categories are you proposing to read him? Remember, before answering, the serious penalties involved, if you get on the wrong side of any one of these lines.

A certain boldness, and even rashness, is necessary now, if we are to maintain the republic. It is true that we can gather some shreds of authority, reminding our interrogators that in 1762 Boswell called Hume, quite simply, 'the greatest Writer in Brittain', and that in *My Own Life* Hume described his 'Love of literary Fame' as 'my ruling Passion'.[1] We can quote his most recent and best biographer, Ernest Mossner, for the opinion that from the beginning Hume 'regarded philosophy as part-and-parcel of literature. To be a philosopher is to be a man of letters: the proposition was received by Hume and the eighteenth century as axiomatic' (p. 63). Yet the republic of letters cannot depend on this kind of authority or precedent. Its laws are immediate and substantial, in the writing and reading of literature, or they are nothing. The proof that now matters is that we can read Hume, sensibly and centrally, as a

---

[1] Boswell, *Private Papers*, ed. Geoffrey Scott and Frederick A. Pottle, vol. 1 (New York, 1928), p. 130; Ernest C. Mossner, *The Life of Hume* (Edinburgh, 1954), Appendix A.

writer, and that this literary emphasis not only does not weaken his importance as philosopher, but is even fundamental to it. We can distinguish two elements of this proof: first, his close and lifelong preoccupation with the *writing* of his philosophy; second, his fundamental interest in the relations between reasoning and experience. Though these questions can properly be separated, for discussion, they are not finally distinct. The first is a matter of style, but it is more, finally (even against some of Hume's ways of putting the question), than the simple delivery of something already complete. The second is a matter of philosophy, but again it is in the end much more than a formal argument, for the relation between reasoning and experience is explored as much in problems of structure and style as in heads and proofs immediately recognizable as such. These related questions, that is to say, come together in the question of the nature of literature, as Hume understood and wrote it.

Two pieces engage our first attention: the autobiographical letter of 1734[1], and the similarly personal but more public analysis—a piece that deserves classic status—at the end of the first book of *A Treatise of Human Nature* (1739–40) (I, iv, vii). In each of them Hume is engaged in a kind of self-questioning which has general importance just because it is personal: the relation between reasoning and experience is being touched at the root.

I was after that left to my own Choice in my Reading, and found it encline me almost equally to Books of Reasoning and Philosophy, and to Poetry and the polite Authors. Every one, who is acquainted either with the Philosophers or Critics, knows that there is nothing yet establisht in either of these two Sciences, and that they contain little more than endless Disputes even in the most fundamental Articles. Upon Examination of these I found a certain Boldness of Temper growing in me, which was not enclin'd to submit to any Authority in these Subjects but led me to seek out some new Medium by which Truth might be establisht. After much Study and Reflection on this, at last, when I was about 18 Years of Age, there seemed to be open'd up to me a new Scene of Thought, which transported me beyond Measure, and made me, wyth an Ardor

---

[1] *Letters*, ed. J. Y. T. Greig, vol. I (Oxford, 1932), p. 13.

natural to young men, throw up every other Pleasure or Business to apply entirely to it. (1734)

The new 'medium', the new 'scene of thought', has all the quality of an experience—a dimension rather than a doctrine— reached, however, by 'study and reflection'. We can describe it in retrospect and abstraction as an option for empiricism:

I found that the moral Philosophy transmitted to us by Antiquity, labor'd under the same Inconvenience that has been found in their natural Philosophy, of being entirely Hypothetical, and depending more upon Invention than Experience. Every one consulted his Fancy in erecting Schemes of Virtue and of Happiness, without regarding Human Nature, upon which every moral Conclusion must depend. This therefore I resolved to make my principal Study, and the Source from which I wou'd derive every Truth in Criticism as well as Morality. (1734)

Yet this option is not in any narrow sense intellectual; it is clearly a decision of the whole being, as indeed the consequences showed. The easy way to connect Hume the thinker with Hume the writer is to illustrate the difficulties of translating the new 'scene of thought' into words:

When one must bring the Idea he comprehended in gross, nearer to him, so as to contemplate its minutest Parts, and keep it steddily in his Eye, so as to copy these Parts in Order, this I found impracticable for me, nor were my Spirits equal to so severe an Employment. Here lay my greatest Calamity. I had no Hopes of delivering my Opinions with such Elegance and Neatness, as to draw to me the Attention of the World, and I wou'd rather live and dye in Obscurity than produce them maim'd and imperfect. (1734)

This is a normal and general difficulty, expressed in the terms of his century: the search for 'such Elegance and Neatness, as to draw to me the Attention of the World' is what the literary pursuit was often and is still often understood to be. Yet something else was happening, in this first creative struggle, and it is Hume's distinction, inquiring into the relation between reasoning and experience at much more than a formal level, to bring it to notice:

I have notic'd in the Writings of the French Mysticks, and in those of our Fanatics here, that, when they give a History of the Situation of their Souls, they mention a Coldness and Desertion of the Spirit, which frequently returns, and some of them, at the beginning, have been tormented with it many Years. As this kind of Devotion depends entirely on the Force of Passion, and consequently of the Animal Spirits, I have often thought that their Case and mine were pretty parralel, and that their rapturous Admirations might discompose the Fabric of the Nerves and Brain, as much as profound Reflections, and that warmth or Enthusiasm which is inseparable from them. (1734)

We hardly need further witness of the kind of passionate inquiry which Hume's thinking was; yet at once, in this letter, we become aware of a tension which is more acute, because more local, than the natural strain on any profound and passionate thinker. It is surely surprising, alike to our preconceptions about Hume's empiricism and to our ordinary sense of his mature style, for which 'coolness' continually suggests itself as a description, to read of that inseparable 'warmth or Enthusiasm' and of that surprising 'parralel Case'. There is a subtlety of reference not wholly separable from confusion, in what is still an unfinished movement of mind: the others are 'Fanatics', and yet 'pretty parralel'. While the phrases hang in the mind, one is reminded of Hume's defence of the third book of the *Treatise*, 'Of Morals', against Hutcheson's criticism that 'there wants a certain Warmth in the Cause of Virtue':

I must own, this has not happen'd by Chance, but is the Effect of a Reasoning either good or bad. . . . Any warm Sentiment of Morals, I am afraid, wou'd have the Air of Declamation amidst abstract Reasonings, and wou'd be esteem'd contrary to good Taste. And tho' I am much more ambitious of being esteem'd a Friend to Virtue, than a Writer of Taste; yet I must always carry the latter in my Eye, otherwise I must despair of ever being serviceable to Virtue. I hope these Reasons will satisfy you; tho at the same time, I intend to make a new Tryal, if it be possible to make the Moralist and Metaphysician agree a little better.[1]

Behind the ordinary dilemma of a philosophical style, itself complicated by an anxious consciousness of contemporary canons of taste, something fundamental to the inquiry itself is here being skirted. It is interesting that in this letter to Hutcheson, Hume uses the analogy with which he ends the *Treatise*: the distinction between the anatomist and the painter.

[1] Mossner, *Life*, p. 134.

At first glance the distinction is commonplace: the anatomist dissects, accurately, to discover the 'most secret Springs and Principles'; the painter describes 'the grace and beauty' of actions; the two functions are different, and must not be confused, though the anatomist can give 'very good advice' to the painter, as can the dissecting metaphysician to the engaging moralist. Yet when we read this analogy, as it is written in the *Treatise*, we can see in the language the tension within which Hume was working. He has reached, by argument, the conclusion that 'sympathy is the chief source of moral distinctions', and now adds, nervously and hopefully:

Were it proper in such a subject to bribe the readers assent, or employ any thing but solid argument, we are here abundantly supplied with topics to engage the affections. All lovers of virtue (and such we all are in speculation, however we may degenerate in practice) must certainly be pleas'd to see moral distinctions deriv'd from so noble a source. . . . (III, iii, vi)

After the heaviness of 'bribe', the tone becomes closer and warmer, as if in oversight, yet the whole movement is conscious, reaching its climax in the moving rhetorical questions: 'Who indeed does not feel an accession of alacrity . . . ?', 'And who can think any advantages of fortune a sufficient compensation for the least breach... ?' When the caution returns, it is already partly discounted:

But I forbear insisting on this subject. Such reflexions require a work apart, very different from the genius of the present. The anatomist ought never to emulate the painter: nor in his accurate dissections and portraitures of the smaller parts of the human body, pretend to give his figures any graceful and engaging attitude or expression. There is even something hideous, or at least minute, in the views of things which he presents; and 'tis necessary the objects shou'd be set more at a distance, and be more cover'd up from sight, to make them engaging to the eye and imagination. An anatomist, however, is admirably fitted to give advice to a painter...

The real question being argued, being *written*, here, is the question of what it is to be a moralist. In the letter to Hutcheson, the metaphysician had been the anatomist, and the moralist the painter. But if the end of all the dissection is the discovery of a human body (to which alone appeal can be made,

not merely to have effect but to make sense, for it is there that
the source of morality resides) then the attention of the
anatomist is the intention of the painter, though the detailed
work of the anatomist seems, while it is being done, 'hideous
or at least minute'. Hume is not departing from analysis,
but reconstituting it, when he moves from 'argument' to
'declamation'. The end of the detailed moral inquiry is properly the moralist actively engaging human sympathy, yet the
tension is still there, from that first and natural fear of 'consulting his Fancy in erecting Schemes of Virtue and Happiness';
and Hume must forbear insisting, renounce any pretension to
the 'graceful and engaging', even while he engages and insists.
In this tension, a whole movement of thought—in effect the
transformation of empiricism—is being slowly and unevenly
brought to light. The moralist must be an anatomist, however
unwillingly, because he would be a painter, but a good painter.

The central document of this tension is, of course, the concluding chapter of the first book of the *Treatise*. Parts of this
chapter have been widely quoted, but the movement of mind
there is so close and subtle that incidental quotation tends to
misrepresent. What is at first surprising, in a work in many
ways so rigorous, is the note of personal confession. It is tempt-
ing to write this down as simple weakness (the young author's
itch to be at himself) or, when we have read more widely in
Hume, and stumbled over his many ironies, to take it as rhetoric
of a subtle kind: the confession of incapacity which in polite
studies is the only authorized way to claim capacity; the for-
bearing to insist as the only polite tone of insistence. But these
elements are at best minor. The confession, in a vital sense, is
the argument, only it is an argument of a new kind.

Thus the language of Hume on the social sense, which in
abstraction one writes down so easily as the basis of his morals,
is immediately arresting. He is 'affrighted and confounded' by
the 'forelorn solitude' into which his line of reasoning has led
him, and can fancy himself 'some strange uncouth monster,
who not being able to mingle and unite in society, has been
expell'd all human commerce, and left utterly abandon'd and
disconsolate. Fain wou'd I run into the crowd for shelter and
warmth; but cannot prevail with myself to mix with such

deformity.' Between the uncouth and the deformed, what?
For 'such is my weakness, that I feel all my opinions loosen and
fall of themselves, when unsupported by the approbation of
others.' It is just this weakness that, as a reasoner, he has to
face: 'After the most accurate and exact of my reasonings, I
can give no reason why I shou'd assent to it; and feel nothing
but a *strong* propensity to consider objects *strongly* in that view,
under which they appear to me.' Assent comes from experience
and habit, which he shares with others, but then this weakness
is a general weakness; the apparent assent of reason is no more
than an illusion in common. The question then is, 'how far
we ought to yield to these illusions?' Imagination is dangerous
to reason, even when it has become common and conventional,
but if we reject it where we can distinguish it as such, and limit
ourselves to the understanding, we shall find that we are left
without any evidence or certainty at all. The contradictions
of all reasoning are then so deep that reasoning itself seems
useless, and the '*intense* view of these manifold contradictions
and imperfections' leads again to that 'Coldness and Desertion
of the Spirit', 'inviron'd with the deepest darkness and utterly
depriv'd of the use of every member and faculty'. At this point,
Hume instances what has often been taken as his way out of
this darkness:

I dine, I play a game of back-gammon, I converse, and am merry
with my friends; and when after three or four hours' amusement,
I wou'd return to these speculations, they appear so cold, and
strain'd, and ridiculous, that I cannot find in my heart to enter into
them any farther.

The sceptic, yielding to fatigue and the demands of his senses,
confirms his scepticism, but this is not at all (as Hume's
enemies would have it) the relapse into philistinism to be
expected from one holding the 'low view' of man. On the
contrary, it is characteristic of Hume, in his long dialogue
between reasoning and experience, to feel and think even when
in apparent flight. His 'animal spirits and passions' have
reduced him to 'this indolent belief in the general maxims of
the world' but the sentiments are recognized as those of 'spleen
and indolence' and the way is prepared for the return to
reasoning, when 'I feel my mind all collected within itself.'

9

Curiosity and ambition give energy again, but behind them there is a more decisive realization: if the questions are indeed cold and strained and ridiculous, there is no final alternative but to go on into them, except the relapse to superstition. The declaration that mattered in Hume's life is then almost casually made: 'Generally speaking, the errors in religion are dangerous; those in philosophy only ridiculous.' Contradiction can be lived with; false belief can not. And the conviction of falseness there is, we notice, assumed. All the arguments on it will come later. The sceptic has arrived at a way of living with his scepticism, and this way, paradoxically, is one of affirmation. For 'a true sceptic will be diffident of his philosophical doubts, as well as of his philosophical conviction'. It is in this way that Hume's essential tension is, if not resolved, negotiated. Here, decisively, is the discovery of how to write. The inquiry will continue, searching always farther into the contradictions and imperfections of reasoning. But the anatomist has now most decisively instructed the painter: an engaged, ironic and warily moving painter. For

we shou'd yield to that propensity, which inclines us to be positive and certain in *particular points*, according to the light, in which we survey them in any *particular instant*. . . . On such an occasion we are apt not only to forget our scepticism, but even our modesty too; and make use of such terms as these, *'tis evident, 'tis certain, 'tis undeniable*; which a due deference to the public ought, perhaps, to prevent. I may have fallen into this fault after the example of others; but I here enter a *caveat* against any objections, which may be offer'd on that head; and declare that such expressions were extorted from me by the present view of the object, and imply no dogmatical spirit, nor conceited idea of my own judgment, which are sentiments that I am sensible can become no body, and a sceptic still less than any other.

The philosophical decision is here, substantially, a choice of style.

Of the connexion between style and belief, Hume was formally as well as substantially aware:

There are certain sects, which secretly form themselves in the learned world, as well as factions in the political; and though sometimes they come not to an open rupture, they give a different turn to the ways of thinking of those who have taken part on either side. The most remarkable of this kind are the sects founded on the different sentiments with regard to the *dignity of human nature*; which is a point that seems to have divided philosophers and poets, as well as divines, from the beginning of the world to this day. Some exalt our species to the skies, and represent man as a kind of human demigod, who derives his origin from heaven, and retains evident marks of his lineage and descent. Others insist upon the blind sides of human nature, and can discover nothing, except vanity, in which man surpasses the other animals, whom he affects so much to despise. If an author possess the talent of rhetoric and declamation, he commonly takes part with the former: If his turn lie towards irony and ridicule, he naturally throws himself into the other extreme.[1]

But this way of putting the matter seems absurdly simple, when we look at Hume's own practice. In the received account of him, the 'turn . . . towards irony and ridicule' is predominant, yet in this matter of the dignity or meanness of human nature, Hume's place is clearly with the former option, though he brings it sharply down to earth. The apparent paradox indicates a more real paradox, which is central to Hume's particular character as a moralist. I have described this as the sceptic who finds a way of affirming, but the point that has now to be taken is that this is more than a marginal outlet—the agreed lapse into particular and local affirmations—and is indeed, in his moral writings, his distinctive kind of achievement.

We should perhaps make here the necessary critical distinction between scepticism and cynicism. Again and again we find Hume's power of argument probing, with a sharpness that can properly be associated with scepticism, a particular kind of idea. But it is remarkable how often this very idea is attacked because it appears to degrade human dignity or capacity. There is a good example in the essay from which I have just quoted:

Now this being a point, in which all the world is agreed, that human understanding falls infinitely short of perfect wisdom; it is proper we should know when this comparison takes place, that we may not

---

[1] *Essays Moral and Political* (London, 1742), 'Of the Dignity or Meanness of Human Nature'.

dispute where there is no real difference in our sentiments. Man falls much more short of perfect wisdom, than animals do of man; yet the latter difference is so considerable, that nothing but a comparison with the former can make it appear of little moment.

It is also usual to *compare* one man with another; and finding very few whom we can call *wise* or *virtuous*, we are apt to entertain a contemptible notion of our species in general. That we may be sensible of the fallacy of this way of reasoning, we may observe that the honourable appellations of wise and virtuous, are not annexed to any particular degree of those qualities of *wisdom* and *virtue*; but arise altogether from the comparison we make between one man and another. When we find a man, who arrives at such a pitch of wisdom as is very uncommon, we pronounce him a wise man: So that to say, there are few wise men in the world, is really to say nothing; since it is only by their scarcity that they merit that appellation.

The difference between scepticism and cynicism could hardly be more marked; indeed Hume's writing is the outstanding instance, in English, where this critical distinction can be read. Those enemies of Hume who have relied on a kind of free association between sceptical thinking and the denial of value, have succeeded only in muddling an experience of genuine complexity. The sceptical character of his theory of human understanding is of course very evident, but the conclusions he consequently drew, on the relations between reasoning and experience, and between fact and value, are, precisely, the theoretical basis of that movement of mind which I have described as the sceptic who learns how to affirm. To rely on the necessary avowals of scepticism (indeed to reduce these calm and deliberate avowals to what can be called 'admissions'), while ignoring the *consequently* firm assertions of value, is simply to dismember the Humean experience.

The complicating difficulty, undoubtedly, has been Hume's attitude to religion, for here (we have still to observe, in twentieth-century England as well as in eighteenth-century Calvinist Scotland) an obstinate kind of questioning, a scepticism, can lead, suddenly, to a cry of fire. Angry prejudices can be released, only to turn suddenly and assume the name and body of love. Yet the major effect of Hume's religious scepticism is surely the abolition of the argument from design, and this enterprise seems expressly conceived as a way of affirming both reason and the limits of reason in our experience of the human condition. I do not know who would now want to identify 'the religious sense' with the (in many ways irreligious) argument from design, but of course the argument presses further: a moral questioning of the consequences of religion as Hume saw it practised and expounded. Here again we have the sceptical thinker arguing against the intolerance which seems to follow from a unitary explanation of life; against the punishment of body and spirit by the kind of self-abasement which seems to follow from the distance of a perfect God; against the hypocrisy which can fill the gap between actual and aspiring belief; against the corruption of philosophy which can follow from its reservation to deductive reasoning from a principle asserted to be beyond reason. In abstraction even, but much more in the body of the writing, this opposition to negations, this denial of the necessity of particular denials, composes itself into a very positive moral account, which the tone most notably confirms. We can certainly instance Hume's penetration and wit in the *Dialogues concerning Natural Religion* (1779)—notably the brilliant part VI ('the world, therefore, I infer, is an animal') —but we can also instance, from the same dialogues, his deeper achievement: the humanity of the extension of scepticism to scepticism itself; the bold and yet intricate imaginative confidence (at first sight so surprising in a moralist, though it would not be surprising in a dramatist or novelist) which allows and controls the award of victory to the defeated Cleanthes. The simple opposition to scepticism hardly knows, in Hume, with what manner of man it has to deal.

The problem, that is to say, emerges again and again as one of *reading* Hume: reading in a wholly literary sense. This is certainly the case, though a very particular case, with *An Enquiry concerning the Principles of Morals* (1751), 'of all my writings, historical, philosophical, or literary, incomparably the best'. All students of Hume will know the kind of summary that can be given of Hume's doctrines in the *Enquiry*, but, without questioning its usefulness, it can still reasonably be asked whether the main purpose of writing or reading the *Enquiry* is to arrive at that kind of summary of conclusions. The unfinished (and also, in some important respects, unstarted) argument between the 'literary' and the 'philosophical' reader of moral essays, might well now be directed towards just this question. It can be put in one way as the familiar critical question of the relation between content and form. The general intricacy of this relation is especially marked in moral writing. The very terms of definition—'moral doctrine', 'moral writing' —contain, if we would look at them, some of the major difficulties. We do not ordinarily believe, in the reading of literature, that the content of a work can, in any adequate way, be represented by summary; or rather, it can be so *represented*, for the agreed and limited purposes of particular discussions, but can only be *found* in a particular structure and sequence of words. The urgency of abstract inquiry, and indeed of doctrine, is certainly such that we have to use representations. But what can then happen, as the representation becomes by habit the content, is that we can find ourselves working with very feeble versions of both doctrine and style. Thus 'doctrine', commonly, is 'conclusion', although that very word ought to remind us of what, from all antecedent stages, has been lost. And 'style', commonly, is reserved to 'expression', all its deep connexions with a process of experience quite lost or forgotten: style indeed as 'such Elegance and Neatness, as to draw to me the Attention of the World', or worse (since the 'attention of the world' is a complicated connexion), style as that which is not there (its presence indicating the taint of literature), or which interferes as little as possible with the expression of doctrine.

No simple description of Hume's style in the *Enquiry* is likely to be adequate. Indeed the fact of variation, in ways of writing as in ways of thinking, seems essential to any full understanding of it. In one sense, the drive of the argument, of the proof, is very certain and even at times overbearing; but equally there are many signs of uncertainty, hesitation, even reverie, and these are gathered up rather than resolved in the final rhetoric of conviction. Thus the austere firmness of the opening, so confident in the clarity of its antitheses and in its promised penetration and synthesis, stands virtually alone in the work, except perhaps for the first appendix, 'Concerning Moral Sentiment'. This is the boldness of conception and proposition, and it is interesting that it is from this opening and appendix that most of the sentences definitive of Hume's doctrines are taken. Yet when he passes to the substance of proof, more of the mind is at once and, as it were, involuntarily engaged. The 'experimental method . . . deducing general maxims from a comparison of particular instances' is in general followed, and has an important effect on the *general* structure of the essay. But in fact, as soon as he begins collecting instances, he touches a different string: he is concerned not only to deduce but to persuade. Consider how early, in the section 'Of Benevolence', he gives the anecdote of the dying Pericles, and not only as an instance in argument but as an instance for the communication of feeling: '*You forget*, cries the dying hero who had heard all. . . .' Whenever this kind of instance occurs to him, Hume's instinct is to make his own feeling about it the proof, and only then to recall and appear to excuse himself—the movement of mind we have seen before:

But I forget that it is not my present business to recommend generosity or benevolence, or to paint in their true colours all the genuine charms of the social virtues. These, indeed, sufficiently engage every heart, on the first apprehension of them; and it is difficult to abstain from some sally or panegyric, as often as they occur in discourse or reasoning. But our object here. . . .

And it is significant that what immediately follows this recall is not a return to deduction, but a reassertion of the immediacy and communication of feelings of just this kind. The argument that our approbation of the social virtues is due at least in part to their utility is introduced, characteristically, with the suasive question—'may it not thence be concluded?'—following a panegyric on 'any humane beneficent man' which ends: 'Like the sun, an inferior minister of Providence, he cheers, invigorates and sustains the surrounding world.' It is difficult to feel that the scrappy assertions which follow the question carry anything more than a small part of the burden of proof, by comparison with the demonstration of Hume's actual range of feelings of this kind: 'The eye is pleased with the prospect of cornfields and loaded vineyards, horses grazing, and flocks pasturing; but flies the view of briars and brambles affording shelter to wolves and serpents.' The very element of convention, in this kind of description of feeling, is, as it were, folded into the proof. Or again: 'Can anything stronger be said in praise of a profession, such as merchandise or manufacture, than to observe the advantages which it procures to society? And is not a monk and inquisitor enraged when we treat his order as useless or pernicious to mankind?' The shift there, from 'society' to 'mankind', is a shift within a unity of feeling which, if it is not wholly communicated, will quickly reveal itself, in the light of deduction, as a bundle of propensities and prejudices. It is again wholly characteristic that when he passes to the summary of his argument on benevolence—'upon the whole, then, it seems undeniable...'—he moves into a kind of language which is not neutrally descriptive but conventionally communicative:

The social virtues are never regarded without their beneficial tendencies, *nor viewed as barren and unfruitful.* The happiness of mankind, the order of society, the harmony of families, the mutual support of friends are always considered as the result *of the gentle dominion over the breasts of men.*

To read these sentences without the phrases I have italicized is to see very clearly, by contrast, how Hume is writing and thinking. For these phrases are clearly not emotional intensifications of the argument. Without them, the argument is not really there. The supposed alternative to benefit, as an explanation of approval, is at once suppressed and swollen, until the phrase serves really to confirm, in feeling, the idea of benefit. The powerful normative and appealing clauses of the second sentence move rhythmically to a result which has already, in effect, been assumed, so that in a way no definition of cause is needed; the sentence, by that stage, has done its work. Yet since definition, clearly, for Hume, is not enough, all the feeling of this part of the inquiry is concentrated into the association of 'dominion' with 'gentle' and 'breasts'.

This is to take only one section of the whole work. There are, as we shall see, further variations. Yet what we can learn here is perhaps decisive. For the point of my observations is not at all to convict Hume of being a thinker who lapses into what is called 'emotive' language. Indeed the assumptions about language which led to the separation of an 'emotive' category seem to me profoundly distorting in any study of communication. Behind them lies that learned and willed separation of writer and reader which itself produces a particular style: in argument, especially, the style that wishes to be no style, or, at second thought, to be elegant. What matters about Hume is that his argument, his doctrine, depends on the same assumptions that we have seen at work in the writing: the shared conventions of humane feeling; the certainty that these are embodied in the common language of approval and disapproval; the conviction that moral activity is the use of this language, and that reasoning is necessary mainly to confirm this use and to expose the inadequacy of other definitions of morals. It is difficult to see how he could have completely established these convictions without embodying them, in practice, in his writing.

That he tried, however, to get outside the assumptions, or rather to demonstrate them by a different kind of writing and thinking, is equally important in any final assessment. The close and strenuous distinction between a mistake of *fact* and one of *right*, in the appendix 'Concerning Moral Sentiment', is only one of many possible examples of the kind of reasoning we can properly call impersonal, and in which Hume's capacity is so evidently of the highest order that it compels respect even in disagreement. Or again he can, even within the drive of his demonstration of moral conventions, pause and reflect with a sudden flexibility of intelligence which is the more remarkable when it has been seen how strong the conventions and the feelings are. A good example of this is the seventh note in section vi, 'Of Qualities Useful to Ourselves', when after a confident account of our sentiments towards rich and poor, as conformable with his theory of moral distinctions, he adds, hesitantly but convincingly, the complexities of these sentiments which in fact confuse the demonstration. In the two final paragraphs of the same section, he introduces, first, an alternative moral dimension, and, second, a sudden relation of conventional regard to different types of society, and each point serves only to disturb what had seemed a too simple and indeed overbearing demonstration; yet it if had indeed been overbearing, the recognitions would not have come. The mood of reverie which comes when contradictions, not so much of propositions as of feelings, are recognized, is always impressive. Near the climax of his argument, in part i of section IX, there is the old tension: 'I must confess that this enumeration puts the matter in so strong a light that I cannot, *at present*, be more assured of any truth which I learn from reasoning and argument. . . .' Yet if the matter is as clear as that, and still men dispute, 'when I reflect on this, I say, I fall back into diffidence and scepticism, and suspect that an hypothesis so obvious, had it been a true one, would long ere now have been received by the unanimous suffrage and consent of mankind'. But what is equally characteristic, in this whole movement of mind, is the brisk resumption, in part ii, of what remains the most difficult part of his proof—the movement from 'approbation' to 'interested obligation'. Even here, however, he slides from a statement of the problem to a rhapsodical solution of it, quickly corrected to more detailed and incisive argument, and then, at the point of final difficulty, the kind of engagement (which is not only persuasive rhetoric) that we have already examined:

Treating vice with the greatest candour and making it all possible concessions. . . .
    That *honesty is the best policy* may be a good general rule, but is liable to many exceptions. And he, it may perhaps be thought, conducts himself with most wisdom who observes the general rule and takes advantage of all the exceptions. I must confess that if a man think that this reasoning much requires an answer, it will be a little difficult to find any which will to him appear satisfactory and convincing. If his heart rebel not against such pernicious maxims, if he feel no reluctance to the thoughts of villany or base-ness, he has indeed lost a considerable motive to virtue; and we may expect that his practice will be answerable to his speculation.

As he considers and rejects the 'secret and successful' breaker of moral laws, the mind of the reader may return uneasily to the simple panegyric on success in part ii of section VI, and to the two inclusions of secrecy in his listing of the social virtues. These lists, throughout, break into many kinds of considera-tion. It is, then, difficult indeed to emerge from our reading and be satisfied with the more easily abstracted definitions.

Indeed, to read for these definitions is to mistake Hume: the 'definitions' depend, empirically, on all the instances and on all the apparent synonyms.[1] Or, to put it another way, the substance of Hume's inquiry is in the whole body of the writing: in the variations, hesitations and contradictions as deeply as in the lines and heads of proof.

In his account of moral activity, which in its main directions is deeply positive and affirmative, Hume seeks to embody two principles: the communication of feeling, which is sympathy, and the engagement of feeling, which is the necessary involvement of man with mankind. A position of this kind inevitably emphasizes conventions: not only is the common language the moral consensus, but also there is a practical equivalence between humanity and society. This element of convention, not only in Hume but in eighteenth-century culture generally, raises certain important critical questions.

It has been suggested, for example, that in his reliance on approval and disapproval as moral criteria, he is opening the way for, and indeed participating in, the degeneration of social morals to the trivial and external concerns of Lord Chesterfield. It is, I think, true that when he is affirming certain kinds of convention, in the language of his period, an evident blandness of tone can take temporary charge: 'He must be unhappy indeed, either in his own temper, or in his situation and company, who has never perceived the charms of a facetious wit or flowing affability, of a delicate modesty or decent genteelness of address and manner.'[2] Certain words in that sentence, 'facetious', 'affability', 'genteelness', are now so heavily compromised that conviction of Hume is almost too easy. Yet a certain smoothing complacency is undoubtedly present: most often, I think, when he feels he is going against the grain of his time, and seeks anxiously to appease it. I find it necessary to remember, when Hume purrs in this way, that in fact, through most of his life, he was challenging some of the central beliefs of his time: indeed, became notorious, lost jobs through pre-

---

[1] Cf. C. W. Hendel's introduction to his edition of the *Enquiry* (New York, 1957), pp. xxvi–xxvii.

[2] *Enquiries*, ed. L. A. Selby-Bigge (Oxford, 1894, enlarged 1902), IX, i, 226. Future references to the *Enquiry* are to this edition.

judice, had his very tomb guarded against desecration. I cannot myself associate a man like that with Chesterfield, though the literary fact remains clear, that at times he sounds so bland and comfortable that he is now paradoxically exposed to a different kind of enemy.

And then, quite apart from this occasional blandness, we have certainly to note a limitation of his mind by temporary social assumptions. It is significant that when in his discussion of benevolence (*Enquiry*, II, ii) he introduces instances of moral feelings modified by 'further experience and sounder reasoning' three out of the four (on charity, tyrannicide, and luxury) seem now profoundly ambiguous. Indeed the reduction of charity to a weakness has the real complacency which in subsequent Poor Law legislation became inhuman and terrible. Much of Hume's political writing is marred in this way, by a too easy acceptance of convention at those points where society was not, after all, equivalent with humanity.

Again, we must certainly remark a limitation of kinds of feeling: the prudential exclusion of intensity and passion; the limitation of responses to suffering; the too easy sneer at enthusiasm: 'A gloomy, hair-brained enthusiast, after his death, may have a place in the calendar; but will scarcely ever be admitted, when alive, into intimacy and society, except by those who are as delirious and dismal as himself' (IX, i, 219). His attack on the 'monkish virtues'—'celibacy, fasting, penance, mortification, self-denial, humility, silence, solitude' (IX, i, 219)—has the disability of so many of his lists: that it is not really discriminating, and that the often bad is confounded with the often good. His argument against them is similarly mixed: that they disqualify from fortune and society, which is simple complacency; and that they 'stupefy the understanding and harden the heart', which is at least arguable of part of the list, and indeed seems to me true.

Yet we must not surrender to an opposite but equal limitation. The social feelings are real, are not merely Chesterfield, and Hume's range, here, is both wide and deep:

Let us consider what we call vicious luxury. No gratification, however sensual, can of itself be esteemed vicious. A gratification is only vicious, when it engrosses all a man's expence, and leaves no ability for such acts of duty and generosity as are required by his situation and fortune. Suppose that he correct the vice, and employ part of his expence in the education of his children, in the support of his friends, and in relieving the poor: would any prejudice result to society ? On the contrary, the same consumption would arise; and that labour, which, at present, is employed only in producing a slender gratification to one man, would relieve the necessitous, and bestow satisfaction on hundreds. The same care and toil that raise a dish of peas at Christmas, would give bread to a whole family during six months. To say, that, without a vicious luxury, the labour would not have been employed at all, is only to say, that there is some other defect in human nature, such as indolence, selfishness, inattention to others, for which luxury, in some measure, provides a remedy; as one poison may be an antidote to another. But virtue, like wholesome food, is better than poisons, however corrected.[1]

This is the best of Hume, and it has been too little emphasized.

Nor can we finally say that, in his attention to social approbation and disapprobation, Hume neglects the self-approval of individual conscience. Indeed, on the very last page of the *Enquiry* he writes: 'Inward peace of mind, consciousness of integrity, a satisfactory review of our own conduct; these are circumstances very requisite to happiness, and will be cherished and cultivated by every honest man who feels the importance of them' (ix, ii, 233). And in his final paragraph, contrasting the pleasures of virtue with the 'empty amusements of luxury and expense', he writes of 'the unbought satisfaction of conversation, society, study, even health and the common beauties of nature, but above all the peaceful reflection on one's own conduct' (xx, ii, 233). The unity of these points of reference is indeed Hume's whole moral appeal.

Yet was this unity possible ? Is the unity not merely conventional ? In answering these questions, we must first take account of one fact, that Hume quite often enters, in his moral and political writings, a distinct kind of social relativism, which of all ways of thinking can be the most dangerous to the simple reliance on convention. At a formal level, the matter can be easily settled. Nobody who has read such essays as 'Of National Characters', 'The Rise of Arts and Sciences', 'Of Commerce', and 'Of Refinement in the Arts', would wish to

---

[1] 'Of Refinement in the Arts', in *Essays*.

accuse Hume of confusing a local and temporary society with universal and historical humanity. On the contrary, he is sometimes a remarkably original contributor to new kinds of relative historical analysis. Yet a genuine ambiguity remains, and it centres, characteristically, upon his use of the word 'society'. Thus he can observe, without difficulty:

In countries where men pass most of their time in conversation and visits and assemblies, these *companionable* qualities, so to speak, are of high estimation and form a chief part of personal merit. In countries where men live a more domestic life and either are employed in business or amuse themselves in a narrower circle of acquaintance, the more solid qualities are chiefly regarded. (VIII, 212)

And he goes on to a comparison of England and France. The distinguishing word here is 'companionable', and indeed, just before this passage he has written:

As the mutual shocks in *society*, and the oppositions of interest and self-love, have constrained mankind to establish the laws of *justice*...: in like manner, the eternal contrarieties, in *company*, of men's pride and self-conceit, have introduced the rules of *Good Manners* or *Politeness*. ... (VIII, 211)

This distinction between 'society' and 'company' seems simple enough to maintain, especially to the modern reader. We are used to 'society' as a general description of the system of common life, and indeed to the abstraction from descriptions of particular systems or societies to a general condition of 'society' as such. But the earliest meaning of 'society' had been 'the company of one's fellows': a description of an immediate relationship between persons. The complexities in the development of 'society' as a word reflect general complexities in actual social development and social philosophy; they are by no means particular to Hume. But because of the nature of his moral thinking, Hume was especially exposed to these complexities and their consequent confusions. For example, when he is discussing 'social virtues'—'humanity, benevolence, lenity, generosity, gratitude, moderation, tenderness, friendship' (IX, i, 226)—he runs together qualities which cover the whole range from directly personal behaviour to public standards. It is not that he fails to recognize the kind of distinction that we would now make, but that, usually, 'society' is for him both the common system of life and the activity of a particular class of persons—in fact a ruling class. His beneficent man is also quite naturally master and employer; in that limited position, social and personal virtues can be seen as often coincident. But this has the disadvantage that his kind of thinking about social values tacitly excludes the experience of those who are not a ruling class, and this is profoundly disabling in a system of morals which depends so fundamentally on *universal* approbation. Further, the comparisons he can make between the moral systems of different societies are not easily extended to comparisons of moral systems within a particular society: the practical point at which his assumption of a moral consensus breaks down. It is interesting that Adam Smith went on to just this question, distinguishing 'two different schemes or systems of morality current at the same time' in 'every society where the distinction of rank has once been completely established'.[1] Hume, unconsciously assimilating 'society', at many points, to a sense not far from a class-based 'company of his fellows', misses what seems to me the central difficulty in his whole argument from consensus. I have made a rough count in the *Enquiry*, and taking 'company of his fellows' as sense *A*, and 'system of common life' as sense *B*, find twenty-five uses of *A* as against 110 uses of *B*, but also, at some critical points in the argument, sixteen uses which are really *A/B*. His further uses of 'political society' (four), 'civil society' (three), 'human society' (nine), 'general society' (one), 'family society' (one), add further complications. The truth is that Hume is trying to generalize and even universalize, in the matter of virtue and society, while retaining within this crucial term not only an unconscious particularity but also, largely unanalysed, the essential complexities of the operative and connecting word.

This point affects, finally, the question of Hume's reference to 'utility' and to the utilitarian tradition. It is clear that he uses the principle of utility as a foundation of morals, and it is in fact the case, against some accounts of him, that he uses, in the *Enquiry*, such characteristic phrases as 'just calculation'

[1] *The Wealth of Nations* (London, 1776), vol. II, pp. 378–9.

and 'the greater happiness' (ix, ii). But it is also clear that his 'utility' is based, not exclusively or even primarily on the separate calculating individual, but essentially on what he took to be general and objective social experience. Further, through the complexity and confusion of 'society' that we have noted, he was able to identify this with general human experience. The 'calculation', that is to say, is made identical, or nearly so, with the actual social process; or, to put it another way, the process of living in society is the calculation, which needs no other and separate principles to determine it. I do not think it is fanciful to see this identification of society with a contained and self-regulating calculation as the reflexion of a particular stage of bourgeois society in which the relation between the market (the obvious model for this process) and the society as a whole could be seen as organic. By derivation, the relationship between personal moral decision and the social process could also be seen as organic. When this identification between the market and the whole society visibly failed to hold, as in the shocks of change immediately after Hume's life, the market element, in the calculation of utility, became abstracted, and society, for the utilitarian moralist, was only the aggregate of abstract individual calculations. From that kind of utilitarianism Hume is quite distinct.

On the other hand, the emphasis on separate individual moral calculation had appeared long before Hume, and was an object of his conscious attack. There is, surely, in a thinker of Hume's quality, never only reflexion. His whole enterprise can be seen as an attempt to restore the identity of social and personal virtues, at a time when the tensions of change had forced and were forcing these apart. That he failed was inevitable; he could only succeed, in his own clear sight, by an unconscious limitation of what was relevant social experience. Yet the enterprise, like Burke's enterprise in the emphasis of community, passed into the stream of thought, beyond its local failure. The complexity, both of Hume and of his actual influence, must surely be seen in this way. As the last great voice of a mature but narrowly based culture, on the edge of transformation by profound social change, the sceptic who wished to affirm, who in his own writing learned how to affirm,

succeeded in articulating modes of scepticism and modes of
affirmation which could work and move even when the living
basis of his own difficult resolution had passed away with his
generation and his society. It is in this sense that we can repeat
Basil Willey's exact description of him as 'the fine flower of the
English (or shall we say the Anglo-Scottish) eighteenth-century
mind'.

8

RADICAL PROSE IN THE LATE
EIGHTEENTH CENTURY[1]

BY MATTHEW HODGART

The field of radical prose style in the late eighteenth century
is a large one. It could be held to include the works of Price
and Priestley; of Francis Place and Major John Cartwright;
of Franklin, even of Jefferson and other American revolution-
aries. One could even call Blake's *Marriage of Heaven and Hell*
a masterpiece of radicalism; and on a different plane Thomas
Holcroft's *Memoirs* contain writing of a high order, especially
his account of his life as a Newmarket stable-boy. But I intend
to discuss only two radical works, Tom Paine's *The Rights of
Man* (1791–2) and William Godwin's *Political Justice* (1793).[2]
I shall try to show that each represents a different radical style
as well as a different type of radical thought; that in each case
there is some connexion between thought and style; and that
each derives much from the fertile genius of Edmund Burke.

Burke, indeed, could be classed among the radicals; an outsider from the Irish tradition, he invented a new analysis of
English politics, and a new style for presenting this analysis.
Until 1790 Paine (1737–1809) did not even consider that Burke
and he were in serious disagreement about essentials; and Paine
derived many of his ideas and some features of his style from
the early speeches of Burke, especially *On American Taxation*
(1774) and *On Conciliation with the Colonies* (1775). Paine's
Common Sense and the first number of *The Crisis* appeared in the
following year and owed much to Burke's defence of the

[1] Acknowledgments are due to the *Bulletin of the New York Public Library*, where
this article first appeared in 1962 in an earlier form.

[2] Thomas Paine, *Representative Selections*, ed. Harry Hayden Clark (New York,
1944, revised 1961); William Godwin, *Enquiry Concerning Political Justice and its
Influence on Morals and Happiness*, ed. F. E. L. Priestley, 3 vols. (Toronto, 1946;
photofacsimile of the 3rd edition corrected, 1798). Future references are to these
editions.

American cause. Paine's radicalism, like Burke's, is practical, concerned with current issues but also rooted in history— history that includes both the narrative of recent events (in which Paine excels) and the account of the developing con- stitution of England (in which he is less adept). Like Burke, he starts from the detailed description of things as they are: the Americans deserve their independence, not only on grounds of justice, but because the Americans live the life they do:

> The scene which that country presents to the eye of the spectator has something in it which generates and enlarges great ideas. Nature appears to him in magnitude. The mighty objects he be- holds act upon his mind by enlarging it, and he partakes of the great- ness he contemplates. . . . The wants which necessarily accompany the cultivation of a wilderness produced among them a state of society which countries long harrassed by the quarrels and intrigues of governments had neglected to cherish. In such a situation man becomes what he ought to be. . . . (p. 173)

That is from Part II of *The Rights of Man*, and except for the melioristic and dogmatic last sentence, it is very much the same in matter and manner as what Burke had said seventeen years earlier. Paine's style, though to a lesser degree than Burke's, is metaphorical and analogical. The images are drawn from his experience: they are usually deeply felt yet carefully worked out; like Burke, he seems to think metaphorically. This is rare enough among radicals, or indeed among politicians. The late James Thurber wrote that 'you can count on your fingers the Americans [i.e. politicians] since the Thomas Paine of "the summer soldier and the sunshine patriot" who have added bright clear phrases to our language'. There is a real experience of campaigning in summer and winter behind that phrase. It is, however, to be contrasted with Paine's other famous phrase, 'he pitied the plumage and forgot the dying bird'. That is a fling at Burke, a parody of Burke's grandest manner, and his way of showing that when pressed he could outdo the master. Paine thought that he himself had 'some talent for poetry' (p. cxii), and he shows a poet's concern for the objects and experiences that lie behind words. There are, I think, very few dead metaphors in his prose, in which respect he contrasts strikingly with Godwin.

Several influences on Paine's style have been traced, such as Benjamin Franklin, and the Dissenting tradition as it appears in secularized form in Price and Priestley. Paine quotes Swift and Milton's prose, both of which left their mark on him, as did the King James Bible, of which his Quaker upbringing had given him an intimate knowledge. We are not surprised to find him mentioning Bunyan's Doubting Castle and Giant Despair. Paine's style is essentially in the tradition of plain argument: as in Defoe and Franklin, the syntax and structure follow the thought. The result is not unlike what Paine calls 'the style of English manners, which borders somewhat on bluntness'. But he had also given the problem of style much consideration. Harry Hayden Clark, in his excellent introduction to his selections from Paine (pp. cviii–cxviii), gives an interesting analysis of the stylistic principles Paine worked from: he shows how Paine aimed at simplicity, boldness, wit, the appeal to feeling (by the use of rhetorical figures), the balance of imagination and judgement, appropriateness of diction and carefully controlled construction. Paine was evidently the most self-conscious of radical stylists, and was successful in reaching a huge audience largely because he had thought so hard about the art of propaganda. All this is certainly correct; but Burke's was the most powerful single influence that Paine underwent. With a wider audience in view, Paine simplified Burke's parliamentary flourishes. Although a narrower thinker and a lesser man than Burke, he was in many ways the same kind of radical: a working statesman, and the friend of statesmen, he was at home in the political world that he was striving to change—and at home in the natural world from which he drew many of his images. Paine may choose to contrast Lafayette's 'generous and manly thinking' with 'Mr Burke's periods' which, he says, finish 'with music in the air and nothing in the heart' (p. 66); but he ends *The Rights of Man* with a Burkeian prose poem:

It is now towards the middle of February. Were I to take a turn into the country, the trees would present a leafless, wintery appearance . . . though some of them may not *blossom* for two or three years, all will be in leaf in the summer, except those which are *rotten*. What pace the political summer may keep with the natural, no human foresight can determine. It is, however, not difficult to perceive that the spring is begun. (p. 233)

If not very remarkable prose, this is not far removed from Burke's organic analogy of the great oak, or from his complex image of Windsor Castle, 'girt with its triple keep of kindred and coeval towers'. Like Burke, Paine perhaps owes something to Milton's *Areopagitica*: 'We reck'n more then five months yet to harvest; there need not be five weeks; had we but eyes to lift up, the fields are white already.'

Although William Godwin (1756–1836) was associated with Paine and other active politicians, and although *Political Justice* did have a considerable political effect, he is a metaphysical revolutionary, drawing the metaphysical distinctions that Burke hated. Nor is Godwin at all at home in the worlds of practical statecraft, history, or even nature. As a consequence his style reflects his abstraction from concrete, sensuous reality; when he does use metaphors they are usually dead ones. Although he seems to have taken over some of Shaftesbury's manner as well as his optimistic notions, one of Godwin's starting-points, both for style and ideas, is assuredly in Burke, but in the Burke of *A Vindication of Natural Society*, which appeared in 1756, the year of Godwin's birth. This is a puzzling early work, which I have not seen adequately explained. Subtitled *A View of the Miseries and Evils arising to Mankind from every Species of Artificial Society. In a Letter to Lord. . . . By a Late Noble Writer*, it purports to be a parody of Bolingbroke's style and ideas; and yet rhetorically and rhythmically it is not very like Bolingbroke's prose; and it does not accurately represent Bolingbroke's Tory views on politics and society, even considered as a *reductio ad absurdum*. (Whether Burke took something of his normal, mature style from Bolingbroke is another question.) What the real impulse behind the *Vindication* was I do not know; but I suspect that the young Burke was more of an anarchist than he would ever have admitted. There are some facetious passages which proclaim loudly their ironic intent, but much of the book, taken out of context, could be read as a classic exposition of philosophic anarchism. Godwin chose to read it thus. Innocent of irony himself, he simply ignored Burke's statement in his preface: 'The design was to show that . . . the same engines which were employed for the destruction of religion, might be employed with equal success for the subversion of government.' Godwin brushed this aside in a footnote full of praise for Burke's treatise, 'in which the evils of the existing political institutions are displayed with incomparable force of reasoning and lustre of eloquence, while the intention of the author was to show that these evils were to be considered as trivial' (I, 13 n.). That was not Burke's intention, but no matter. Godwin, as he himself admits, and as his editor F. E. L. Priestley demonstrates, lifted most of his arguments about and illustrations of the calamities of political history straight out of the *Vindication*; and later uses Burke's material about monarchy and aristocracy, only disagreeing with Burke slightly about democracy, which Godwin thinks not excessively worse than no government at all. Since he admired the abstract, non-sensuous, latinate diction, and the heavy, articulated construction used by Burke, he copied these too. Here is an extract from the *Vindication*:

For as *subordination*, or in other words, the reciprocation of tyranny and slavery, is requisite to support these societies; the interest, the ambition, the malice, or the revenge, nay even the whim and caprice of one ruling man among them, is enough to arm all the rest, without any private views of their own, to the worst and blackest purposes; and what is at once lamentable, and ridiculous, these wretches engage under those banners with a fury greater than if they were animated by revenge for their own proper wrongs.

Apart from the oratorical anaphora and a note of violence in 'wretches', this could easily be Godwin and not Burke writing. What makes *Political Justice* so tiring to read is that Godwin follows or exaggerates even minor tricks of the style of the *Vindication*: for example, many sentences are divided into two members; almost every significant adjective or noun has its doublet. 'Whim and caprice', 'worst and blackest'—that kind of doubling in the passage I have here quoted appears in almost every paragraph of Godwin's; he will even write 'calm and tranquil', or 'disinterested and impartial'. Most tediously, his sentences tend to finish with the same pattern of a double thud, e.g. '. . . the wildest dreams of delirium and insanity' (II, 136, 137, 141).

Godwin has many profound insights into politics and ethics, and on re-reading him I have been surprised to see how often I found him convincing. But he does make it hard for his admirers. His metaphors, for instance, are usually moribund: 'Moral considerations swallow up the effect of every other accident . . . the slow and silent influence of material causes perishes like dews at the rising of the sun' (I, 42). I cannot see a mouth swallowing there, nor yet 'the dews of yon high eastern hill'. Godwin's diction is peculiarly inappropriate to many of his topics; he is fond of describing the horrors of war, poverty, earthquakes, and a favourite illustration is the amputation of a limb. But such horrors are strikingly unrealized: 'their distorted countenances, their mutilated limbs, their convulsed and palpitating flesh' (II, 175) leaves us cold, compared with, say, Johnson's moving description of suffering in his review of Soame Jenyns. This extreme debility of description and imagery springs from Godwin's almost total rejection of the real worlds of history and of nature. He quotes Burke on the miseries of history only to prove that we can learn nothing from history except that it is miserable; it is only what man *can become* when he transcends history that matters. He even rejects the comforting myth of the Golden Age, so congenial to eighteenth-century Whigs: we are to think only of the future. He ignores the practical problems of statesmanship, concerned with patching up this imperfect world, in favour of the absolute claims of truth, virtue, justice. 'The universal exercise of private judgment is a doctrine so *unspeakably* beautiful, that the true politician will certainly feel *infinite* reluctance in admitting the idea of interfering with it' (I, 181–2), and by that he means, of descending to particular cases. The body of experience which sustains Burke's and Paine's mature styles is to Godwin not only trivial but somehow vulgar.

Godwin chooses the first quotation made in *Political Justice* from another book on the miseries of political history, namely the fourth book of *Gulliver's Travels*. It might seem surprising to find him in agreement with the greatest of Tories, but later on there is another allusion which explains his admiration: 'To assert, in a firm and resolute manner, the thing that is not, is an action from which the human mind unconquerably

revolts' (I, 352). Godwin here stands revealed as a true
Houyhnhnm. Not only is he incapable of suspecting that Swift
may have been ironical about the horses, but Godwin utterly
rejects irony as a weapon, because it involves saying the thing
that is not. There is one mildly funny passage in *Political
Justice* about the symbolism of the royal sceptre, there is a
ridiculous quotation from Tertullian which he describes as
'humerous', but of true irony there is none. This is because,
it would seem, all irony demands some kind of compromise
with the world, and so irony goes the way of metaphor and
sensuous description. At his best, as in some of his political
pamphlets, Godwin achieves a Houyhnhnm-like boldness and
simplicity; at his worst he retreats into an abstract diction
which shuts out the disturbing complications of reality. He
then takes refuge, as other politicians of the left and the right
have done, in the heavy, latinate and oratorical style which
established itself in the mid eighteenth century. Both the best
and the worst can be illustrated from the halves of a single
sentence: 'If every man today would tell all the truth he knew,
it is impossible to predict how short would be the reign of
usurpation and folly' (I, 333).

That Godwin owed much to Burke he did not deny. In a
generous tribute added to the third edition, after Burke's death,
Godwin praises Burke's 'vividness and justness of painting' and
'wealth of imagination'—and here he is evidently speaking of
the mature works rather than of the *Vindication*. Justice, however, compels him to add that 'their exuberance subtracts, in
no inconsiderable degree, from that irresistibleness and rapidity
of general effect, which is the highest excellence of composition'
(II, 545-6 n.).

Neither Godwin nor Paine attained 'the highest excellence
of composition'. Only occasionally in Paine, and hardly ever
in Godwin, do political theory and propaganda achieve the
autonomy of literature, as they do in Milton, Swift or Burke.
They are still read for their importance in the history of ideas,
and sometimes for their ideas; but they deserve a place in the
history of style, if only because they show the diverse effects of
two traditions in English radicalism.

9

WORDSWORTH AND THE EMPIRICAL PHILOSOPHERS

BY HUGH SYKES DAVIES

It is generally allowed that writers of the stature of William Wordsworth (1770–1850) meant what they said, that an indispensable base of their stature was their 'sincerity'. But it is much less commonly assumed that they said what they meant. The common reader, usually having but little experience in exact uses of complex language, is unperceptive of such uses in what he reads; and even the critic, with a greater personal experience of them, still falls by so far short of great writers in this respect that he is liable to underrate the precision of what is on the page before him—moreover, since a little looseness here and there enlarges the scope and need for his own comments, he is rather tempted to find it. Wordsworth is specially liable to this rather loose reading, to this infusion of one's own meaning into a writer's own words. He is still not far removed in date, and few of his terms give the clear signal of obsolete unintelligibility which sends the reader perforce to a glossary or a dictionary. His vocabulary, moreover, was characteristically central, free from erudition or oddity, 'a selection of the language really spoken by men'. Few of his words draw any attention to themselves, but many of them deserve and require close attention nevertheless, indeed much the more because their superficial easiness fails to give warning of their full force.

The words for which this close attention is required at the moment are the first two in a well-worn phrase from a well-known stanza, which has fallen into the rather unhappy role of summing up much of what Wordsworth had to say:

> One impulse from a vernal wood
> May teach you more of man,

Of moral evil and of good,
Than all the sages can.

('The Tables Turned', 21–5)

'Impulse' is perhaps the simpler of the two. It is one of a group
of words, not in themselves uncommon or recondite, which
were taken up into the Wordsworthian meditation, and so
moulded by its pressure that they came to bear a characteristically personal meaning in his poetry. There is, for example, a
powerful use of it in *The Prelude* of 1850:

Thus my days are past
In contradiction, with no skill to part
Vague longing, haply bred by want of power,
From paramount impulse not to be withstood. . . . (1, 237–40)

It is also used to describe the influence upon Ruth's wayward
husband of the more dangerously stimulating aspects of an
exotic climate—'The wind, the tempest roaring high, The
tumult of a tropic sky':

Whatever in those climes he found
Irregular in sight or sound
Did to his mind impart
A kindred impulse, seemed allied
To his own powers, and justified
The workings of his heart.

('Ruth', 127–32)

Any careful reader of Wordsworth's poetry will, of course,
become sensitized to the special force of a word like this, by
the normal reaction of the mind to recurrence and context. It
did not escape his first careful reader, for in the Dejection Ode,
Coleridge wrote:

Those sounds which oft have raised me, whilst they awed,
And sent my soul abroad,
Might now perhaps their wonted impulse give. . . . (17–19)

The poem was originally addressed to Wordsworth, and it
seems clear that Coleridge had not missed the special meaning
which the word would naturally bear in this context. It is the
clearer because his usual way of using it was very different.

Wordsworth used 'impulse' thirty-nine times in his poetry, Coleridge ten times: Cowper three, Shelley seventeen times, and Keats not even once. By themselves, such figures mean a little, but not very much, for the number of occurrences of any particular word in any one writer will depend partly upon how much he wrote; the more words he set to paper, the larger the score for any one word. What is of much greater significance is the difference between the word as usually used by Coleridge and the others, and as used by Wordsworth. For them, excepting only the passage just quoted from Coleridge, it was always with the meaning of impulse as opposed to deliberate reflexion, as in the phrase 'to act on impulse'. For him, it meant not an inexplicable eddy *within* the human spirit, but a movement stirred in it from *without*, an influence upon the individual of some force in the outer universe. His use of it was indeed personal, in the sense that it was unlike that of his contemporaries, but not wholly novel, for the term had been commonly used by theologians in the seventeenth century to describe the influence upon man of good or evil spirits; the *Oxford English Dictionary* cites the title of a treatise published in 1701, *Discourse of Angels . . . also something touching Devils, Apparitions, and Impulses.*

There are many other words which make the same kind of demand in reading Wordsworth properly: 'insight', 'power', 'paramount', 'simplicity' are examples. All of them had served as habitual rallying-points in his thought and feeling, and had acquired to some extent a meaning peculiar to him. For the most part, however, this will reveal itself, of itself, by the accumulation of contexts, and if it does not, then the concordance—the first and incomparably the best succedaneum and prop for our infirmities as readers—will make the revelation for us. The case is otherwise with the first word of the phrase 'one impulse'. Here is a word so deceptively simple that in no context will the mind dwell much on it, still less feel the need to strengthen its grasp of it by recourse to the concordance or dictionary. It is one of those small, frequently used words with which it seems impossible to go far wrong. Nor is it possible, but the trouble with words of this kind, used by a writer at once of high precision and of great complexity, is that many readers, while not going far wrong with them, do not go

far enough right with them either. There is a striking example
in one of Prospero's speeches:

> . . . these our actors,
> As I foretold you, were all spirits, and
> Are melted into air, into thin air.
>
> (*The Tempest*, iv, i)

Here 'thin' as applied to air is so simply appropriate that no
reader can ever have gone far wrong with it. But he may not
have gone very far right with it either, and the annotators do
little to help him on his way, for they do not direct his attention
to the doctrine, so well known to Shakespeare and his audience,
concerning the manner in which spirits, both good and bad,
become visible to man. The trick was done, according to the
best authorities, by thickening or densifying air to such an
extent that it had shape and colour; and when the time had
come to disappear, this thickened air was allowed to resume its
normal thinness. Very little harm is done here if the full
meaning is not taken: it is quite another matter in Donne's
'Aire and Angels', where failure to grasp the same doctrine
can be quite ruinous. To miss the full significance of 'one' in
Wordsworth's poem may not be quite ruinous, but it is damaging enough.

There is not much excuse for missing it, even if the poem—
or worse still, the stanza—is read in isolation. For the word is
given the place of greatest possible emphasis, first in the first
line of the stanza, with a stronger stress than the norm of the
metre would confer upon it: how much stronger can be felt if
you try the effect of 'An impulse. . . .' Moreover it is, by that
firmness of draughtsmanship in sentence-structure so characteristic of Wordsworth, made to balance antithetically against
the word 'all' in the last line. The syntactic shape involved,
in fact, is quite a common one, and very like that of the
deplorably similar lines:

> Sound, sound the clarion, fill the fife,
> Throughout the sensual world proclaim,
> One crowded hour of glorious life
> Is worth an age without a name.
>
> (Thomas Mordaunt, 'Verses written during the War
> 1756–63')

Certainly Wordsworth cannot be accused of having muffed his meaning, even for the reader on the run. For one who takes the poem together with those written at about the same time, the significance of 'one' is put beyond doubt by this couplet:

> One moment now may give us more
> Than years of toiling reason;
> ('To my Sister', 25–6)

where nearly the same thought is matched by precisely the same placing of the word at the beginning of the stanza, with the same metrical emphasis. And the more extensive reader of Wordsworth will readily recognize in it a brief statement of that doctrine of 'spots of time' which makes the climax of book XII, itself the climactic book of *The Prelude*.

But while the significance of 'one' ought not to be missed in this context, it is easier to miss the fact that it was in sharp contradiction with the teaching of the empirical philosophers about human experience. Wordsworth himself never much emphasized, nor even clearly stated, this contradiction. Perhaps he was never quite clearly and emphatically aware of it, for what he was contradicting was not one of their formal doctrines, but rather an unexpressed assumption or implication running through them, and it was quite possible for him to believe that he wrote in general harmony with their formal doctrines, without his observing that he was in sharp disagreement with what they implied.

In their determination to show that all ideas, all thought, all the works of the mind were derived from sensory experience and from nothing else, the empirical philosophers from Locke onwards were led to present the mind as essentially passive and inactive. This is the purport of the three revealing images in which Locke describes it; first, as a cabinet, 'The senses at first let in particular ideas, and furnish the yet empty cabinet . . .'; second, as blank paper, 'Let us suppose the mind to be, as we say, white paper, void of all characters, without any ideas, how comes it to be furnished ?'; third, as a dark room,

. . . external and internal sensation are the only passages that I can find of knowledge to the understanding. These alone, as far as I can discover, are the windows by which light is let into this dark room. For methinks the understanding is not much unlike a closet wholly shut from light, with only some little opening left to let in external visible resemblances or ideas of things without: would the pictures coming into such a dark room but stay there, and lie so orderly as to be found upon occasion, it would very much resemble the understanding of a man in reference to all objects of sight, and the ideas of them.[1]

With these images, and their implications, Berkeley, Hume and Hartley would not have disagreed.

They would also have accepted in a general way Locke's further statement, contrasting the initial passivity of the mind with its subsequent activity: 'But as the mind is wholly passive in the reception of all its simple ideas, so it exerts several acts of its own, whereby out of its simple ideas, as the materials and foundations of the rest, the other are framed' (II, xii, 1). Even in this activity, however, Locke did not allow the mind much autonomy, for he saw the formation of complex ideas from simple ones as profoundly conditioned by sensory experience and its patterns. Thus in what he calls 'the notice that our senses take of the constant vicissitude of things' such relations as cause and effect, contiguity, identity and diversity are suggested by experience itself. And their most powerful mode of suggestion is recurrence, for if simple ideas often occur together, they will set up associations between them, some natural and 'reasonable', others resting only on chance and custom:

ideas that in themselves are not at all of kin, come to be so united in some men's minds that it is very hard to separate them; they always keep in company, and the one no sooner at any time comes into the understanding, but its associate appears with it; and if they are more than two which are thus united, the whole gang, always inseparable, show themselves together. (II, xxxiii, 5)

The same pattern of recurrence in sensory experience is the groundwork of Locke's view of language:

If we should inquire a little farther, to see what it is that occasions men to make several combinations of simple ideas into distinct and, as it were, settled modes, and neglect others which, in the nature

[1] *An Essay Concerning Human Understanding* (London, 1690), I, ii, 15; II, i, 2 and xi, 17.

of things themselves, have as much an aptness to be combined and make distinct ideas, we shall find the reason of it to be the end of language; which being to mark or communicate men's thoughts to one another with all the despatch that may be, they usually make such collections of ideas into complex modes, and affix names to them, as they have frequent use of it in their way of living and conversation, leaving others which they have but seldom an occasion to mention loose, and without names that tie them together. . . . (ii, xxii, 5)

Among Locke's chief successors, Berkeley alone had little to say about the role of recurring experiences, not because he took a different view of the formation of complex ideas, but because he was too exclusively concerned with the result of the process in forming universal terms and abstract ideas to bother much about the process itself.[1] In Hume, on the other hand, the recurrences of experience became quite central, for his view of causality depended entirely on the mental effects of the 'constant conjunction' of sensations, 'the repetition of like objects in like relations of succession and contiguity', 'the coherence and constancy of certain impressions'.[2] Indeed in one curious passage he remarks that mere recurrency can reverse the usual rule that

ideas of the memory are more *strong* and *lively* than those of the fancy. . . . This is noted in the case of liars; who by the frequent repetition of their lies, come at last to believe and remember them, as realities; custom and habit having in this case, as in many others, the same influence on the mind as nature, and infixing the idea with equal force and vigour. (ii, v)

Hartley again, though for somewhat different purposes, laid the greatest stress on the role of recurring sensations in mental life. His basic propositions on association are full of phrases such as these:

Let the sensation A be often associated with each of the sensations B, C, D, &c. . . . A, impressed alone, will, at last, raise b, c, d, &c. all together, i.e. associate them with one another. . . . All compound

---

[1] *A Treatise Concerning the Principles of Human Knowledge* (London, 1708), Introduction, 18.
[2] *A Treatise of Human Nature* (London, 1739–40) part ii, sections vi and xiv; part iv, section ii.

impressions A + B + C + D, &c. after sufficient repetition leave compound miniatures a + b + c + d, &c. which recur every now and then from slight causes. . . .[1]

His definition of memory is: 'The rudiments of memory are laid in the perpetual recurrency of the same impressions, and clusters of impressions' (prop. xc). And of the imagination, he says: 'The recurrence of ideas, especially visible and audible ones, in a vivid manner, but without regard to the order observed in past facts, is ascribed to the power of imagination or fancy' (prop. xci).

In all these sentences, and in the expositions of which they are part, it is steadily assumed, though nowhere quite explicitly stated, that experience tends to be continuous and homogeneous: that it flows in through the senses upon the mind with an unremitting and undifferentiated force, no one piece of it being of greater importance than another. It is further stated, and explicitly, that the more complex mental structures made up from sensations are not the product of any autonomous activity in the mind, but are suggested to it by the frequent recurrence of some sensations in 'gangs' and 'clusters' amid 'the constant vicissitude of things'. To the mind conceived as quite passive, without any power to choose among or to modify sensations, all sensations must be equal, save that mere frequency of occurrence would draw attention to some rather than others.

But though this was the steady assumption of the empirical philosophers, they were too sensible, too acute observers to overlook some facts not altogether consistent with this view of mind and experience. They mentioned them, at least, and however cursorily did their best to reconcile them with their over-riding conceptions. Locke, for example, notes that ideas may be fixed in the memory by 'attention' and 'pleasure or pain' as well as by 'repetition', and that 'in remembering the mind is often active', especially when 'roused and tumbled . . . by some turbulent and tempestuous passion' (II, x, 3 and 7). He describes the effect of selective attention quite fully:

How often may a man observe in himself, that whilst his mind is intently employed in the contemplation of some objects, and

[1] *Observations on Man* (London, 1749), part I, prop. xii.

curiously surveying some ideas that are there, it takes no notice of impressions of sounding bodies made upon the organ of hearing with the same alteration that uses to be for the producing the idea of sound ! A sufficient impulse there may be on the organ; but it not reaching the observation of the mind, there follows no perception. (II, ix, 4)

He might well have added—had he not been Locke—that a mind intent upon proving one thing can be singularly incurious about the implications of some of the proofs it uses, and by way of illustration, he need have gone no further than his own incuriosity about the possibility that sensations might sometimes get into the memory without the intervention of conscious perception.

A still more remarkable example of the same incuriosity is to be found in Hume's proof of his distinction between memory and fancy as depending only on the relative faintness of ideas in the latter:

It frequently happens, that when two men have been engaged in any scene of action, the one shall remember it much better than the other, and shall have all the difficulty in the world to make his companion recollect it. He runs over several circumstances in vain; mentions the time, the place, the company, what was said, what was done on all sides; till at last he hits on some lucky circumstance, that revives the whole, and gives his friend a perfect memory of everything. (II, v)

It is indeed a curious illustration of the blinkered selectiveness of even the best minds, that Hume should have been capable both of making this observation, and of making nothing of it, of just dropping it when it had served the immediate purpose of his argument, without for a moment wondering what was the nature and mode of operation of this one 'lucky circumstance', whence came its special evocative power, what aspect of the original experience might have given this special force to it, and above all, whether this kind of behaviour did not flatly contradict his habitual assumptions about the equality of sensations in their impact on the mind.

The aspect of Wordsworth's relation with the empirical philosophers which specially concerns me will by now have become apparent. So far as the notion of 'impulse' goes, he was in general agreement with them, and his use of the word is not very different from the way it is used in the last quotation from Locke.[1] But in his insistence upon the potential significance of '*one* impulse', of one experience rather than a host of others, he was in agreement only with Hume's observation, and in sharp disagreement with his assumptions about the texture of experience.

Wordsworth was able to make notable advances on the theories of the empirical philosophers simply because he was better than they were at their own game. The ultimate basis of their theories had always been the same—observation by introspection. Thus Locke, in the last quotation, begins 'How often may a man observe in himself'; Berkeley regularly makes remarks like this 'Whether others have this wonderful faculty of *abstracting their ideas*, they best can tell: for myself I find indeed I have a faculty of imagining, or representing to myself ideas of those particular things I have perceived . . .' (introduction, 10); and Hume equally often says such things as this: 'I believe it will not be very necessary to employ many words in explaining this distinction. Every one of himself will readily perceive the difference betwixt feeling and thinking' (I, i, 1). Very many of their observations were, of course, just and accurate, and Wordsworth found the same things in himself. But many of his observations were still more just, more profoundly penetrating, and in some of them he made discoveries which they had overlooked—or passed by without perceiving their significance.

In his discovery that human experience was not evenly continuous and homogeneous, and that amidst its normal flow there were incidents of a quite different quality in determining the growth of the mind, he was perhaps helped by the fact that his own mode of experiencing things was specially sensitive to

[1] One of the most notable pioneers in this field was Arthur Beatty, in *William Wordsworth: his Doctrine and Art in their Historical Relations*, University of Wisconsin Studies in Language and Literature, no. 24 (Madison, 1927). We owe much to it, but there were perhaps times when Professor Beatty overstated his case, and one of them was his claim that the 'one impulse' stanza 'is exactly the same as the statement of Locke: "The mind is wholly passive in the reception of all its simple ideas"' (p. 126).

the isolated, in time or in space.[1] Here is a small selection from
the many instances that might be given:

> And one coy Primrose to that Rock
>   The vernal breeze invites.
> ('The Primrose of the Rock', 5-6)

> Yet, Lady! shines through this black night,
> One star of aspect heavenly bright.
> (*The White Doe of Rylstone* (1815), 1356-7)

> And suddenly, behold a wonder!
> For One, among those rushing deer,
> A single One, in mid career
> Hath stopped. . . .
> (*ibid.* 1641-4)

> Fair as a star, when only one
> Is shining in the sky.
> ('She dwelt . . .', 7-8)

> Behold her, single in the field,
> Yon solitary Highland Lass!
> ('The Solitary Reaper', 1-2)

> Well might it please me more to mark and keep
> In Memory, how that vast abiding-place
> Of human creatures turn where I might was sown
> Profusely sown with individual sights.
> (*The Prelude*, ms.E, 1839, VII, 598 f.)

> there, in silence, sate
> This One Man, with a sickly babe outstretched
> Upon his knee. . . .
> (*The Prelude*, 1850, VII, 607-9)

---

[1] An outlying example of the same interest in isolated things occurs in *A Guide through the District of the Lakes,* ed. E. de Selincourt (London, 1906), p. 38: 'In the bosom of each of the lakes of Ennerdale and Devockwater is a single rock, which, owing to its neighbourhood to the sea, is—The haunt of cormorants and sea-mew's clang, a music well suited to the stern and wild character of the several scenes!' The tip of the rock in the midst of Lake Ennerdale is still to be seen, despite the raising of the level of the water by the Corporation of a small town by the name of Whitehaven which uses the lake as a reservoir. Visible preparations are now being made for a further vandalism of the same kind, which will submerge the rock completely. Its main purpose, so it is said locally, will be to provide water for a chemical manufactory.

There is a Yew-tree, pride of Lorton Vale,
Which to this day stands single, in the midst
Of its own darkness. . . .
Of vast circumference and gloom profound
This solitary Tree!
('Yew-Trees', 1–3, 9–10)

      A single Tree
There was, no doubt yet standing there, an Ash. . . .
(*The Prelude*, 1805, VI, 90–1)

But there's a Tree, of many, one,
A single Field which I have looked upon. . . .
('Ode: Intimations of Immortality', 51–2)

I love a public road: few sights there are
That please me more; such object hath the power
O'er my imagination since the dawn
Of childhood, when its disappearing line,
Seen daily afar off, on one bare steep
Beyond the limits which my feet had trod
Was like a guide into eternity.
(*The Prelude*, 1805, XII, 145–51)

But the central record of this sensitiveness to the 'one', the isolated sight or moment, and the most profound comment upon it, is at the end of book XII of *The Prelude*. This miserably truncated quotation from the final autobiographical passage will serve to bring out what is most relevant in it for the present purpose:

      I went forth
Into the fields, impatient for the sight
Of those led palfreys that should bear us home;
My brothers and myself. There rose a crag,
That, from the meeting-point of two highways
Ascending, overlooked them both, far stretched;
Thither, uncertain on which road to fix
My expectation, thither I repaired,
Scout-like, and gained the summit; 'twas a day
Tempestuous, dark, and wild, and on the grass
I sate half-sheltered by a naked wall;
Upon my right hand couched a single sheep,
Upon my left a blasted hawthorn stood . . .
      Ere we to school returned,

That dreary time,—ere we had been ten days
Sojourners in my father's house, he died,
And I and my three brothers, orphans then,
Followed his body to the grave. . . .
And, afterwards, the wind and sleety rain,
And all the business of the elements,
The single sheep, and the one blasted tree,
And the bleak music from that old stone wall,
The noise of wood and water, and the mist
That on the line of each of those two roads
Advanced in such indisputable shapes;
All these were kindred spectacles and sounds
To which I oft repaired, and thence would drink,
As at a fountain; . . .
                    (*The Prelude*, 1850, XII, 289–301, 305–9, 317–26)

In this, perhaps the most powerful, revealing, and also perplex-
ing of the experiences which Wordsworth reports in *The
Prelude*, there is no need to expatiate on the importance of
isolated moments—often containing within themselves isolated sensations such as 'the single sheep, and the one blasted
tree'. And it is impossible to improve on Wordsworth's own
generalizing comment upon such experiences and their place
in the growth of the mind:

There are in our existence spots of time,
That with distinct pre-eminence retain
A vivifying Virtue, whence, depress'd
By false opinion and contentious thought,
Or aught of heavier or more deadly weight,
In trivial occupations, and the round
Of ordinary intercourse, our minds
Are nourished and invisibly repair'd. . . .
This efficacious spirit chiefly lurks
Among those passages of life in which
We have the deepest feeling that the mind
Is lord and master, and that outward sense
Is but the obedient servant of her will.
Such moments, worthy of all gratitude,
Are scatter'd everywhere, taking their date
From our first childhood: in our childhood even
Perhaps are most conspicuous.
                    (*The Prelude*, 1805, XI, 258–65, 269–77)

All that need be added, perhaps, is the obvious hint that here too Wordsworth should be allowed to have said what he meant, as well as meaning what he said. These special 'spots of time' are indeed 'moments scattered' among many other moments and tracts of time of a different character. They are not part of the more usual texture of experience, for which the account given by the empirical philosophers will serve pretty well. And they are distinguished from it above all by their capacity for isolated and instant action, with long continued effects, whereas in the other type of experience, such effects are dependent upon constant repetition.

Most of his other elucidations of his discovery are to be found in his poetry, and above all in *The Prelude*, rather than in his prose. But there was one statement about it which he made in conversation with De Quincey worth recalling, for it shows how skilful and careful an observer of his own mental processes he had become. He and De Quincey had walked up from Grasmere to Dun Mail Rise, hoping to intercept the carrier bearing a newspaper containing critical news of the Peninsular War. At last, after midnight, they gave up hope:

At intervals, Wordsworth had stretched himself at length on the high road, applying his ear to the ground, so as to catch any sound of wheels that might be groaning along at a distance. Once, when he was slowly rising from this effort, his eye caught a bright star that was glittering between the brow of Seat Sandal and of the mighty Helvellyn. He gazed upon it for a minute or so; and then upon turning away to descend into Grasmere, he made the following explanation: 'I have remarked, from my earliest days, that, if under any circumstances the attention is energetically braced up to an act of steady observation, or of steady expectation, then, if this intense condition of vigilance should suddenly relax, at that moment any beautiful, any impressive visual object, or collection of objects, falling upon the eye, is carried to the heart with a power not known under any other circumstances. Just now, my ear was placed upon the stretch, in order to catch any sound of wheels that might come down upon the lake of Wythburn from the Keswick road; at the very instant when I raised my head from the ground, in final abandonment of hope for this night, at the very instant when the organs of attention were all at once relaxing from their tension, the bright star hanging in the air above those outlines of massy blackness fell suddenly upon my eye, and penetrated my capacity of apprehension with a pathos and a sense of the infinite, that would not have arrested me under other circumstances'. He then went on to illustrate the same psychological principle from another instance; it was an instance derived from that exquisite poem, in which he describes a mountain boy planting himself at twilight on the margin of some solitary bay of Windermere, and provoking the owls to a contest with himself, by 'mimic hootings,' blown through his hands. . . . Afterwards, the poem goes on to describe the boy as waiting—waiting with intensity of expectation—and then, at length, when, after waiting to no purpose, his attention began to relax—that is, in other words, under the giving way of one exclusive direction of his senses, began suddenly to allow an admission to other objects—then, in that instant, the scene actually before him, the visible scene, would enter unawares 'with all its solemn imagery'.[1]

It is, of course, possible to doubt whether De Quincey recollected what Wordsworth had said with complete accuracy—he was writing some thirty years after the event. But it is much harder to doubt that he had remembered vividly both the occasion, and the gist of what Wordsworth had said, for it is so well consonant with what he said elsewhere of these 'spots of time', so entirely in harmony with the most convincing autobiographical passages of *The Prelude*—not least with that last quoted. And in this more prosaic description, the essential isolation of these moments, their difference from the usual texture of experience, emerges with special clearness.

It is hard to resist asking the question, even if it be probably unanswerable, which was the more nearly accurate description of experience, Wordsworth's or the philosophers'. Very possibly, of course, different people tend to experience things in different ways: it is easy to imagine that Locke's tenor of life was pretty different from Wordsworth's. But it is certainly worth remarking that one of the most influential of later observers, Freud, reached substantially the same conclusion as Wordsworth. To him also it became clear—at first much to his surprise—that certain perceptions or sensations had a far greater power on the growth of the spirit than others, that they were comparatively few, but in some cases decisive for its

---

[1] De Quincey omitted this passage from his edition of 1853, and Masson followed him. It is taken from *Tait's Edinburgh Magazine*, VI (1839), p. 94.

future development. It was lucky for Freud that, together with his own acuteness and intelligence as an observer, Vienna provided him with so many so-called 'neurotics'—of whom, as he said himself, 'there were only too many in our society'.[1] And it was even more fortunate for Wordsworth that the material which fell under his notice was so much more normal, so that he could concern himself with the more rewarding problems of the natural, the undistorted growth of the spirit. Allowing for this difference, however—the difference between using normal and pathological subjects for observation—the agreement in the basic findings is remarkable. One of the earliest and clearest of Freud's tributes to the power of single occurrences was in a paper written in 1892, in collaboration with Breuer:

The disproportion between the many years duration of an hysterical symptom and the single occurrence which evoked it is similar to that which we are accustomed to see in traumatic neuroses; it was quite frequently in childhood that the events occurred, producing a more or less grave symptom which persisted from that time onwards.[2]

His later works are full of repetitions and enlargements of this discovery, and this will serve to illustrate the many that might be made:

our hysterical patients suffer from reminiscences. Their symptoms are residues and mnemic symbols of particular (traumatic) experiences. . . . Not only do they remember painful experiences in the remote past, but they still cling to them emotionally; they cannot get free of the past and for its sake they neglect what is real and immediate. This fixation of mental life to pathogenic traumas is one of the most significant and practically important characteristics of neurosis.[3]

Freud, then, has reported unambiguously in the same sense as Wordsworth, that mingled with the normal texture of experience, there are a few experiences of an altogether special character, which may cause long-lasting damage to the personality. His discovery was, in fact, simply the obverse of Wordsworth's—that in the formation of the normal human personality,

[1] My Contact with Josef Popper-Lynkeus (1932), trans. in Collected Papers, vol. v (London, 1950), p. 295.
[2] On the Psychical Mechanism of Hysterical Phenomena, trans. in Collected Papers, vol. I (London, 1924), p. 25.
[3] Five Lectures on Psycho-Analysis, trans. (London, 1957), pp. 16–17.

not all experiences count equally and evenly, but that some 'spots of time' have 'distinct pre-eminence' and 'retain' it.

One of the differences between the normal and the pathological reaction to these moments is suggested by an observation in another of Freud's early papers, on *Screen Memories* (1899):

... there are some people whose earliest recollections of childhood are concerned with everyday and indifferent events which could not produce any emotional effect even in children, but which are recollected (*too* clearly, one is inclined to say) in every detail, while approximately contemporary events, which on the evidence of their parents moved them intensely at the time, have not been retained in the memory. Thus the Henris mention a professor of philology whose earliest memory, dating back to between the ages of three and four, showed him a table laid for a meal and on it a basin of ice. At the same period there occurred the death of his grandmother which, according to his parents, was a severe blow to the child. But the professor of philology, as he now is, has no recollection of his bereavement; all that he remembers of those days is the basin of ice.[1]

It is unneccessary to point the similarities between the situation of the professor and Wordsworth's recollections of the death of his father. It is, of course, the differences that matter: that Wordsworth remembered his bereavement completely, no less than 'the single sheep, and the one blasted tree', and that he had, on the whole, richer things to remember in connexion with his grief than a basin of ice. He was in no danger of becoming a professor of philology.

Whether the empirical philosophers be in the right, or Wordsworth and Freud, a writer who is at all concerned with the growth of human spirits cannot but plump for the one or the other. For they suggest, even impose, very different methods of description. A writer who himself experiences things, and believes others to experience them, in the way described by the philosophers will tend to be attracted by the method of 'stream of consciousness', or *monologue intérieur*, for by its means he can best represent the undifferentiated flow of sensations, and the thoughts and feelings they provoke, with their eddies of recurrence and conjunction. One of the earlier descriptions of this

---

[1] *Collected Papers*, vol. v (London, 1950), p. 50.

method in the novel reads (as it well might, considering the ancestry of the writer) like latter-day Locke:

> Examine for a moment an ordinary mind on an ordinary day. The mind receives a myriad impressions—trivial, fantastic, evanescent, or engraved with the sharpness of steel. From all sides they come, an incessant shower of innumerable atoms; and as they fall, as they shape themselves into the life of Monday or Tuesday, the accent falls differently from of old; the moment of importance came not here but there; so that, if a writer were a free man and not a slave, if he could write what he chose, not what he must, if he could base his work upon his own feeling and not upon convention, there would be no plot, no comedy, no tragedy, no love interest or catastrophe in the accepted style, and perhaps not a single button sewn on as the Bond Street tailors would have it. Life is not a series of gig lamps symmetrically arranged; life is a luminous halo, a semi-transparent envelope surrounding us from the beginning of consciousness to the end. Is it not the task of the novelist to convey this varying, this unknown and uncircumscribed spirit, whatever aberrations or complexity it may display, with as little mixture of the alien and external as possible?[1]

If life is indeed like this, then this would no doubt be the right way, or one of the right ways, of describing it, even if it led to the kind of artistic difficulty discussed by Stuart Gilbert in his study of *Ulysses*. Quoting (and translating) from a perceptive French critic, he says:

> The necessity of recording the flow of consciousness by means of words and phrases compels the writer to depict it as a continuous horizontal line. . . . But even a casual examination of our inner consciousness shows that this presentation is essentially false. We do not think on one plane, but on many planes at once. . . . The life of the mind is a symphony. It is a mistake or, at best, an arbitrary method, to dissect the chords and set out their components on a single line, on one plane only. . . . But in the silent monologue, as transposed into words by Joyce, each element seems of equal importance, the subsidiary and the essential themes are treated as equivalent, and an equal illumination falls upon those parts which were, in reality, brightly lit up, and those which remained in the dark background of thought.[2]

[1] Virginia Woolf, 'Modern Fiction', in her *The Common Reader* (London, 1925), p. 189.
[2] Stuart Gilbert, *James Joyce's Ulysses* (London, 1952) (revised), pp. 27-8.

But over and above the artistic difficulty—that of overcoming the sheer tedium of an undifferentiated stream of consciousness —there may be the much more fundamental objection that it is based upon a wrong psychology, an inadequate description of human experience: as it certainly is if Wordsworth and Freud are more right than the philosophers.

On the other hand, a writer inclined to agree with Wordsworth and Freud will need to find the means of describing the more crucially formative moments and impulses of his own mind, and the minds he wishes to represent. The unselectiveness, the evenness of the 'stream of consciousness' may serve him occasionally for preparatory and explanatory passages of experience, for those in which the climactic events are prepared and presaged; but for the climactic events themselves, for the crucial 'spots of time', his technique will need to be more traditional, for it cannot but select, shape, and pose almost in isolation those moments which were so highly selected, so specially shaped and isolated in experience.

It would be easier to discuss this mode of presentation, in its contrast with the 'stream of consciousness', if there were an accepted term to describe it. One was suggested, long ago, by De Quincey in an autobiographical exploration quite like *The Prelude* in its quality, though not, of course, in degree of merit. Describing one of the most profoundly formative moments of his own life, he tells how he had crept into the room where lay the dead body of a dearly loved sister, and had found it full of sunlight. He notes other reasons why, for him at that period of his childhood, thoughts of death and images of summer had become intermingled:

And, recollecting it, I am struck with the truth, that far more of our deepest thoughts and feelings pass to us through perplexed combinations of *concrete* objects, pass to us as *involutes* (if I may coin that word) in compound experiences incapable of being disentangled, than ever reach us *directly*, in their own abstract shapes.[1]

Perhaps it is now too late for De Quincey's coinage to be put into circulation. The term 'imagery' seems to have taken on roughly the same work, and much more besides. But also

---

[1] *Autobiographical Sketches* (Edinburgh, 1853), ch. ii (from *Blackwood's Magazine*, 1845); *Collected Writings*, ed. David Masson, vol. I (Edinburgh, 1889), pp. 38–9.

somewhat less, for it tends, in itself and for the careless user, to emphasize only one element in such crucial experiences, that of sensation. It does poor justice to the elements of thought and feeling needfully present in them, and no justice at all to the essential involvement, *involution*, of the thought and feeling in the sensory experience, and of it in the thought and feeling. De Quincey's term would far more surely suggest the Wordsworthian view of human experience, and the nature of the literary techniques appropriate to it.

It would also point to an awkward reflexion which seems to follow from this view of experience. If it is commonly true, at least of some people, that the growth of the mind is discontinuous, depending often on comparatively few crucially formative involutes; and if these experiences are indeed correctly described as depending upon some special conjunction of an inner state and some outward circumstance, then it follows that chance, destiny, fate—whatever synonym seems most euphemistic— has the power of intervening in the very formation of the human personality. Wordsworth himself seems to have warded off such a conclusion, and Basil Willey aptly elucidates his apparent rejection of it:

> In the celebrated 'spots of time' passage at the end of book XII of *The Prelude*, he says explicitly that of all the recollections which hold for him a 'renovating virtue', he values most those which record moments of the greatest self-activity, those which 'give knowledge to what point, and how, the mind is lord and master, outward sense the obedient servant of her will'; recollections, that is, which show the mind 'not prostrate, overborne, as if the mind were nothing, a mere pensioner of outward forms—' (as in sensationalist philosophy), but in its native dignity, creating significance in alliance with external things.[1]

But there is also throughout Wordsworth's writing the somewhat contrary belief that in such moments, one outward form is not just as good a servant as another, that some have the property of constituting more profitable, more healthy 'spots of time' than others. To give but one example, when Coleridge described himself, in 'Frost at Midnight', as having suffered a little from the environment of his childhood, from having been

[1] *The Seventeenth Century Background* (London, 1934), p. 302.

'rear'd in the great city, pent 'mid cloisters dim,' Wordsworth cordially agreed with him, and contrasted Coleridge's experience with his own:

> the gift is yours,
> Ye winds and sounding cataracts! 'tis yours
> Ye mountains! thine, O Nature! Thou hast fed
> My lofty speculations; and in thee,
> For this uneasy heart of ours, I find
> A never-failing principle of joy
> And purest passion.
> Thou, my Friend! wert reared
> In the great city, 'mid far other scenes.[1]

And there can be no doubt at all that the general tenor of his writing is to the effect that some concrete objects will serve in the making of 'involutes' far better than others. Once he put the point down in very plain prose. It was in the 1815 preface, in his explanation of that classification of his poems which has proved such a doubtful blessing to his admirers and editors, in a comment upon that very poem about the boy and the Winander owls which he had mentioned to De Quincey on Dun Mail Rise. Despite the curious attempt in the last lines to turn the poem into a kind of elegy, the 'boy' had, of course, been himself, and in the earliest surviving draft the pronouns make this quite clear.[2] Evidently, however, he had long felt that the experience described was unlikely to be understood or accepted as weighty enough to form the only substance of a separate poem. Probably for this reason he had added the graceful, but entirely unforceful elegiac fiction—just to round the thing off, as it were, into a more customary shape.[3] Yet the original experience recorded had always seemed to him to be a specially clear and demonstrative example of the workings of the imagination, and he therefore placed it first, in his new

---

[1] *The Prelude* (London, 1850), II, 445–53; cf. VI, 264–274. where the same contrast is drawn at greater length.

[2] The ms. is printed in *The Prelude*, ed. E. de Selincourt (Oxford, 1959) (revised by Helen Darbishire), pp. 639–70. These lines will exemplify the real identity of the boy: 'And when it chanced/That pauses of deep silence mocked my skill/Then often, in that silence, while I hung. . . .'

[3] Hence the failure of the devoted Wordsworthians to identify the lad; cf. de Selincourt's note to *The Prelude*, v, 397–8.

arrangement, among Poems of the Imagination, but with this much help to the reader in the preface:

... in the series of Poems placed under the head of Imagination, I have begun with one of the earliest processes of Nature in the development of this faculty. Guided by one of my own primary consciousnesses, I have presented a commutation and transfer of internal feelings, co-operating with external accidents, to plant, for immortality, images of sound and sight, in the celestial soil of the Imagination.[1]

'Accidents', then, and what is more 'external' accidents, can enter into the most intimate moments of the formation of the spirit. It seems to be an unavoidable consequence of Wordsworth's view of experience, however he may have tried to avoid it, that sometimes it may matter very much what we chance to be seeing, hearing, or touching at a crucial moment of thought and feeling. It would be much more comfortable to believe, with the philosophers, that fate and destiny work upon us more smoothly, with lesser impulses more thinly spread, and altogether less intimately. Perhaps, for philosophers, that is how they do work.

[1] *The Poetical Works of William Wordsworth*, ed. E. de Selincourt, vol. II (Oxford, 1944), p. 440.

10

COLERIDGE AND THE VICTORIANS

BY GRAHAM HOUGH

When Coleridge died in 1834 it must have seemed to the world of letters but one more faint expiration in a general eclipse. The great writers of his own generation, even those of the generation succeeding his own, were dead or silent, and the luminaries of the mid-century were as yet hardly visible above the horizon. And as for Coleridge himself, the work on which his fame had been built was already far in the past. His best poetry was written by 1802, and most of his criticism by 1817. It looks like a parallel, though less prolonged, to Wordsworth's 'fifty years' decay'. And long before his death his older friends had decided that it was so. Hazlitt wrote in *The Spirit of the Age* in 1825: 'Mr Coleridge, by dissipating his [mind], and dallying with every subject by turns, has done little or nothing to justify to the world or to posterity the high opinion which all who have ever heard him converse, or known him intimately, with one accord entertain of him.' He goes on to paint the picture of an age in which 'Monarchy was at variance with' Genius; and Genius had therefore to be crushed. The philosophers, 'the dry abstract reasoners', submitted to these reverses pretty well;

But the poets, the creatures of sympathy, could not stand the frowns both of king and people. . . . They did not stomach being sent to Coventry, and Mr Coleridge sounded a retreat for them by the help of casuistry and a musical voice. 'His words were hollow, but they pleased the ear' of his friends of the Lake School, who turned back disgusted and panic-struck from the dry desert of unpopularity, like Hassan the camel-driver,
> And curs'd the hour and curs'd the luckless day
> When first from Shiraz' walls they bent their way.
They are safely inclosed there. But Mr Coleridge did not enter with them; pitching his tent upon the barren waste without, and having no abiding place nor city of refuge!

De Quincey, in an article in *Tait's Magazine* just after Coleridge's death, uses much the same sort of language; and the opinion lingered on till our own day. E. K. Chambers could conclude his life of Coleridge in 1938 with the sentence: 'So Coleridge passed, leaving a handful of golden poems, an emptiness in the heart of a few friends, and a will-o'-the-wisp light for bemused thinkers.'

Yet anyone whose reading takes him among early Victorian biography and memoirs will find something very different from this elegiac note. He will be astonished at the frequency with which Coleridge's name crops up. Carlyle's *Life of Sterling* (1851), Mill's *Autobiography* (1873), Newman's *Apologia* (1864), the lives of F. D. Maurice and Julius Hare—they all tell a very different story. The difference is most clearly announced in Mill's two celebrated essays, on Bentham (1838) and Coleridge (1840): 'Jeremy Bentham and Samuel Taylor Coleridge—the two great seminal minds of England in their age.' He defines the situation as follows:

The name of Coleridge is one of the two English names of our time which are likely to be oftener pronounced, and to become symbolical of more important things, in proportion as the inward workings of the age manifest themselves more and more in outward facts. . . . If it be true, as Lord Bacon affirms, that a knowledge of the speculative opinions of men between twenty and thirty years of age is the great source of political prophecy, the existence of Coleridge will show itself by no slight or ambiguous traces in the coming history of our country; for no one has contributed more to shape the opinions of those among its younger men, who can be said to have opinions at all.

F. D. Maurice dedicates his *Kingdom of Christ* in 1842 to Derwent Coleridge, the poet's son, and refers to 'the influence which your father's writings are exercising on the minds of this generation'. Twenty years ago, he says, the name of Coleridge was so unpopular that men feared to be associated with it. Now the various parties which only differed in the degree of their dislike for him are scrambling for a share of his opinions. And Julius Hare dedicates *The Mission of the Comforter* (1846) 'To the honoured memory of Samuel Taylor Coleridge, the Christian Philosopher', and refers to himself as 'one of the many pupils whom his writings have helpt to discern the sacred concord and unity of human and divine truth'. When we consider the great influence exercised by Hare at Cambridge, and by Maurice at both Oxford and Cambridge and later in the capital, we cannot suppose that such judgements stood unsupported.

The explanation of these two strangely divergent sets of opinions is that they are not directed to the same object. It is not, as we might suppose, a sectarian or a party matter. Tributes to Coleridge's power come from all shades in the spectrum of nineteenth-century thought. So do the repinings over his dissipated energies. But there are two Coleridges to be considered. The earlier Romantic generation was naturally concerned with Coleridge the poet and the critic of poetry; and in this they have been followed by the majority of literary students to our own time. His Victorian admirers were interested chiefly in the Coleridge of the Highgate days—the inspired table-talker, the speculative thinker, the religious and political philosopher. Mill's encomium refers to the author of the *Lay Sermons* (1816–17), *Aids to Reflection* (1825), *On the Constitution of Church and State* (1830), and the two posthumous publications, the *Literary Remains* (1836–9) and *Confessions of an Inquiring Spirit* (1840). Readers of 'The Ancient Mariner', of the Wordsworth chapters in the *Biographia*, amateurs of Imagination and Fancy, have on the whole agreed to leave the dust on these volumes undisturbed, and it is this massive body of work that E. K. Chambers dismisses in a regretful phrase.

It is true that we are not even yet in a position to give Coleridge's philosophical writing the attention it could properly claim. In spite of much recent work—a first edition of the *Philosophical Lectures* by Miss Coburn (1949), an edition of the *Treatise on Method* by Miss Snyder (1934), and much else besides, there is still unpublished material. Textual divergencies in the common reprints are baffling. Nineteenth-century studies will be immensely served by the complete critical edition of Coleridge's work now projected. Nevertheless the general lines of Coleridge's speculative thought are tolerably well known. If E. K. Chambers' bemused thinkers wish to stabilize the will-o'-the-wisp light that dances before them they may turn to the first chapter in Basil Willey's *Nineteenth Century Studies* (1949), to Shawcross's introduction to *Biographia* (1907), and to Mill's hundred-year-old essay. But they will find little about Coleridge in the standard histories of philosophy. There are several reasons for this. In English culture Coleridge is the chief representative of an important phase of European thought. But in the larger European perspective he is not an original thinker. He is an eclectic derivative of German idealism. The movement he inaugurated was not long continued; it was not followed up by the professional philosophers; and the demands that his thought could satisfy were ultimately met by a more effectively produced and better advertised article imported direct from Germany towards the end of the century. So that Coleridge remains the first of the great nineteenth-century 'thinkers' rather than a philosopher in the strict technical sense. And it is in non-philosophical circles, or unprofessionally philosophical circles, between his own death and the Oxford Hegelianism of the seventies and eighties that we are to look for his widest influence.

The general purpose of Coleridge's speculative writing is (to put it in the briefest form) to establish a school of modern English philosophic idealism to counteract the scepticism and empiricism of the eighteenth century. His originality and his measure of success are a matter of debate. He said himself that the essentials of his philosophical system were complete before he went to Germany in 1798, before he ever made the acquaintance of German transcendentalism. Others have suggested that his system is actually a cento of borrowings from Kant and Schelling, many of them unacknowledged. Others again allege that he never properly understood Kant, and produced only distortions and misinterpretations of the Critical Philosophy. Surely none of these can represent the whole truth. Coleridge was soaked in Platonism and neo-Platonism from his earliest literate years; he had expounded Plotinus and Porphyry at school. After a sojourn in the dry territory of the associationists he returned to his true spiritual home via Berkeley—or one version of Berkeley. He was aware of obligations to the mystics[1] and to the Schoolmen[2]; he was acutely conscious of a

[1] *Biographia Literaria*, ch. ix.   [2] *Statesman's Manual*, appendix E.

tradition of idealist and Platonic thought in England—what he called 'the spiritual platonic old England', of which Sidney, Shakespeare, Bacon and Wordsworth were the representatives; contrasted with 'commercial G. Britain',—'with Locke at the head of the Philosophers & Pope of the Poets'.[1] When he made the acquaintance of Kant, he said, it at once 'invigorated and disciplined my understanding'; and when he came to Schelling 'I first found a genial coincidence with much that I had toiled out for myself, and a powerful assistance in what I had yet to do'.[2] The genial coincidence extends to several pages simply translated and incorporated into his own work; but in essence there is no reason to doubt this account of the matter. He found in the Germans a cast of mind sympathetic to his own and a parallel historical mission; he found some new ideas and above all a powerful armoury of new logical and epistemological weapons which, be it admitted, he was hardly likely to have developed for himself. And though he was immensely learned, he was not a scholar in the modern sense; he used ideas and terminology to suit his own turn and was not particular to acknowledge obligations. In fact the critical side of Kantian philosophy largely passed him by. His kind of idealism was more Platonic than Kantian and more Christian than either, for the regulative principle of all Coleridge's philosophical activity was to make his idealist thought a secure base for Christianity, for contemporary Christianity.

To this end he finds it necessary to reject the 'white paper' psychology of Locke and the mechanistic account of mental operations given by the associationists; and to adopt something like the doctrine of innate ideas. He makes much of the distinction between two faculties of the human mind, Understanding and Reason—concepts which he certainly met in the German transcendentalists, but just as certainly had found much earlier in some part of the Platonic tradition that he followed so assiduously. Understanding judges of phenomena and forms generalizations from them; Reason perceives directly truths not accessible to the senses. Precisely what illuminations

---

[1] *Notebooks*, ed. Kathleen Coburn, vol. II (New York, 1961), no. 2598, a note written in the summer of 1805.

[2] *Biographia Literaria*, ch. ix.

Reason brings is not always clear, but the primary truths of natural religion—God, freedom and immortality—are among them. The most compendious accounts of the matter are to be found in appendix C of *The Statesman's Manual* and appendix A of *Aids to Reflection*.

In political philosophy Coleridge looks to the Idea of the State, believing that there is a form to which the actual British constitution tends, even a form to which all civil society must tend. He finds this in the reconciliation between permanence and change, and seeks to embody each of these in a particular institution of the state. Permanence is to be found chiefly in the landed interest, which should be embodied in the House of Lords; change in the personal interest, i.e. the professional, industrial and commercial part of the nation, which should be embodied in the House of Commons. And the whole is to be, not a Benthamite free-for-all of competing individualities, but an organic whole in which each part can alone find fulfilment. This all sounds familiarly Burkean but, as Mill pointed out, it is far less founded on mere prescription and the status quo, and would involve a far more radical reformation of the eighteenth-century House of Commons than anything that Burke could contemplate; more radical, we might add, than what actually occurred in 1832. Yet it is a Tory and paternal, not a Whiggish and individualist radicalism; already the political voices of Carlyle, of Ruskin, of Young England, can proleptically be heard.

Coleridge is perhaps most original in his view of the Church. He holds that its specifically religious function is from the political point of view a side-issue. To him the main function of the Church as a human institution is the advancement of knowledge, the instruction and civilizing of the nation. The Church includes the whole of the 'clerisy', the universities as well as the parish clergy, and for its maintenance a portion of the national wealth is properly set aside. Whatever the realities may have been, we have only to recall the secular and social aspirations of the Oxford Movement to see how powerful this ideal of an almost theocratic learned establishment was to be in the years to come.

We are now approaching the core of Coleridge's thought, the religious philosophy to which all was subordinated. The function of the Church is to teach not only religion but secular wisdom as well, for the two are ultimately one. The aim of Coleridge's religious writing is to show that all the central doctrines of Christianity, all the sacraments and traditional devotional observances, are deducible, with the aid of revelation, from the constitution of the human mind itself. In other words, to base Christian apologetics not on history or authority but on the intuitions of Reason. Since we are discussing the history, not the validity, of Coleridge's ideas, we need say nothing for the moment about the feasibility of this attempt. The point to emphasize is that in making it Coleridge was showing an almost prophetic awareness of the religious needs of the next age. Basil Willey has cogently pointed out[1] that by the time the attacks on traditional Christianity were launched, the defensive positions were already laid down—by Coleridge. He was aware, astonishingly early, of the historical criticism of the Scriptures and all that it was to imply; and he was conscious that the prime foundations of eighteenth-century natural religion—physico-theology and the argument from design— were to him unsatisfying and were not likely to remain long undisturbed.

The preliminary statement to the *Confessions of an Inquiring Spirit* asks:

I. Is it necessary, or expedient, to insist on the belief of the divine origin and authority of all and every part of the Canonical Books as the condition or first principle of Christian Faith?

II. Or, may not the due appreciation of the Scriptures collectively be more safely relied on as the result and consequence of the belief in Christ; the gradual increase—in respect of particular passages— of our spiritual discernment of their truth and authority supplying a test and measure of our own growth and progress as individual believers, without the servile fear that prevents or overclouds the free honor which cometh from love?

The question was well timed to meet the coming science of Tübingen. Coleridge was of course aware of earlier German 'higher criticism', but its impact on England was hardly felt till after his death. Strauss's *Leben Jesu* appeared in 1835 and was translated by George Eliot in 1846. Once that dangerous

---

[1] *Nineteenth Century Studies* (London, 1949), p. 31.

solvent had begun to work, the old Paleyan 'evidences' from miracle and prophecy were to seem but slender supports, and it is not surprising that the Coleridgean line of argument should be the necessary and inevitable recourse. Paley in particular with his positivist apologetic—a pseudo-historical defence of revelation, a mechanistic defence of natural religion—was Coleridge's particular opponent, and much of the polemic in *Aids to Reflection* is directed against him and his school.

I more than fear the prevailing taste for books of natural theology, physico-theology, demonstrations of God from Nature, evidences of Christianity, &c., &c. Evidences of Christianity! I am weary of the word. Make a man feel the want of it; rouse him, if you can, to the self-knowledge of his need of it; and you may safely trust it to its own evidence.[1]

The case was similar with the pressure of evolutionary thought. Lyell's *Principles of Geology* appeared in 1833, *Vestiges of Creation* in 1842. Tennyson read them both, and like many another was quick to realize that this train of discovery and speculation was forcing a withdrawal from the old teleological position, the belief in the Divine Mechanic. Again, Coleridge's *Aids* were found powerful—not in refuting what could not be refuted, but in removing the whole debate to another ground, the ground of religious experience. As Coleridge himself put it: 'In order to non-suit the infidel Plaintiff, we must remove the cause from the Faculty that judges according to Sense, and whose judgments therefore are valid only on Objects of Sense, to the Superior Courts of Conscience and intuitive Reason!'[2]

The need of Coleridge's assistance was soon, then, to become obvious. It was perhaps called for most of all by the growth of a Benthamite ideology, with its unhistorical and analytic view of society, individualism and utilitarianism in ethics, laissez-faire in economics—the whole outlook of a progressive, increasingly industrial country. The later Wordsworth too had foreseen this and feared it. But what besides mere obstruction had the traditionalists to set against it? There was of course Burke. But for the temper of post-Reform-Bill England Burke was too much the champion of mere prescriptive establishment. Coleridge in *The Friend*, and more systematically in *On*

[1] *Aids to Reflection*, Conclusion.   [2] *Ibid.* p. 233.

the Constitution of Church and State, was doing more than defend what happened to have come about. He was providing a possible form of nineteenth-century conservatism with a strong philosophical basis; and his influence might have been longer-lived if modern conservatism had not preferred to get along without one. To young men in the thirties and forties, acutely conscious that much of the most powerful intelligence of the time was working towards a Benthamite extinction of existing institutions and beliefs, yet also conscious of a profound allegiance to their religion, to the national church, to much of the traditional social pattern, Coleridge came as a godsend. They felt in their hearts that the rising ideology was wrong, yet they were unable to demonstrate its wrongness intellectually. He placed weapons in their hands, and more than that, he provided them with an example. As Julius Hare pointed out, the personal testimony of Coleridge to the possibility of a Christian philosophy and of a view of society based upon it was immensely influential. For Coleridge had the capacity (sometimes looked at askance, but necessary, it appears, to all great teachers) of communicating his belief even to those who only imperfectly understood its grounds.

The surviving records of his Highgate conversation alone make this clear. The oral channel was probably the one through which most of the Coleridgean influence originally worked. Carlyle in his life of Sterling affords a grudging but convincing testimony to the power exercised by Dr Gilman's resident sage. But ideas in nineteenth-century England, more, probably, than either before or since, were disseminated by the universities. How many phases of nineteenth-century thought turn out to be emanations from some powerful tutor or university preacher? The movement that centred in Newman is the obvious example. But the influence of Jowett at Balliol, later that of Thomas Hill Green, even that of Walter Pater, were not dissimilar. And the radiating influence of F. D. Maurice at Cambridge was only second in importance to the Oxford Movement itself. Maurice was not a frequenter of Coleridge's Highgate circle, but Julius Hare was. And Hare soon became the recognized exponent of Coleridgean ideas in Cambridge. He also became F. D. Maurice's tutor at Trinity and contributed much to the formation of his mind—a formation so effective that he even (an extreme example of tutorial partiality) expressed the opinion that there had been no such mind since Plato's. And his influence continued after Maurice went down. As Edward FitzGerald tells us, it was still active in expounding the ideas of Coleridge and 'the German school' to the next, the Tennysonian, generation of undergraduates.

Maurice was, if not the actual founder, the most powerful foundation member of the celebrated Apostles Club, and very much responsible for its ethos. It is an ethos which is a little difficult to define, since it contained its share of uncertain youthful exploration; but its general direction seems fairly consistent. It can best be described as a religious liberalism, but not a reductive liberalism; not one which tries to explain away traditional dogma, but rather to show its necessity by showing its essential congruity with the needs of the human spirit. This was allied with much general philosophic and scientific curiosity; a devotion to the poetry of the Romantic generation; and in spite of a (not uncommon) sympathy with other peoples' revolutions, a fundamental acceptance of the traditional structure of English society and its ways of life. The Apostles in fact translated into terms of a younger university generation the essentials of Coleridgean thought. Arthur Hallam has spoken of the enormous influence exercised by Maurice through the foundation of this society.[1] The reason for it is obvious. It provided a middle way between infidel philosophic radicalism and the dogmatic traditionalism of the Oxford Movement. If we were to trace the long-range influence of this type of Broad Churchmanship we should probably be justified in speaking of a Cambridge movement equal in extent (though not in sharpness of definition) with its more famous rival.

Maurice's influence however was not confined to Cambridge. Having gone down because of a scruple over signing the Articles, he later overcame it and went up to Oxford. There again he made his influence felt, and there Coleridgean ideas were in any case not unknown: for Thomas Arnold, in many ways the Oxford counterpart of Maurice, had been greatly

[1] Hallam Tennyson, *Tennyson: a Memoir* (London, 1897), vol. I, p. 43.

affected by Coleridge in his early days. Indeed his view of the Church could well be called a practical version of the Coleridgean ideal. Maurice's influence was soon to extend beyond the universities. On leaving Cambridge he undertook the editorship of *The Athenaeum*; and it was at this time that John Stuart Mill made his acquaintance. Coleridge and Bentham are making a cautious *rapprochement*, and the seed of the two famous essays is sown. Mill, if he does not indulge in any incautious comparisons with Plato, is yet said to have called Maurice the ablest and subtlest logician in Europe. There is a passage in *On Liberty* (1859) about a refined and deeply conscientious theological thinker 'who spends a life in sophisticating with an intellect which he cannot silence, and exhausts the resources of ingenuity in attempting to reconcile the promptings of his conscience and reason with orthodoxy, which yet he does not, perhaps, to the end succeed in doing'. It is sometimes thought to refer to Newman, but was almost certainly written with Maurice in mind, for it is so closely paralleled by the references to him in the *Autobiography*. There was, Mill says, 'more intellectual power wasted in Maurice than in any other of my contemporaries. Few of them certainly have had so much to waste. Great powers of generalization, rare ingenuity and subtlety, and a wide perception of important and unobvious truths. . . .' After citing 'his noble origination of the Christian Socialist movement', Mill goes on to acknowledge Maurice's relation to Coleridge and his own debt to the Coleridgean school:

The nearest parallel to him, in a moral point of view, is Coleridge, to whom, in merely intellectual power, apart from poetical genius, I think him decidedly superior. At this time, however, he might be described as a disciple of Coleridge, and Sterling as a disciple of Coleridge and of him. The modifications which were taking place in my old opinions gave me some points of contact with them; and both Maurice and Sterling were of considerable use to my development (ch. v).

Coleridge's part in modifying the rigours of Utilitarianism is thus established. What is more surprising is to find him in a similar though more ambiguous relation with the Oxford Movement. In 1839, in an article in *The British Critic*, Newman cites Coleridge as one of the influences that prepared the way for the success of the Tractarians—

a very original thinker who, while he indulged a liberty of speculation which no Christian can tolerate, and advocated conclusions which were often heathen rather than Christian, yet after all instilled a higher philosophy into inquiring minds than they had hitherto been accustomed to accept. In this way he made trial of his age, . . . and succeeded in interesting its genius in the cause of Catholic truth.

He reprinted this in the *Apologia*; but in other places he does a good deal of hedging about the actual influence of Coleridge on his thought. Late in life he denied that he had ever read a line of Coleridge; but this is evidently a failure of recollection. T. D. Acland wrote to Newman in 1834 about his own 'Coleridgean reveries', how he would have feared to present their results to Newman's severer mind. But on reading a page of Newman on the Arians he decided that 'after all, poor Coleridge was not so bad a fellow if well used'; and was rejoiced to find that something like a Coleridgean view 'had obtained the sanction of a calm mind like yours'.[1] This hardly suggests that Newman could be supposed to be entirely ignorant of Coleridge's thought; yet in his own *Chronological Notes* for 1835, a year later, he remarks that he then for the first time read some of Coleridge's work—'and I am surprised how much that I thought mine is to be found there'.[2] All this suggests that the effect of Coleridge on Newman was an ambiguous one; and his whole relation to the Oxford Movement was to remain so. Hare and Maurice both remark on a general tendency to father Tractarianism on Coleridge, and both deny the charge. However, it continued to be made; and we have the paradox that Coleridge to the fully-formed Tractarian appears as an accidentally useful ally, but in himself an almost libertine and infidel speculator; while to Low Churchmen he appears as so extreme a sacramentalist as to put him in the Tractarian camp.

The explanation, I think, can be found in a slightly later reference by Newman. Coleridge, he says, looked 'at the

[1] T. D. Acland to Newman, 11 May 1834; *Letters and Correspondence of Newman*, ed. Anne Mozley, vol. II (London, 1891), p. 39.
[2] Wilfrid Ward, *The Life of Cardinal Newman* (London, 1912), vol. I, 58 and n.

Church, sacraments, doctrines, etc., rather as symbols of a philosophy than as truths—as the mere accidental type of principles'.[1] To the Low Churchman and to certain types of Broad Churchman, Coleridge's scrupulosity about 'the Church, sacraments, doctrines, etc.' is almost indistinguishable from that of the Oxford reformers: yet to a mind like Newman's, acutely and sensitively perceptive of the real basis of Coleridge's thought, his concern to found doctrine on the intuitions of Reason rather than on the *ipse dixit* of Revelation appears mere philosophical shadow-boxing. The practical tendencies of Coleridge's work may indeed have been very close to Newman in his Anglican days; but there was nevertheless a real duality. To take an analogy from the moral sphere, it is the difference between the man who says 'It is wrong because it is forbidden' and the man who says 'It is forbidden because it is wrong'. Though such men may for long tread the same path, the difference between them is in the end probably irreconcilable. I am inclined to think, however, that the effects of Newman's readings in Coleridge were deeper and longer lasting than he supposed. No student of Coleridge can read *A Grammar of Assent* (1870) without feeling how much of its central argument is, whether consciously or not, a re-statement of Coleridgean principles.

'It is a mystery: and we are bound to believe the words without presuming to enquire into the meaning of them.' That is, we believe in St Paul's veracity; and that is enough. Yet St Paul repeatedly presses on his hearers that thoughtful perusal of the Sacred Writings, and those habits of earnest though humble enquiry which . . . would lead them 'to a full assurance of understanding εἰς ἐπίγνωσιν (to an entire assent of the mind; to a spiritual intuition, or positive inward knowledge by experience) . . . (pp. 56–7).

This is Coleridge, from *The Statesman's Manual*; and it is paralleled with remarkable closeness by Newman's distinction between different kinds of assent, different motives to assent; and his notion of the final act of assent by a spiritual intuition which he calls, in a coinage that might well be Coleridge's own, the illative sense.

[1] Wilfrid Ward, *The Life of Cardinal Newman* (London, 1912), vol. 1, p. 49 n.

In general, as the century goes on, the influence of Coleridge becomes diffused. Much that was once clearly recognizable as his becomes common property. At this he would not have been surprised, for he himself had spoken, in one of his odd images, of truth as a 'divine ventriloquist', and implied that it was a matter of indifference through whose mouth it was uttered.[1] Such a diffusion, with a consequent vulgarization, is indeed the fate of any widely influential thinker. It would be beyond the scope of a short essay to do more than indicate some of these diffractions of the Coleridgean light; and often the connexions are not traceable in detail. Perhaps one of the most unexpected tongues on which a form of Coleridgean doctrine can be heard is that of Disraeli. For all the flash and glitter and unreal romanticism, it is hard not to recognize in the political programme of Young England something like a stagy version of Coleridge's political theory. The social detail and the close following of particular political combinations in *Coningsby* (1844) tend to obscure the resemblance, but take some fair summary of the ideological purport of the novel (Cazamian's, for example), and the kinship appears with surprising plainness.

A Whig aristocracy, egoistic and devoid of any traditional sentiment; an energetic middle class, solely absorbed in the pursuit of wealth; men of reason, cold-blooded sophists, deceiving theorists, the economists, the utilitarians, have destroyed the vital harmony which imparted its health to the British body politic. They have divided class from class, individual from individual. . . . What is required is that in religion, obedience, charity, in the generous emotions of veneration and respect, there should be revived again the system of feudal equality of vassals before their suzerain, the medieval liberty of the subject in his relation to his prince and his father. The Church, endowed with the spiritual power, will play her part in this general accord, which will re-establish justice through love.

I know of no evidence that Disraeli had studied Coleridge, and the immediate agency that stands behind his ideas is no doubt that of Carlyle. But the emphasis on the Church is hardly Carlylean; and given Disraeli's open-minded curiosity

---

[1] *Biographia Literaria*, ch. ix.

for all the winds of contemporary opinion it is not unlikely that he was affected by Coleridge's *Constitution of Church and State*. Divorced as he was by race and social position from the educational and clerical hierarchy, there is nevertheless one passage in *Coningsby* on the development of the young hero's political opinions (book II, ch. vii), that indicates a real awareness of the channels by which such views as Coleridge's were diffused:

They came no doubt from the Universities. They were of a character, however, far too subtle and refined to exercise any immediate influence over the minds of youth. To pursue them required much previous knowledge and habitual thought. They were not yet publicly prosecuted by any school of politicians, or any section of the public press. They had not a local habitation or a name. They were whispered in conversation by a few. A tutor would speak of them in an esoteric vein to a favourite pupil, in whose abilities he had confidence, and whose future position in life would afford him the opportunity of influencing opinion.

But this is little more than surmise. What is much clearer is the effect of Coleridge's religious thought on Tennyson's *In Memoriam* (1850). I have written of this elsewhere,[1] and what has been said above about Maurice and the Apostles indicates the personal channels of communication. The general direction of *In Memoriam* is to abandon the hope of basing religious apologetic on Paleyan natural theology—

> I found Him not in star or sun,
> Or eagle's wing or insect's eye—

and to fall back on a philosophy of religious experience. It was neither in Tennyson's nature, nor appropriate to his poem, to deploy an elaborate Coleridgean metaphysic; and no doubt his solution—

> the heart
> Stood up and answered 'I have felt'

—is a far less reasoned thing than what is to be found in *Aids to Reflection*. But it moves in the same direction, and it is I believe quite certain that Coleridge is its ultimate source.

[1] 'The Natural Theology of *In Memoriam*', *Review of English Studies*, XXIII (1947).

The most obvious successor of Coleridge as a religious thinker is Matthew Arnold. In view of Thomas Arnold's Coleridgean associations, and the son's avowed continuation of his father's task, there can be no difficulty about the lines of communication. *Literature and Dogma* (1873) can well be regarded as *Confessions of an Inquiring Spirit* done over again for the eighteen-seventies. The object is the same—to introduce a truer method of interpreting Scripture; but Arnold was aiming at a wider public, and that was perhaps the reason, for all Coleridge's intellectual prestige, that he found so much of the work still left to do. Like Coleridge, Arnold advocates the abandonment of an untenably literal interpretation of the Bible for a more generous and heartfelt reading of its spirit. But there are significant differences, and they go to show that in the course of its passage through the century Coleridge's teaching had lost a great deal of its philosophical armament. Coleridge had a persistent and vigorous sense that religion can and should be justified by the deepest speculative activity of the human mind, even if its final sense is something that goes beyond speculative activity. Arnold tends to ignore speculative activity altogether, and everywhere adopts an attitude of ironically modest scepticism towards metaphysics. Arnold would base religion almost entirely on moral experience, and this is a narrower thing than Coleridge's attempt; moral experience as Arnold understands it—mainly a matter of *conduct*—is a narrower thing than Coleridge's appeal to the intuitions of Reason. The popular conception of Arnold in his own day as a kid-gloved dilettante is wildly unjust, a trivial reaction to certain aspects of his polemical manner; but perhaps there is a germ of truth in the feeling that Arnold's 'culture' is not a weighty enough vehicle for the arduous approach to religion, that it is not something universal, not common to humanity as such, that it is too much conflated with the style and accidental customs of a class and an educational tradition, too much the affair of a particular civilization at a particular moment of its history. Can *literary tact* really be a decisive tool in approaching the documents of religion ? Is not Arnold's founding of religion on morality a putting of the cart before the horse ? And is not the amendment 'morality touched with emotion' a mere attempt to disguise this fundamental reversal of values ? However clearly Arnold spoke to his age by producing a more accessible version of Coleridgean apologetic, his attempt is at bottom a less serious thing than Coleridge's. And though solemnity is not seriousness, the sometimes unhappy 'vivacities' with which his discourse is interspersed perhaps suggest a less profound level of engagement.

The two main questions that can be raised about the later bearing of Coleridge's thought are first its effectiveness, secondly its value. The first has been answered by our preceding illustrations. Contrary to a popular belief, Coleridge was evidently an extremely effective expository and controversial writer, and a genuinely inspiring force on the generations that succeeded him. The second question is more difficult. Anything that generates intellectual and moral activity in others must have value: and to go beyond this is to go beyond my range. Nothing I can say about the validity of his kind of argument is likely to have much weight or importance, but it seems better to say what I think. Coleridge's whole conception of the nature of the human person was antecedently a Christian-Platonic one. To show, as he seeks to do, that a nature so conceived can only be satisfied by a Platonized Christianity is an elaborate argument in a circle. And even this argument has its gaps. The darkest apprehensions of Newman's imagination could not have foreseen anything like the Bishop of Woolwich, but it is plain that he sees Coleridge as moving in this direction. It is hard to make comparisons between such different intellectual planes, but perhaps he was right. For all the deep seriousness and subtlety of argument, there does seem to be a fatal *non sequitur* in Coleridge's position. Even if we concede that his analysis of the fundamental requirements of the human spirit is in fact fundamental, what is never made out is that they must lead to Christianity. That they can accommodate Christianity may be admitted: but that they entail it, which is what Coleridge would have us believe, is never shown at all. Nor do I see that his apologetic methods could ever be the finally appropriate ones for a religion so inveterately historical. But perhaps we should regard his endeavours in another light. He and those like him in the nineteenth century were essentially engaged in maintaining a continuity—continuity between a faith, with its historic expression, that has entered too deeply into the life of western civilization ever to be expunged or merely abandoned, and a new secular, technical conception of society which seems to have little room for it. Their purpose was to maintain continuity by re-statement—an activity that is perpetually necessary in many fields if the fabric of civilization is not to show dangerous fissures. In religious thought this process appears to be still going on. How closely the ultimate re-statement will resemble the original deposit of belief is not yet apparent.

11

NEWMAN AND THE ROMANTIC SENSIBILITY

BY JOHN BEER

He asks what I *mean*; not about my words, not about my arguments, not about my actions, as his ultimate point, but about that *living intelligence*, by which I write, and argue, and act. He asks about my Mind and its Beliefs and its Sentiments. . . .[1]

John Henry Newman (1801–1890) was among those English thinkers who regard the human mind not simply as an instrument for the functioning of the reason, but as an organ through which the whole man expresses himself. Much of its activity he took to be subtle and scarcely definable—an intuitive response to present surroundings or a distillation of past experience. The mind, he said, 'makes progress not unlike a clamberer on a steep cliff, who, by quick eye, prompt hand, and firm foot, ascends how he knows not himself, by personal endowments and by practice, rather than by rule'.[2] But a mind which is so delicately attuned to its surroundings will reflect, more than commonly, the past interplay between the individual and his environment. We cannot understand such a man unless we see him against the intellectual currents of his own time: in the case of Newman himself this automatically entails taking some account of the Romanticism which dominated the artistic and intellectual world of his youth.

Romanticism was not confined to literature, music and the arts; it had intimate connexions with the religious life of the time. In the middle of the eighteenth century, the attempt to harness rational activity to the service of orthodox religion had begun to die out in dryness and deadness. The failure of a

---

[1] Newman on Charles Kingsley's attack, *What, then, does Dr Newman mean?* (London, 1864); *Apologia*, ed. Wilfrid Ward (London, 1913), p. 99.

[2] *Sermons, Chiefly on the Theory of Religious Belief, Preached before the University of Oxford* (London, 1843), p. 252.

'reasonable' religion to bring about moral improvement had led many preachers to adopt a more directly emotional approach, an appeal to the language of the heart. And while Methodists and Evangelicals were exercising every possible appeal to the feelings of their audiences, there grew up a literature of sensibility which was to exercise a decisive influence on the nature of romanticism. Poets, too, adopted the 'appeal to the heart', whether or not their poetry was written from a religious point of view.

Newman himself seems at first sight remote from such an atmosphere. His writings on the doctrine of development and his *Essay in Aid of a Grammar of Assent* (1870) suggest, superficially, a formal mind, content to treat theological questions with rigorous logical analysis. Yet the testimony of his contemporaries is different. Matthew Arnold's is the best known:

Who could resist the charm of that spiritual apparition, gliding in the dim afternoon light through the aisles of St Mary's, rising into the pulpit, and then, in the most entrancing of voices, breaking the silence with words and thoughts which were a religious music,—subtle, sweet, mournful?[1]

Some free-thinkers of the time shared Arnold's emotion. George Eliot was strongly affected by the *Apologia pro vita sua* (1864) as 'the revelation of a life—how different from one's own, yet with how close a fellowship in its needs and burthens —I mean spiritual needs and burthens'. A month later she wrote to a correspondent that it

breathed much life into me when I read it. Pray mark that beautiful passage in which he thanks his friend Ambrose St John. I know hardly anything that delights me more than such evidences of sweet brotherly love being a reality in the world. I envy you your opportunity of seeing and hearing Newman, and should like to make an expedition to Birmingham for that sole end.[2]

And Mark Pattison wrote to Newman in old age:

The veneration and affection which I felt for you at the time you left us are in no way diminished, and however remote my intellectual

---

[1] Arnold, *Discourses in America* (London, 1885), pp. 138–40.
[2] Letters to Sara Hennell, 13 July and 28 August 1864; *The George Eliot Letters*, ed. Gordon S. Haight, vol. IV (New Haven, 1954), pp. 158–9, 160.

standpoint may now be from that which I may presume to be your own, I can still truly say that I have learnt more from you than from anyone else with whom I have ever been in contact.[1]

Even Newman's adversaries responded warmly to his personality. In 1875 he published a reply to Gladstone on the Immaculate Conception which offended some Ultramontanes of his own church, including W. G. Ward; yet a friend of Ward's expressed her conviction that 'if he met you face to face he would burst into tears and you would come to more understanding than now seems possible'.[2] And Gladstone himself, on the same occasion, wrote that Newman's style always had 'an exciting effect on him, and made him wish to shout and do something extravagant'.[3]

The peculiar charm which impressed his contemporaries in such varying ways has some of its roots in Newman's own youth. His early writings betray, from time to time, a powerful sensibility—so powerful that its workings sometimes seemed like a revelation. In a memorandum of 1819, he wrote of the feeling aroused in him by one of the most poignant of sounds:

Sunday evening bells pealing. The pleasure of hearing them. It leads the mind to a longing after something, I know not what. It does not bring past years to remembrance; it does not bring anything. What does it do? We have a kind of longing after something dear to us, and well known to us—very soothing. Such is my feeling at this minute as I hear them.[4]

In a letter of 1827 to his mother he broke off unexpectedly into a semi-humorous rhapsodic passage which yet has a certain intensity:

Does the sea blossom? Are green leaves budding on its waters, and is the scent of spring in its waves? Do birds begin to sing under its shadow, and to build their nests on its branches? Ah! mighty sea! Thou art a tree whose spring never yet came, for thou art an evergreen.
There is a pastoral![5]

[1] Meriol Trevor, *Newman*, vol. II (London, 1962), p. 620.
[2] *Ibid.* II, 516.
[3] *Ibid.*
[4] Newman, *Letters and Correspondence*, ed. Anne Mozley, vol. I (London, 1891), p. 52.
[5] *Ibid.* I, 163.

A year later he described a ride to Cuddesdon, after the death
of his sister Mary:

The country . . . is beautiful; the fresh leaves, the scents, the varied
landscape. Yet I never felt so intensely the transitory nature of this
world as when most delighted with these country scenes. And in
riding out today I have been impressed more powerfully than before
I had an idea was possible with the two lines:

> Chanting with a *solemn* voice
> Minds us of our *better choice.*

I could hardly believe the lines were not my own, and Keble had
not taken them from me. I wish it were possible for words to put
down those indefinite, vague and withal subtle feelings which quite
pierce the soul and make it sick. Dear Mary seems embodied in
every tree and hid behind every hill. What a veil and curtain this
world of sense is! beautiful, but still a veil.[1]

In 1831, when on holiday in Devonshire, he wrote of a different,
more languorous and delicious mood.

. . . really I think I should dissolve into essence of roses, or be
attenuated into an echo, if I lived here. . . . The rocks blush into
every variety of colour, the trees and fields are emeralds, and the
cottages are rubies. . . . The exuberance of the grass and foliage is
oppressive, as if one had not room to breathe, though this is a
fancy. . . .[2]

Similar feelings about the world are to be found in his early
poems, one of which bears the title 'The Trance of Time'.
Few contemporary poems, indeed, appealed more strongly to
the Victorians than 'The Pillar of the Cloud', for it contains a
nostalgia that takes in both past and future:

> And with the morn those angel faces smile
> Which I have loved long since, and lost awhile.

But despite this highly developed sensibility, Newman was
less drawn to the Romantic poets than one might have expected.
He had a liking for individual poems, such as Wordsworth's
'Ode on the Intimations of Immortality', but the general
poetic achievement of Wordsworth, Coleridge, Keats and Shel-

---

[1] Newman, *Letters and Correspondence*, ed. Anne Mozley, vol. 1 (London 1891),
p. 184.
[2] *Ibid.* 1, 242–3.

ley did not attract him. On the contrary, his favourite writers of the period were Southey and Scott. It was not simply their sense of romantic adventure that he liked, rather that their work displayed a combination of romance and righteousness.[1]

Newman was always suspicious of any movement which allowed romance to reign unchecked. In his youth, his father had remarked to him: 'Take care; you are encouraging a morbid sensibility and irritability of mind,'[2]—and the admonition no doubt remained with him. His tastes in music followed the same pattern. Beethoven he greatly admired; but he disliked later romantic composers, such as Brahms and Mendelssohn, preferring Mozart and the music of the eighteenth century.[3] And his love of nature was held in rein. Life, he remarked to Aubrey de Vere, was 'full of work more important than the enjoyment of mountains and lakes'.[4]

Virtue was more important than beauty. In youth, indeed, he thought it more important than religion, and argued against his schoolmaster in favour of Pope's *Essay on Man*. 'What, I contended, can be more free from objection than it? Does it not expressly inculcate "Virtue alone is happiness below"?'[5]

One of Newman's best expressions of the correspondence between the world of natural beauty and that of natural virtue comes in his sermon 'The Second Spring', where he describes the second in terms of the first:

. . . Fair as may be the bodily form, fairer far, in its green foliage and bright blossoms, is natural virtue. It blooms in the young, like some rich flower, so delicate, so fragrant, and so dazzling. Generosity, and lightness of heart, and amiableness,—the confiding spirit, the gentle temper, the elastic cheerfulness, the open hand, the pure affection, the noble aspiration, the heroic resolve, the romantic pursuit, the love in which self has no part,—are not these beautiful?[6]

But the older Newman pursues his metaphor relentlessly. If natural virtue grows to flower and fruition like natural beauty,

[1] I owe the phrase to Stanley T. Williams; cf. his *Studies in Victorian Literature* (New York, 1923), pp. 230–1.
[2] *Letters and Correspondence, op. cit.* I, 126.
[3] Trevor, *op. cit.* II, 635–6.
[4] Quoted in *A Tribute to Newman*, ed. Michael Tierney (Dublin, 1945), pp. 352–3.
[5] *Letters and Correspondence*, I, 22.
[6] Newman, *The Second Spring* (London, 1852), p. 10.

it also resembles it in its inevitable decay and death. Morose-
ness, cynicism and selfishness supervene. Permanence must be
sought elsewhere.

Had Newman not been haunted by a quest for permanence,
his path might have been more straightforward. He might have
remained in Oxford, and exercised his talents in the appeal to
righteousness, leaving to his contemporaries an echo of verbal
music and a sense of the sweetness of virtue. That, indeed, is
how Pater *did* remember him: and when Newman left Oxford it
was Pater more than any other man who evoked the lost ghost
of his inner sensibility.

But Newman was looking for permanence and stability, and
looking for them with an unusual pertinacity. Richard Whately
of Oriel remarked of him that he had the clearest mind he
knew[1]; and this clarity of mind, coupled with a strongly
developed sense of reality, made him both quick to perceive
self-contradictions and unwilling to rest content in any position
which involved them.

When he was elected Fellow of Oriel in 1822, he found himself thrust into a group of minds unusually active in the Oxford
of the day. Men such as Copleston and Whately, closely connected with the new liberal movement in theology, confronted
Newman with their sharp analytic arguments. As time passed,
he became aware of another group of liberals, emanating from
Cambridge, who were Kantian and Platonic rather than
Aristotelian, and who acknowledged a common debt to the
writings of Coleridge.[2] In 1833, during his Mediterranean
tour, he visited Coleridge's friend, John Hookham Frere;[3]
other figures in the movement included J. C. Hare and John
Sterling. Newman's statement that he did not read Coleridge
until 1835 may be taken as correct—there is evidence to suggest
that he was restrained for a long time by the fact that Coleridge
was separated from his wife; but he must have been previously
aware of Coleridge's teachings and their import. When he did
read Coleridge's writings, he received a powerful intellectual

---

[1] Trevor, *op. cit.* I, 48.
[2] Cf. Charles R. Sanders, *Coleridge and the Broad Church Movement* (Durham,
N.C., 1942), p. 14.
[3] Gabrielle Festing, *J. H. Frere and his Friends* (London, 1899), p. 242.

stimulus. He recorded his surprise on finding 'how much I thought mine, is to be found there'.[1] And he immediately seized upon what seemed to him the crucial point in Coleridge's thinking—his advocacy of religious symbolism. The following January he wrote of Sir James Stephen that, on his first impression, he was 'too much of a philosopher, looking (in Coleridge's way) at the Church, sacraments, doctrines, &c, rather as symbols of a philosophy than as *truths*. . . .'[2] A few years later, in the *British Critic*, there appeared that well known characterization of Coleridge (later reprinted in the *Apologia*) as 'a very original thinker, who, while he indulged a liberty of speculation, which no Christian can tolerate, and advocated conclusions which were often heathen rather than Christian, yet after all instilled a higher philosophy into inquiring minds, than they had hitherto been accustomed to accept'.[3]

The fact that he found so many of his own ideas in the writings of a 'liberal' theologian no doubt disturbed Newman. One reason for the coincidence was that the two men shared a liking for the earlier Anglican divines; the interests with which they approached them were, however, different. Coleridge was more interested in the divines of the later seventeenth century, and their quest for a reconciliation between Revelation and Reason. In their time, the *via media* of the Anglican Church had begun to take on a different significance. Devised originally as a political expedient to reconcile Protestants and non-papist Catholics, it offered a principle of toleration which could be extended into other fields. To some divines of the time, fascinated by the ordered universe of Newton, it had seemed natural to suppose that an investigation of the Creation under the auspices of the Church must both display the benevolence of the Creator and reveal a fully integrated universal reality, in which reason and revelation would be finally reconciled. Their tolerance of scientific investigation was a new sort of 'middle way'.

During the eighteenth century the possibility of such an integration receded; the 'reality' of religion was relegated by most people to the sphere of the 'heart'. Coleridge, however,

---

[1] Cf. Graham Hough, p. 186 above; Newman, *Letters and Correspondence*, vol. II, p. 39 n.   [2] *Ibid.* II, 156.   [3] *Apologia*, ed. Ward, p. 195.

had endeavoured to rescue the cause of a more fully integrated reality. Without quite rejecting the contemporary cult of sensibility, he had passed beyond it, lending his weight to the belief that the ultimate order of nature was intimately related to the structure of Christian doctrine, and that a proper language of symbols would reveal the fact.

If Coleridge's attempt was a quixotic one, it had two points in its favour: it was true to his own imaginative experience as a poet, and it was not hopelessly contradicted by the science of his time. But as the nineteenth century proceeded, it became clear that the investigations of scientists would take them far away from the possibility of such an immediate integration. Any attempt to reconcile reason and revelation would be likely to make more evident the split in 'reality' which scientific investigation was daily producing.

How far Newman perceived this it is hard to say; what is certain is that he rejected Coleridge's attempt to approach Christianity by way of a symbolism derived from sense-experience. He rejected it as he had rejected his own early romantic yearnings. Reality was not to be discovered by exercising the sensibility; reality, for the mass of men, must be closer to their whole experience, more directly available.

On this basis, however, realism was not to be discovered in 'orthodox' Protestantism either. Contemporary Biblical scholarship was beginning to sap the absolute authority of the Bible. Newman returned to the Laudian divines of the early seventeenth century, with their stress upon the authority of the Church as such, and sought to use the *via media* in the more traditional way, as a means of reconciling the present Protestant church with its Catholic heritage.

In one respect he was pursuing another strand of Coleridge's thought. Coleridge, in the body of his thinking, had from time to time emphasized the importance of 'organic unity'. Human institutions and movements, he thought, should be viewed not as mechanisms with a particular functional purpose, but as organisms, growing originally from some basic idea and gradually unfolding, like a flower, in various implications. Institutions ought not to be attacked or destroyed without reference to their original Idea.

The same principle was employed by Newman in the elaboration of his doctrine of 'development'. Newman, however, was more preoccupied with the importance of self-consistency in the organism. Coleridge, pursuing his metaphor, saw his organic principle triumphantly at work in the symbiosis of Church and State. Newman, for whom the Idea of the Church necessarily contained the idea of its own authority, felt that the lives of ecclesiastical and secular organisms could not be wedded. The Church of England, by forfeiting its authority to the state, had departed from its own original 'Idea'. It had lost its 'reality' as a church.

The word 'reality' is important. For Newman, the question was not simply one of belonging to a self-consistent institution, but of preserving his own status as a real human being in a real society. This need provides one key to the events of the crucial period when he was reconsidering his religious position. His secession to Rome in 1845, which has seemed to many the working of a massive intellectual integrity, moving majestically in a line laid down by the dictates of its own working, has appeared to others as the result of mere pique at his rejection by the majority of contemporary Anglicans.

There *was* a subjective element in Newman's secession, but when one takes into account the acute realism of his nature, subjective and objective elements dovetail together more closely than one might have expected. The rejection of Newman's doctrine of Anglicanism by the mass of his contemporaries could not but strike at his own sense of personal identity. He was aware of the fact. In July 1843 he wrote to Mrs Froude, 'I feel it so difficult to bring out what I would say, that when I attempt it, I become unreal'; in November 1844, he wrote to Keble, 'I feel myself very unreal'.[1] And this in turn made him sensitive to the whole question of reality, more quick to perceive those elements in Anglicanism which were consistent neither with the idea of the Church, as he conceived it, nor with the world around it.

Viewed in these terms, Newman's conversion can be seen as the removal from a faith under which his sense of reality had

[1] G. H. Harper, *Newman and Froude* (Baltimore, 1933), p. 12; *Correspondence of Newman with John Keble and Others, 1839–45* (London, 1917), p. 352.

gradually been undermined to a faith which restored it. Instead of a church which was wary of its own catholicism, he moved into a church which sat in calm assurance of its own authority. The power of this central reality was enough to destroy any doubts which he might have entertained concerning particular points of doctrine. The apparent self-contradictions of Anglicanism were replaced by the massive self-consistency of Rome.

It is hard to understand the purely intellectual element in Newman's conversion without considering this fact. The *intellectual* occasion, his re-examination of the Monophysite controversy and his realization that the Anglicans were now in a position similar to that occupied by the Monophysites many centuries before, need not have produced the change: he could have continued to argue that the Monophysite church had been wrong and the Anglican right. What now impressed Newman, however, was the sense of an enduring reality in the Roman body. 'Rome was where she now is.'[1] Just as he had exclaimed, when he saw Sicily, 'It *is* a country', so now as he entered the Roman church he found himself feeling, 'This *is* a religion'.[2]

But Newman's move was not simply concerned with his own sense of personal reality or with his sense of the reality of the Church. The question of 'reality' went deeper, affecting the whole of Christian faith and practice. Newman was setting his face against the tendency, which had grown steadily stronger since the disrupted cosmology of the Renaissance, to push the reality of religion inside the individual. He had long felt that, if religion was real, it could not be expressed merely in certain inward qualities of the soul: it must have external existence and authority.

Early in 1835 he had made the point in a sermon entitled 'Self-Contemplation', where he drew a distinction between two views of doctrine—between

the ancient and universal teaching of the Church, which insists on the Objects and fruits of faith, and considers the spiritual character of that faith itself sufficiently secured, if these are as they should be;

[1] *Apologia*, ed. Ward, p. 211.
[2] *Letters and Correspondence*, I, 408; *Apologia*, ed. Ward, p. 394.

and the method, now in esteem, of attempting instead to secure directly and primarily that 'mind of the spirit', which may savingly receive the truths, and fulfil the obedience of the Gospel.

He explained his distinction further in a letter to Lord Lifford:

... If an awakened sinner asked an ancient believer what he must do to be saved, he would answer (I consider): 'Look to the Word Incarnate, look to the Holy Trinity, look to the Sacraments, God's instruments, and break off your sins, do good whereas you have done evil.' But I conceive one of the modern school, without denying this, would for the most part drop it, and say instead: 'Your heart must be changed; till you have faith, you have nothing; you must have a spiritual apprehension of Christ; you must utterly renounce yourself and your merits and throw yourself at the feet of the Cross, etc. . . .'[1]

Newman's rejection of this second tradition was based partly on moral grounds: what set out to be a rejection of self actually led to greater concentration on the self: '. . . a man thus minded does not simply think of God when he prays to Him, but is observing whether he feels properly or not; does not believe and obey, but thinks it enough to be conscious that he is, as he thinks, warm and spiritual. . . .'[2]

For Newman, this reliance on an 'inner' reality was dangerous. But the question may still be raised: why, in his search for an objective reality, did he stop at Roman Catholicism? His near-contemporary Mark Pattison followed a very similar course in early life: from the puritanism of his upbringing, he emerged to the idea of the Church and then, for a time, to join the Tractarians; but he finally moved outside the church altogether. To quote his own account:

I passed out of the Catholic phase, but slowly, and in many years, to that highest development when all religions appear in their historical light, as efforts of the human spirit to come to an understanding with that Unseen Power whose pressure it feels, but whose motives are a riddle.[3]

Newman he criticized for not moving into this wider sphere.

[1] Letter of 12 September 1837, first published in Newman, *Autobiographical Writings*, ed. Henry Tristram (New York, 1957), p. 141.
[2] *Lectures on Justification* (London, 1838), p. 378.
[3] Mark Pattison, *Memoirs* (London, 1885), pp. 327–8.

Newman assumed and adorned the narrow basis on which Laud had stood 200 years before. All the grand development of human reason, from Aristotle down to Hegel, was a sealed book to him. There lay a unity, a unity of all thought, which far transcended the mere mechanical association of the unthinking members of the Catholic Church; a great spiritual unity, by the side of which all sects and denominations shrink into vanity.[1]

Pattison is being unfair: Newman was perfectly aware of the 'grand development of human reason', but unwilling to allow it supreme authority. The fact of his antipathy remains. He is said to have disliked George Eliot, for example, both for her realism and her agnosticism: he could not endure the novels of natural fact.[2] He was not one of the great Victorian 'seekers after truth', but saw himself in a different role. His poem 'The Pilgrim', written about himself, ends, 'Yet kept he safe his pledge, prizing his pilgrim-lot'.[3]

If we regard Newman as a 'pledged pilgrim' we see him more clearly. But at this point the literary critic has least to say. He can only expose the various places in which Newman speaks of the need for fixed principles. Certain principles are given to man and 'virtue' consists in holding fast to them. A good deal of the argument in the *Grammar of Assent*, for example, rests on presupposing the universality of the Conscience in all men. There is an equal insistence upon the importance of the Will in the struggle towards faith. But these conceptions of the nature of man are by no means arbitrarily reached; they reflect Newman's own personal experience. They also reflect his feeling for reality. There is a telling moment in his novel, *Loss and Gain* (1848), when one character remarks of another, 'I don't like Lord Newlights: he seems to me to have no principle, that is, no fixed, definite religious principle. You don't know where to find him.'[4] For Newman, the 'reality' of a person lies in the existence of such a point of fixity.

Conscience, will and principle: these are the stakes which

---

[1] Mark Pattison, *Memoirs* (London, 1885), p. 210.
[2] S. T. Williams, *op. cit.* p. 230.
[3] *Verses on Various Occasions* (London, 1896), p. 61.
[4] Newman, *Prose and Poetry*, ed. Geoffrey Tillotson (London, 1957), p. 180. Further references to the novel are to this edition; my text is that of the 6th edition (1874).

Newman drives into the uncertain universe of nature in order to create the firmer structure that he needs. There is thus an element of the 'given' in his thinking, which is not subjected to the questioning of thought. In the same way, there is an inflexibility, a formal note in his writing, which precedes the play of intelligence. The 'pledged pilgrim' has set his face as a flint.

So far, we have seen Newman in a predicament common to young men of the Romantic period: torn between the attractions of the inner world of sensibility and the demands of the world around them, and forsaking the one world in favour of the other. The pattern is not unfamiliar. The world of sensibility is unified but also self-enclosing; after a certain point the world at large seems to offer a superior reality.

Newman had found his 'superior reality' in a religious quest which led him finally to the Roman Catholic Church. We still need to explain why he found that church so satisfying and why he was never tempted to move from it. And as we look for an explanation, we find that only half the story has been told. The other half, which is to be found in the pages of his novel, *Loss and Gain*, adds to our sense of Newman's uniqueness.

The fact is that, although Newman distrusted the contemporary cult of sensibility, he was too honest to reject completely so powerful a part of his own experience. And when he came to write the story of a conversion to Rome, he endowed his hero, Charles Reding, with a nature of extreme sensibility. From the beginning, he limited the possible development of that sensibility by setting him in surroundings, both at home and in Oxford, which were dominated by good sense and good humour; but he also gave Reding a basic seriousness which refused to be budged by the gentle probings of his family's humour. Thus a delicate balance is struck: Reding's sensibility is automatically limited in scope, and yet the fact of its existence is a note of his peculiar vocation. Moreover, realism informs his sensibility from the beginning of the novel. At one point he responds negatively to his mother's suggestion that he should go for a walk.

'It makes me melancholy,' said Charles. 'What! the beautiful autumn makes you melancholy?' asked his mother. 'Oh, my dear mother . . . I like spring; but autumn saddens me.' 'Charles always says so,' said Mary; 'he thinks nothing of the rich hues into which the sober green changes; he likes the dull uniform of summer.' 'No, it is not that,' said Charles; 'I never saw anything so gorgeous as Magdalen Water-walk, for instance, in October; it is quite wonderful, the variety of colours. I admire, and am astonished; but I cannot love or like it. It is because I can't separate the look of things from what it portends; that rich variety is but the token of disease and death.' 'Surely,' said Mary, 'colours have their own intrinsic beauty; we may like them for their own sake.' 'No, no,' said Charles, 'we always go by association; else why not admire raw beef, or a toad, or some other reptiles, which are as beautiful and bright as tulips or cherries, yet revolting, because we consider what they are, not how they look?' 'What next?' said his mother, looking up from her work; 'my dear Charles, you are not serious in comparing cherries to raw beef or to toads.' 'No, my dear mother,' answered Charles, laughing, 'no, I only say that they look like them, not are like them.' (pp. 248–9)

Charles's mother has her place in the total effect. Despite her comic misunderstanding, she has a groundbass of good sense which helps to confirm from one angle the argument which Charles is advancing. Charles is refusing to accept any kind of isolated aestheticism: beauty must play its part in a larger pattern of reality. His note of melancholy grows however, and with it a note of foreboding for the future happiness of the family.

'Come, Mary,' he said, 'give us some music, now the urn is gone away. Play me that beautiful air of Beethoven, the one I call "The Voice of the Dead".' 'Oh, Charles, you do give such melancholy names to things!' cried Mary. 'The other day,' said Eliza, 'we had a most beautiful scent wafted across the road as we were walking, and he called it "The Ghost of the Past"; and he says that the sound of the Eolian harp is "remorseful".' 'Now, you'd think all that very pretty,' said Charles, 'if you saw it in a book of poems; but you call it melancholy when I say it.' 'Oh, yes,' said Caroline, 'because poets never mean what they say, and would not be poetical unless they were melancholy.' (p. 250)

The conversation is carried on at a light, domestic level, but Charles's seriousness emerges continually: elsewhere another aesthetic *motif* is introduced, through which the yearning note in his personality can be more fully expressed:

'Charles has some theory, then, about scents I'll be bound,' said his father. . . . . 'You're right, papa, in this instance,' said his mother; 'I know he has some good reason, though I never can recollect it, why he smells a rose, or distils lavender. What is it, my dear Mary?' '"Relics ye are of Eden's bowers,"' said she. 'Why, sir, that was precisely your own reason just now,' said Charles to his father. 'There's more than that,' said Mrs Reding, 'if I knew what it was.' 'He thinks the scent more intellectual than the other senses,' said Mary, smiling. 'Such a boy for paradoxes!' said his mother. 'Well, so it is in a certain way,' said Charles; 'but I can't explain. Sounds and scents are more ethereal, less material; they have no shape—like the angels.'

Later he continues:

'Scents are both complete in themselves, yet do not consist of parts. Think how very distinct the smell of a rose is from a pink, a pink from a sweet-pea, a sweet-pea from a stock, a stock from lilac, lilac from lavender, lavender from jasmine, jasmine from honeysuckle, honeysuckle from hawthorn, hawthorn from hyacinth, hyacinth—' 'Spare us,' interrupted Mr Malcolm; 'you are going through the index of London!' 'And these are only the scents of flowers; how different flowers smell from fruits, fruits from spices, spices from roast beef or pork-cutlets, and so on. Now, what I was coming to is this—these scents are perfectly distinct from each other, and *sui generis*; they never can be confused; yet each is communicated to the apprehension in an instant. Sights take up a great space, a tune is a succession of sounds; but scents are at once specific and complete, yet indivisible. Who can halve a scent? they need neither time nor space; thus, they are immaterial or spiritual.' 'Charles hasn't been to Oxford for nothing,' said his mother, laughing and looking at Mary; 'this is what I call chopping logic!' (pp. 166–7)

There is a peculiar irony in calling this speech, 'chopping logic': nothing could be further from the atmosphere of Aristotelian analysis than the content of Charles's speech. And the speech itself reverberates through the rest of the novel. The description of the power of scents as 'intellectual' shows Charles's indulgence of sensibility at its most extended; but Newman's hand is on the line, winding carefully—for Charles's love of scents also marks him as a man with a strong spiritual sense and a feeling for wholeness. His family has no need to go beyond its own immediate experience, but he will continue to search for a reality which he can not merely possess (as the

senses 'possess' a landscape) but be possessed by (as the senses
are 'possessed' by a scent). Much as he loves his family, he
misses *that* note in them. He misses it when he attends his
father's church on Sunday——

. . . there were the old monuments, with Latin inscriptions and
strange devices, the black boards with white letters, the Resurgams
and grinning skulls, the fire-buckets, the faded militia-colours, and,
almost as much a fixture, the old clerk, with a Welsh wig over his
ears, shouting the responses out of place. . . . (p. 164)

Newman states affection, but the action of the language suggests the cold and the grotesque, and it is this reaction which will
work more deeply in Charles's mind. And, as his pilgrimage
continues, Newman takes up the image of scent again. By an
ingenious twist of the imagery, it is suggested that Reding is not
only discovering the 'possessing experience' that he has been
longing for, but that that experience is a transforming and
unifying element in his personality, so that others respond to
him as his senses respond to scents.

He could not escape the destiny, in due time, in God's time . . . he
could not ultimately escape his destiny of becoming a Catholic.
And even before that blessed hour, as an opening flower scatters
sweets, so the strange unknown odour, pleasing to some, odious to
others, went abroad from him upon the winds, and made them
marvel what could be near them, and made them look curiously
and anxiously at him, while he was unconscious of his own condition. Let us be patient with him, as his Maker is patient,
and bear that he should do a work slowly, which he will do well.
(p. 227)

It is the boldest rhetorical stroke in the novel; it is also one
of the subtlest. Newman is meeting any dilemma inherent in
the recognized power of the sensibility by suggesting that the
sensibility is itself transformed in the process of conversion. He
can then go forward to the final moment of acceptance, when
Charles finds himself in the possession of a 'deep peace and
serenity of mind, which he had not thought possible on earth':

It was more like the stillness which almost sensibly affects the ears
when a bell that has long been tolling stops, or when a vessel, after
much tossing at sea, finds itself in harbour. It was such as to throw

him back in memory on his earliest years, as if he were really beginning life again. But there was more than the happiness of childhood in his heart; he seemed to feel a rock under his feet; it was the *soliditas Cathedræ Petri*. He went on kneeling, as if he were already in heaven, with the throne of God before him, and Angels around; and as if to move were to lose his privilege. (p. 351)

The renewal and confirmation of the innocent sensibility of childhood is followed immediately by the asserted note of 'adult reality'—the note of solidity and permanence.

In pursuing the theme of 'superior reality' in the novel, however, Newman is sometimes in great danger of overstating his case, particularly when he is indulging his comic vein. He constantly contrasts the seriousness of the Roman Catholics with the amateurism of the Tractarians. When Reding and his friends go to see a newly restored church, for example, the word 'pretty' is used with telling effect. 'It was as pretty a building as Bateman had led them to expect, and very prettily done up. There was a stone altar in the best style, a credence-table, a piscina, what looked like a tabernacle, and a couple of handsome brass candlesticks. . . .' When Charles inquires as to the *use* of these things, however, he discovers that they have none—they are there because traditionally they always were (pp. 120–1). The comic note is reinforced later in the novel, when Charles finds his friend White, a former advocate of clerical celibacy, standing in a religious shop with his chattering wife, who is urging him to buy various items for the adornment of their church and rectory (pp. 145–6, 304–7).

Such scenes are good as comedy, but the criticism of Anglicanism which they suggest is hardly justified. The same objection applies even more strongly to a curious scene at the end of the novel. Charles Reding, on the point of conversion, has been assailed by a succession of individuals who have tried to convert him successively to 'the Holy Catholic Church assembling in Huggermugger Lane', or a new sect which is 'all scriptural', or Judaism, or the Truth Society, or 'the New Jerusalem' (pp. 326–41). In the next but one chapter, Newman turns away to describe, soberly and dispassionately, an order known as the Passionists, the members of which practise self-chastisement, always with some spiritual end. Newman's aim

14

is evidently to suggest, after the turmoil of the previous incidents, a group of men who carry their religion into practice sacrificially; but the effect is likely to be different on the average reader, to whom the Passionists may seem as eccentric as the sects previously described. Newman's hint that they carry out their religion in a more real manner hardly carries conviction, in view of the hardships sometimes suffered by Protestants for their faith. It is a point at which Newman demands a greater sympathy for Roman Catholic practice than he is likely to find in a disinterested reader.

Loss and Gain is a rhetorical novel, the central aim of which is to suggest that the Roman Catholic Church alone is 'truly' religious. Protestant practice ends in tea-meetings, the Tractarian in the acquirement of tasteful church furnishings. Newman's intellectual performance is less striking here than in the *Apologia*. What stays with the reader, however, is not the 'argument' of the novel, but the impression of the hero's religious nature. Newman is able, from his own experience, to pass beyond the intellectual progression of Reding (which in any case ends in an act of will) and to present a young man of naturally religious disposition passing through the world of contemporary religious experience.

Newman himself was such a man. In the *Apologia*, he records how religious beliefs and belief in a supernatural order had taken a fast hold on his imagination from childhood. His early belief in the reality of his own imagination was as strong as Wordsworth's.

I used to wish the Arabian Tales were true: my imagination ran on unknown influences, on magical powers, and talismans. . . . I thought life might be a dream, or I an Angel, and all this world a deception, my fellow-angels by a playful device concealing themselves from me, and deceiving me with the semblance of a material world.[1]

He also records how his early conviction that he was 'elected to glory' fell in with these beliefs and made him 'rest in the thought of two and two only supreme and luminously self-evident beings, myself and my Creator. . . .'

[1] *Apologia*, ed. Ward, pp. 105–6.

The use of the word 'luminous' is significant. An imagery of light runs through Newman's work. Like Coleridge, he uses the emblem of God as the sun to suggest a universe governed by a divine order of harmony and light. The image remains constant, from the wistful 'Lead Kindly Light' of his early poetry to Reding's acceptance of the truth as a reality veiled by clouds.[1] It is there, importantly, in *The Dream of Gerontius* (1866), a work which in some ways epitomizes Newman's literary achievement. Formally and stylistically, the poem breaks no new ground whatever. There are not even the experiments in the rhetoric of sentiment which one finds in the great Victorian poets. But behind the formality lurks imaginative vision. The ecclesiastical orders and hierarchies of heaven and hell are the framework for the expression of a mystical interpretation of the soul's place in the universe. This imaginative power comes through the language, even if it does not wholly possess it. The light-imagery, for example, is no cliché, but expresses subtly the relation of the soul to the divine—until finally it is 'consum'd, yet quicken'd, by the glance of God'.

In other works, the romantic sensibility is allowed further play: it was the sense of this romanticism, rigidly contained and controlled, that made him so attractive to his contemporaries. His rejection of the cult of sensibility in no way involved a denial of the demands of the heart. On the contrary, his prime charge against the Anglicanism of his youth was that there had been so little 'to satisfy and retain a young and earnest heart'.[2]

The appeal to the heart reaches its climax in the sermon, 'The Parting of Friends', preached at Littlemore on 25 September 1843, soon after Newman had resigned from the church of St Mary the Virgin in Oxford. The references to himself and his sorrow are made obliquely, in the third person; but the most heart-rending passages of the Authorized Version are used with a power which makes the subordination of the personal note all the more poignant.

The tenderness which Newman will not indulge in the

---

[1] Newman quotes this incident in a letter; cf. G. H. Harper, *Newman and Froude* (Baltimore, 1933), p. 208.

[2] *Apologia*, ed. Ward, p. 398.

cultivation of art or in the presence of natural beauty, is invoked as a necessary element in human relations. In his remarks on the definition of a gentleman, the presence of sympathy is central to all the characteristics which he requires.[1] His own need for the sympathy of others was marked. His chief regret in not being married, he recorded, was the lack of a constant resource of sympathy.[2] In a moment of bitter loneliness, writing of an old blue cloak he had kept for nearly twenty years, he even confessed: 'I have so few things to sympathize with me, that I take to clokes.'[3] The character of Agellius in his novel *Callista* (1856) has been taken as a self-portrait:

He was lonely at home, lonely in the crowd. He needed the sympathy of his kind; hearts which might beat with his heart; friends with whom he might share his joys and griefs; advisers whom he might consult; minds like his own, who would understand him—minds unlike his own, who would succour and respond to him. (ch. iii, p. 22)

To the Victorian mind, the imagery of sensibility in human relations naturally found its focus in the idea of 'home'. The home was the institution which might protect and sustain those human feelings which were rejected by the logic of a rational and commercial world. Newman's own career was shaped by the quest for a still more permanent 'home'—one which would combine the intimacy of his childhood surroundings with the reality of a self-sufficient order, interpreting the universe. When his hero, Charles Reding, first discusses his religious doubts with his sister Mary, he tells her: '. . . many things have happened to me, in various ways, to show me that I have not a place, a position, a home, that I am not made for, that I am a stranger in, the Church of England' (p. 253).

Mary immediately grasps the practical implication, and sees that he will become a Roman Catholic; but Charles's major preoccupation is elsewhere: '. . . wherever I go, whomever I talk with, I feel him to be another sort of person from what I am. I can't convey it to you; you won't understand me; but

[1] *Discourses on University Education* (Dublin, 1852), pp. ix, 327–31.
[2] Trevor, *op. cit.* I, 235.
[3] *Autobiographical Writings*, p. 138.

the words of the Psalm, "I am a stranger upon earth", describe what I always feel.'

The exchange between the two is central. Charles's sense of alienation contains within itself the potentiality of much more than a conversion to Roman Catholicism; but Mary perceives intuitively that, in the logic of his circumstances, this is the course which he will pursue. It is the only one which will give him both a sense of reality and a ground for the emotions which possess him.

In this context, at least, Newman has his place in a romantic tradition—that of the sensibility reaching towards permanence. Like Wordsworth, he 'longs for a repose that ever is the same'.[1] On one of the two occasions when he quotes from Cowper, the poet of sensibility *par excellence*, it is to express this very yearning. Charles Reding concludes a painful discussion with Mary on the possibility of change in their mutual affection by reciting some lines which, he says, remind one that 'there is One *only* who cannot die, who never changes, only One . . .

> Thou art the source and centre of all minds,
> Their only point of rest, Eternal Word.' (p. 170)

What Wordsworth looked for in the cultivation of household virtues, Newman sought in the Roman Catholic Church. There was a domesticity in his Catholicism which surprised his contemporaries. His fellow Roman Catholics could not understand his reluctance to proselytize. While the London Oratory of St Philip set out to achieve dramatic results, he remained at Birmingham with his small group of fathers, out of the limelight. He did not even particularly desire that their own number should be increased. And when, in old age, he became a Cardinal, his one request was that he might remain in his small community.

Contemporary romanticism did not always end in the quest for permanence, however. There was another tradition of romanticism, more vitalistic in tendency, which, seeing man as a child of the earth and an involuntary disciple of his own imagination, sought to use those resources for the renewal of

---

[1] 'Ode to Duty', l. 40.

humanity. This tradition, which comes to the fore in the writings of Blake, ran just below the surface in the early writings of Coleridge and helped to shape the literary achievement of Keats.

Newman had little feeling for that tradition, but so long as he remained a questing Anglican, calling on his church to resume the glories of a former age, he remained distantly connected with it, and so stood as a symbolic figure for many. When he submitted to the Roman Catholic Church, he severed that bond with his contemporaries for ever. Even while he was moving into the formal, enclosing reality offered by the older body, therefore, he was forfeiting some of his former personal identity. In a bleak moment many years later, he acknowledged the loss:

O how forlorn & dreary has been my course since I have been a Catholic! here has been the contrast—as a Protestant, I felt my religion dreary, but not my life—but, as a Catholic, my life dreary, not my religion. Of course one's earlier years are (humanly speaking) best—and again, events are softened by distance—and I look back on my years at Oxford & Littlemore with tenderness—and it was the time in which I had a remarkable mission—but how am I changed even in look! till the affair of No 90 and my going to Littlemore, I had my mouth half open, and commonly a smile on my face—& from that time onwards my mouth has been closed and contracted, and the muscles are so set now, that I cannot but look grave and forbidding.[1]

The moment of dreariness passed. In the following year, the publication of the *Apologia* began that movement of sympathy on the part of Protestants and Catholics alike which gave him a unique position of affection and trust in his later years. His life as a Roman Catholic grew warmer and richer.

But the validity of that self-analysis remains: and it explains why we still see Newman as a great but isolated individual, a lighthouse on a rock rather than a beacon towards which we can steer. That extraordinary balance of intellect and emotion, that play of sensibility within a firm but formal intellectual structure draws us near in respect but not home in acceptance.

[1] *Autobiographical Writings*, pp. 254–5.

Some years ago, in a perceptive literary analysis, Walter E. Houghton took a sentence from the *Apologia* and showed how it diverges from the normal pattern of Victorian prose by the undertow of reluctance in its arguments.[1] Where John Stuart Mill would have dealt fairly but briskly with objections, Newman employs the phrase 'in spite of . . . in spite of' to register his unwillingness to disagree. The bond of sympathy with his opponents as human beings is overcome only by his relentlessness in pursuit of truth as he envisages it:

> Though I neither was so fond (with a few exceptions) of the persons, nor of the methods of thought, which belonged to this new school, as of the old set, though I could not trust in their firmness of purpose, for, like a swarm of flies, they might come and go, and at length be divided and dissipated, yet I had an intense sympathy in their object and in the direction of their path, in spite of my old friends, in spite of my old life-long prejudices. In spite of my ingrained fears of Rome, and the decision of my reason and conscience against her usages, in spite of my affection for Oxford and Oriel, yet I had a secret longing love of Rome the author of English Christianity, and I had a true devotion to the Blessed Virgin. . . .

The passage is typical. The sense of a pressure of sensibility against the rigid demands of intellect, conscience and will is the most characteristic note in Newman's style. That pressure is intense in the account of his departure from Oxford:

> I slept on Sunday night at my dear friend's, Mr Johnson's, at the Observatory. Various friends came to see the last of me; Mr Copeland, Mr Church, Mr Buckle, Mr Pattison, and Mr Lewis. Dr Pusey too came up to take leave of me; and I called on Dr Ogle, one of my very oldest friends, for he was my private Tutor, when I was an Undergraduate. In him I took leave of my first college, Trinity, which was so dear to me, and which held on its foundation so many who had been kind to me both when I was a boy, and all through my Oxford life. Trinity had never been unkind to me. There used to be much snap-dragon growing on the walls opposite my freshman's rooms there, and I had for years taken it as the emblem of my own perpetual residence even unto death in my University.

[1] Walter E. Houghton, *The Art of Newman's Apologia* (New Haven, 1945), pp. 50–53; cf. *Apologia*, ed. Ward, pp. 260–1.

On the morning of the 23rd I left the Observatory. I have never seen Oxford since, excepting its spires, as they are seen from the railway.[1]

Newman's account includes one partly esoteric reference. The use of the snapdragon as an emblem of his perpetual residence in Trinity does not fully make sense until one turns to an early poem of Newman's on the subject. In 'Snapdragon', written in 1827, the flower is used as an emblem of the virtue of humility which Newman takes as an ideal——

> Mine, the Unseen to display
> In the crowded public way.[2]

The reference to a college life becomes explicit in the last lines of the poem:

> Ah! no more a scentless flower,
> By approving Heaven's high power,
> Suddenly my leaves exhale
> Fragrance of the Syrian gale.
> Ah! 'tis timely comfort given
> By the answering breath of Heaven!
> May it be! then well might I
> In College cloister live and die.

The imagery of scent is precisely that which is used in Newman's later work. Just as the snapdragon releases its scent at the touch of the breeze, so the humble nature, submitting, is gifted with a fragrance which possesses it and is evident to the outside world. A sensuous experience (Newman smelling the snapdragon outside his college room) is transformed into an emblem of virtue, and it will eventually, in *Loss and Gain*, become a symbol of religious faith.

The images used in the remainder of the passage are realistic and direct: nevertheless they too, for the twentieth-century reader, assume a symbolic significance. It is symbolic that Newman should leave the Observatory, for it was the astronomers who first found a footing for scientific investigation in the medieval universities. Even the railway has its place in the picture. Mark Pattison relates how, after Newman's

---

[1] *Apologia*, ed. Ward, p. 327.
[2] *Verses on Various Occasions*, p. 21.

secession, the long period of acute religious controversy was succeeded by an extraordinary calm; and when the fellows were stirred to excitement again, two years later, it was the coming of the Railway Age that aroused them. ('Speculative theology gave way to speculation in railway shares.') When religious controversy and railway mania were alike forgotten, the university turned its attention to the furtherance of scientific investigation.[1] The picture of Newman being carried past the spires of Oxford by an engine of the new technology is an emblem of the age.

It is also an emblem of Newman's personal drama. When he saw Oxford from the train, he was looking at the place where his own identity had been most vivid, and where he could have given his talents most fully. To have remained in Oxford as it was, however, would have been to enclose himself in a walled garden of sensibility: his religious quest for permanence must have died into an aestheticism that circled in its own harmonies, leaving no road open to action. The romantic sensibility of the time, in its search for a satisfactory universe, always confronted the possible fate of being trapped in an echoing music of self-enclosure.

From that fate Newman was immune: his immunity is enacted in the very passage before us. The snapdragon is left as an esoteric symbol; the observatory, the spires, the railway are all part of a factual narrative which is recited as baldly as possible. The moment of greatest emotional indulgence ('even unto death') is guarded by the language of the Authorized Version.

He had achieved an immunity, not a solution. The major romantic quest—the reconciliation of the human, imaginatively and physically, with the new world of scientific investigation—remained. But what is fascinating in Newman is the *extent* of his Romanticism, the degree of his acknowledgement. The principles by which he had achieved that controlled recognition of the contemporary mind are enshrined in two Latin phrases. From the cultivation of sensibility he had endeavoured to remove all self-indulgence by an exclusive concentration on personal relationships within an ordered

[1] Mark Pattison, *Memoirs*, pp. 235–9.

social framework. Both the assertion and the limitations are suggested in the motto which he chose for himself as cardinal: *Cor ad cor loquitur.* He had sought for truth, but had rejected the idea that one could find an ultimate truth in nature, or any symbol of truth in the human mind, apart from revelation. Both the search and the rejection are expressed in his chosen epitaph: *Ex umbris et imaginibus in veritatem.*

12

JOHN STUART MILL

BY NOEL ANNAN

Why should those who love and study English literature read Mill? It is not quite enough to say that everyone who is moved by Victorian poetry and novels and who tries to criticize them should enlarge his understanding of the age by becoming acquainted with its philosophers. It is not even enough to point out that literature is concerned among other things with morality and society, and that Mill (1806–1873) wrote about both. But what did he write that compels a critic or a student to study him? Since the war four Cambridge critics have answered this question, and perhaps it is of interest in passing to note that their answers were given in response to the challenge that teaching literature makes. In literary studies—unlike the natural sciences—the best research often springs from the delight and the despair of teaching.

Basil Willey's memorable essay on Mill[1] sprang from the lectures that he gave for the paper on the English Moralists in the English Tripos. In it he painted the picture of a man continually forced to repudiate the principles on which he founded his philosophy of life. We must, he said, admire the honesty of the utilitarian rationalist who had seen the errors of his creed; but is it not all the more pathetic that Mill was unable to cut himself adrift from it? To attempt to inject feeling into the adamantine doctrines of Bentham was praiseworthy; but what did the attempt amount to? Mill in the *System of Logic* (1843) set down the rules for establishing a science of society, but then had to admit that his elaborate structure neglected all that is most valuable and strange and curious in man. Mill was a perfectionist, yet the *Political Economy* (1848) led inescapably to a scene where the mass of men were forced to live on the brink of starvation. His lofty injunctions to them to reform and improve society were a

[1] Basil Willey, *Nineteenth Century Studies* (London, 1949), pp. 141–86.

mockery when improvement was limited by the operation of the iron law of wages. How odd that Mill, the evangelist of progress, was so terrified by the rise in population that he argued in favour of arresting the growth in productivity and of settling for a static State! He praised liberty, he asserted that the individual must not be engulfed by the tide of vulgar prejudices and deplorable social conventions; yet what hope was there of preserving individuality when in the same breath he declared that all the tendencies of the times ran against it, and when his own better judgement made him move slowly towards socialism? It was all very well to pronounce that the gross utilitarian morality of self-interest was inadequate and could not be reconciled with the principle of promoting the greatest happiness of the greatest number, but in performing his dissection of utilitarian ethics he so mangled the carcass that he left a shambles. Finally, when we turn to observe what Mill made of religion, the maze of contradiction that meets our eyes reveals why all along the line he failed. His religion is devoid of what matters most in religion. It is devoid of love.

All through his life, like some ungifted Moses, he had tried to strike water out of dry rocks—altruism out of self-love, liberty out of bondage—and now here, in culminating frustration, he tries to draw faith out of reason. The rod taps and taps; the rock yields no drop; while—hidden from his short-sighted eyes—the spring bubbles up close at his back. If any proof were needed of St Paul's proposition that by wisdom (reasoning) no man finds God, here is an admirable one.

It is sad yet fitting that one so grave, so grey, so like a power-loom, with lack-lustre eye, so full of joyless knowledge, 'his earnest, exemplary face turned persistently in the wrong direction', should display an incomprehension in discovering Christianity that becomes almost sublime in its perversity.

That was in 1949. A year later F. R. Leavis published his introduction to Mill's essays on Bentham and Coleridge.[1] It was born out of his exasperation with the syllabus of the English Tripos and the lack of discipline that enfeebled back-ground studies to literature. The reconciliation that Mill made between what he called 'the two great seminal minds of the

---

[1] F. R. Leavis, *Mill on Bentham and Coleridge* (London, 1950), pp. 1–38.

age' was magnificent. The mind that saw both these doctrines as necessary and complementary was—unlike Coleridge's—a disciplined mind. It was the mind of a man of integrity whose 'intellectual distinction is at the same time a distinction of character'. Mill, moreover, was a great representative figure of the Victorian age, and Leavis proceeded to trace an educational trail that would lead the student from Mill to George Eliot, who shared Mill's belief in the Religion of Humanity. The trail led past the far less important Carlyle and Sterling, moved in sight of F. D. Maurice, the Broad Church movement and early socialism, to link Mill's own leanings to socialism with a social scientist of the next generation—Beatrice Webb. *My Apprenticeship* was the corollary to the *Autobiography* (1873). Having made this connexion, the student would recall that Mill and Beatrice Webb both rejected materialism and believed that men and women should dedicate their lives to service and high seriousness: in a sense, Beatrice Webb's life was the child of Mill's denunciation of the subjection of women. Yet he would also note the strength of the hold that Benthamism exercised over Mill. For though it is true that Benthamism inspired the movement for reform, it was also inextricably entangled with Adam Smith's economics. The student therefore must hold in his mind not only the image of Mill, the dedicated modifier of utilitarianism. He must also retain the judgement that Dickens passed on 'enlightened' utilitarianism through the character of Gradgrind in *Hard Times*.

Eight years passed. Then, in exploring how the notion of culture had arisen in England and how writers related it to society, Raymond Williams returned to Mill.[1] In his view Mill had recognized well enough what Coleridge was doing. He understood that the social philosophy which ran in rivulets through the morass of Coleridge's writing fed a theory of culture. In this theory culture did not mean the acquisition of a cultivated mind: it was not an eighteenth-century aristocratic virtue, a facet of the personality that enabled a man to move at ease in polite society. Coleridge thought of culture as a vision of life or a moral habit. But Mill, though he was to develop Coleridge's idea of the clerisy or intellectual élite, made

---

[1] Raymond Williams, *Culture and Society 1780–1950* (London, 1958), pp. 49–70.

nothing of Coleridge's notion of culture. He remained in-
→ tellectualist in manner and in method. If in his youth he
appreciated that Bentham and Coleridge should be reconciled,
as he grew older he moved further from reconciling them. The
notion of culture entails fusing entities. Mill did not fuse anything, he opposed sets of abstract principles one against the
other, never realizing that doctrines become alive only through
what they are attached to and through what they pronounce
to be valuable, never realizing that values are 'different orders
of expression which arise from different ways of life'. It was
characteristic of Mill—and of the English—to think of political
activity as a pendulum that swings between two extremes.
This mechanical metaphor reveals their misunderstanding of
life because it shows how they thought of life as a series of
disjointed parts and not as a whole. And this same disjunction
appears in Mill's view of art. His *Autobiography* indeed described his realization in youth that to work for social reform
was by itself an inadequate ideal: man needed poetry as a
source of inward joy and a perennial source of happiness to
sustain him when the treacheries of politics betrayed him. But,
Williams objects, this was to make poetry a substitute for
feeling. Once again Mill was operating by posing antitheses:
feeling versus mind; subjective, intuitive apprehensions versus
logical, mechanical reasoning. He never learnt from Coleridge
that what men needed was not merely to enlarge the mind by
recognizing differences. They needed to change their mode of
thought by reasoning, not from abstracted experience cast into
principles but from their own living, hard, personal experience.
It was this that should mould their attitude to social institutions. What, after all, was Mill but a more humane utilitarian
with all the desperate inadequacies of that creed?

The disastrous inadequacy of utilitarian ethics was again
one of the themes of Dorothea Krook's book, which appeared
in 1959. She discerned three main traditions in moral thought,
of which the basest was the worldly utilitarian ethic of Aristotle,
Hobbes or Hume, which substituted self-sufficiency, or fear, or
sympathy for love as the central moral concept.[1] Yet she singled

[1] Dorothea Krook, *Three Traditions of Moral Thought* (Cambridge, 1959), pp.
181–201.

Mill out not as the exemplar of utilitarian morality but as a humanist who made perfectly legitimate criticisms of the Christianity of his day. She set out to rescue him on this score from Basil Willey's strictures. It was true that Mill was too much the social scientist and too little the humanist to be flexible or imaginative enough. But, at any rate, he did not fall into the complacent morality of the club-man that made Hume's morality so despicable. He might criticize Christianity in a wooden way, but if he had got hold of the wrong end of the stick he was surely holding it by the same end as the Victorian Christian apologists. It was they who repeated the two-centuries-old arguments for the existence of God from a First Cause or from Design or from Consciousness or from the General Consent of Mankind. It was they who entangled themselves in moral dilemmas by declaring God omnipotent and then maintaining that his mercy must be limited to the Elect. If Mill was disabled from understanding the innermost meaning of Christianity, he at least did a good job of demolition in pulverizing these arguments. But he went further. He asked questions which must be asked by those who are serious. He asked what fundamental needs of the human spirit were supplied by Christianity and how far it redeemed men's corrupt consciousness. When, for instance, he considered the claim for immortality, his scrupulous honesty admitted that there was nothing in human knowledge or experience to disprove it— and that therefore it might be true. He also admitted that the terror of death was a reality and that the only possible way of diminishing it was to improve society so that more human beings could lead happy lives. 'They who have had their happiness can bear to part with existence; but it is hard to die without having lived.' Dorothea Krook did not deny Mill's limitations. His scientific habit of mind—a habit which— imposes disastrous restrictions when the mind is working on moral problems—impeded the spiritual resources that undoubtedly lay within him and produced a thin gruel of humanism that was infinitely less impressive than that of Arnold; but he had grace within him.

Now, different as these four accounts of Mill are, they have certain things in common. All praise Mill's conversion to

Coleridge, Wordsworth and the life of the spirit: all welcome his recognition that happiness cannot be attained by making it the direct end: all deplore the backsliding towards utilitarianism and laissez-faire. To Basil Willey the spectacle is pathetic, to Leavis it is an example of distinction in moral bearing, for Williams and Dorothea Krook it demands both sympathy and regret that a man who understood so many of the limitations of the creed that he inherited could not break through it to perceive the moral profundities that it concealed. All of them see in Mill an illustration of what social philosophers might be if only they would expose themselves to the full experience of literature and life that criticism analyses. They judge Mill by his criticism of his age—what he thought were its vices, what virtues he particularly prized and what he conceived to be the purpose of life: they judge him by his answers.

But is it really apposite to judge Mill solely in terms of culture? He worked in a philosophical tradition that is not susceptible to judgements of this kind. Very severe criticism can be made of him as a philosopher; but although he may not sound as impressive as the sages who prophesied over the bones of Victorian culture, he contributed certain notions which are as important as any of theirs. Mill adorns a famous tradition of thought and he cannot be seen in perspective until we stop regarding him as the man who tried and failed to spiritualize utilitarianism. He was not merely the heir to Bentham. He stood at a turning-point in the history of ideas when the social sciences were beginning to detach themselves from philosophy. He stood at the end of a tradition of thought which was established by Hobbes and Locke, and he looked far more to the past than forward to the future. What had begun as an exploration in the mid-seventeenth century of the political conditions that would enable a minority to be free developed into a systematic analysis of society and of human behaviour. In this newly constructed model of the world, the older hierarchical society of feudal obligation and custom and Christian duty disappeared and was replaced by a bustling collection of individuals, each free to own and to accumulate an unlimited amount of property and wealth, each free to pursue his own goals, none owing duties to another apart from those imposed by law, none deflecting himself from the pursuit of his own goals in order to conform to the purposes of others. Each man was responsible for his actions and chose the means to achieve his ends, but each chose different ends because he had been given freedom of conscience. Why then was there not chaos? The famous answer given by Locke was that there existed in Nature a law of the natural identity of interests, whereby men did not consciously co-operate or pursue a common end but where the efforts of each striving on his own behalf were reconciled with the efforts of everyone else. What clinched this argument was the work of the classical economists. For the first time one aspect of human behaviour was analysed as a system of interrelated variables that embodied all sorts of factors such as tariffs, price-levels or the division of labour, and it appeared to be established that men, by pursuing their own self-interested diverse ends, could in fact achieve a common end, i.e. the highest level of wealth possible. It was, as a theory, immensely satisfying, because it explained social behaviour in terms of individual psychology and hence in terms of personal behaviour; it was coherent, in that literature, philosophy and scientific inquiry seemed for a time all to be moving in harmony; and it was heartening, in that it suggested that, as education spread and men grew wiser, they would choose their goals and the means to achieve them in a rational and scientific manner. Above all, it settled what to the pioneers of the model in the seventeenth century seemed all-important, namely the problem why order and not chaos in society would ensue if men were free to choose their own goals at random— for instance to dissent in religion.

Theories, however water-tight and convincing, generate their own doubts, and the positivist theory of social behaviour was no exception. If Hartley provided it with a more rigorous conception of psychology, Hume almost destroyed it by his separation of fact and value. Godwin carried it to the brink of absurdity by arguing that, if men's interests were really identical, then unnatural institutions such as Church and State could be abolished, since education would provide men with all the knowledge that they needed to understand the situation in which they lived. Meanwhile Malthus and Ricardo began to paint a gloomier picture of the economics of competition, and doubted whether competition alone was sufficient to stabilize social relations: perhaps, after all, everything could not be explained in terms of rational self-interest, perhaps social institutions such as marriage, property and custom were also required to explain why men behaved as they did. Against these doubts could be set Bentham's brilliant, clear and simple explanation of the principles that governed institutions and their reform—principles which were sustained by an analysis of human behaviour. Until Mill's time every theoretical weakness that was exposed seemed to find its counter in some new exposition of part of the theory. What finally put the theory into a hopeless state of confusion were social events which it could not explain satisfactorily in its own terms. These events were the population explosion and the effects of the industrial revolution on the lives of human beings. Now it was no longer self-evident that order could be maintained by putting political power into the hands of a small number of property-owners. Now men could no longer believe that whatever economic inequalities were produced by the operations of the market were more than outweighed by the political equality that the freedoms won in the seventeenth century guaranteed. Society was being transformed by industrialism and it was inevitable that the way it worked and the behaviour of the human beings in it would also be transformed.

This revolution in thought is, of course, associated first and foremost with the name of Marx. It was Marx who denied that social phenomena could be reduced to laws about human nature. Mill, standing at the end of the positivist explanation of social behaviour, was still arguing that since men make their own environment and traditions, their institutions and customs must be explicable in terms of the mind and of human nature. For how else had they arisen other than through men's will? Every institution had a motive behind it, everything was purposeful or it could not have been instituted by man. Even though the purpose that lay behind a custom or tradition or institution had long been forgotten or had been perverted, one had only to discover the original motive in order to provide an explanation. This was the theory that Marx destroyed. 'It is

not the consciousness of man that determines his existence—
rather it is his social existence that determines his consciousness.' Man was the product of society and a slave to the
impersonal laws of history that governed society.

What then did Mill contribute to this remarkable tradition
of thought which had shown such coherence and vitality ? His
writings, in particular *The System of Logic* during the fifties and
sixties, captured the minds of a strong minority among the
young men of those decades, and when he died one of them
canonized him as the 'saint of rationalism'. But does the saint
still work miracles ? His treatise on logic, the great counter-
blast against Whewell's intuitionism, was less revolutionary
than it seemed at first sight, technically only slightly more
interesting than was Whateley's work and slightly less interesting than those of De Morgan, Venn or Boole. His inquiry into
the methods of the natural sciences was certainly more original
once he had set aside his argument about causation and had
seen that tests, prediction and probability theory were the
important concepts in the logic of the natural sciences. But the
greater part of his work was connected with the social sciences,
and here he added little. His *Political Economy* ran into many
editions, but it made no contribution of importance to any
part of economics. He did not appreciate the part that mathematics or statistics were to play in economics or in social
inquiry. In common with most contemporary social philosophers, including Marx, he thought his task to be the discovery
of the laws that governed human behaviour and the progress
of society. He admitted that, in order to be significant, *a priori*
deductions from abstract principles must be checked against
empirical data obtained by observing history. But he realized
neither how detailed and statistical such observations had to
be if they related to the present, nor how boldly and powerfully
they had to be analysed if they were extracted from the
past. His *a priori* studies derived, as we have seen, from the
positivist theory that all social events are ultimately the product
of human motives, and the analysis that he made of history was
feeble in comparison with that of Marx, Hegel or even the
utopian socialists or Comte.

There is indeed a feebleness and timidity in Mill. He has

not the same courage as his predecessors in the positivist tradition. He has not their assurance that even when they were criticizing the tradition in which they worked they were enhancing it. Nor has he their political confidence that reforms which were to give reality to popular rights, such as the right to vote, would not destroy order and prosperity. To some critics these limitations seem to be virtues. Gertrude Himmelfarb, for instance, argues that there are two Mills: the blinkered radical under the spell of Harriet Taylor, who repudiated his youthful criticisms of utilitarianism and wrote the dogmatic essays on Liberty and the Utility of Religion; and the mature man who returned to the spirit of the essays on Bentham and Coleridge and wrote the works on Representative Government and Theism.[1] Yet if we set Mill's anxieties about the effect of democracy against those of Tocqueville, or his analysis of government and finance against Bagehot's *English Constitution* and *Lombard Street*, we must admit that he is neither as profound as the first nor as independent as the second. Mill works away plugging holes, reorganizing his defences, admitting defects, modifying virtues, patching and darning. It is not in this way that advances in philosophy or the social sciences are made. Nor do these modifications and criticisms of radicalism impress. Many of them, such as plural voting, were the sort of safeguards that were put forward by the Whigs and Liberal-conservatives whom he despised. Others, such as proportional representation, produced in practice the very opposite of what Mill desired. Although Mill was often trying to see through the formulae of radicalism to discover what would make government not more democratic but better, and although he deplored individuals pursuing their own personal or class interests, he never understood the play of social forces. If his essays had been really searching criticisms of the styles of life in his times, surely one of them would have been concerned with urbanization and industrialization and their appalling problems? He applied Tocqueville's analysis of democracy in America to England, oblivious for the instant of the immense strength of aristocratic and upper-middle-class power. He

[1] *Essays on Politics and Culture by J. S. Mill*, ed. Gertrude Himmelfarb (New York, 1962).

could not imagine that for the next hundred years the intellectual minority, which he was so concerned to protect, was in danger not of being stifled by the masses but of being gelded by the upper classes.

Imagination! *That* has never been the quality that comes first to mind when one reads the rationalist philosophers. There is no need to tell again the failings of the middle-class liberal thinkers. They did not understand that their political reforms would in practice have the effect of transferring power from an aristocracy to a plutocracy. They ignored the destruction by the cash nexus of whatever gains had been made by political action in achieving equality. Their non-historical and dehumanized creed could not take account of the new historiography of dynamic history and daemonic man. Their reform programme of mechanized devices and governmental adjustments was inadequate to meet the new formulations of power politics and revolution. Finally, in psychology they neglected the startling notion of the Unconscious whether it operated in individuals or in the mass. Beside the German Idealists or the utopian socialists, or the Marxists or the historians, Mill seems deplorably unoriginal and uninventive, staid and sedate. He seems to be fiddling with small methodological points or constitutional and financial reforms.

And yet, however much at first sight the Cambridge critics' assessment of Mill seems to be substantiated, a shadow falls across it. Is empirical philosophy or social science susceptible to their cultural criteria? Is Mill primarily intending to advocate a style of life? It is true that a philosopher's style—the way he constructs his system, the way he moves from premises to conclusions, perhaps the metaphors he uses—can be as personal a statement of reality as a poem. Plato, St Augustine, Hobbes and Hegel composed unforgettable dramas concerning the nature and purpose of life. But not all philosophy is concerned with penetrating reality. Indeed most philosophers start their inquiries not in order to answer the riddle of the universe but because they are puzzled by specific logical or epistemological problems, such as induction or meaning; and some such as Mill, who concern themselves with ethics or social theory, indignantly deny that they are ontologists or meta-physicians. Those who study literature should admit that many philosophers do not believe that anything profitable can be said about the whole of life. Critics have a predisposition to prefer metaphysicians because, like poets, they appear to speak to our present condition. Empirical philosophers and social scientists, on the other hand, come to transitory conclusions that are superseded the day after tomorrow. They are the victims of time; but that does not mean that they can be shrugged off—they have made too many damaging criticisms of metaphysics.

There is indeed an innate antagonism between the cultural mode of thought that critics employ and the operations of empirical philosophy and social science. The artist, the meta-physician and the critic who judges them, are all trying to obtain a single vision of life, the empiricist to place life under a prism so that he can study its component parts. The Cam-bridge critics suggest that if Mill had only broken with utili-tarianism he would have been less the slave of abstraction, more able to fuse the insights of Bentham and Coleridge instead of laying them side by side. But this is not so. In Victorian times it became no longer possible for a rationalist philosopher to fuse the various recognized ways of analysing what human beings do. Gradually new academic disciplines were hardening and becoming autonomous and could no longer be subsumed under a super-theory of knowledge. All they could do was occasionally to lighten one another's darkness. The Victorian intelligentsia were puzzled and distressed that this appeared to be so, and they were all too apt to applaud efforts to re-establish the unity of knowledge. Mill made such efforts, but in retrospect it is as just to criticize as to praise him for making them. For in attempting to reconcile Coleridge with Bentham, or good with democratic government, or agnosticism with theism, Mill so far from becoming a better became a worse social scientist.

Social scientists can work only within the concepts and tech-niques of their own discipline. Alfred Marshall introduced into his *Principles of Economics* many high-sounding passages about thrift and self-reliance and poverty; and these admirable senti-ments may have inspired him to tackle the problem of the redistribution of wealth. But they did not affect the logic of his economic theory; the passages could be removed and the theory would be unaffected. Keynes believed that capitalism was grossly inefficient and unemployment a blot upon civilization, but it took long years of controversy and experiment to hammer out the *General Theory*, which did not rely as a theory on moral considerations. As a contribution to social science, Mill's revision of utilitarian ethics—except in so far as it produced confusion—is irrelevant. His successors were far more to the point. They recognized utilitarian ethics for what it was: either it was a matter of technical philosophy to be treated with great rigour as Sidgwick and Moore treated it; or it was a shorthand common-sense guide to political and social reform, not purporting to cover the whole of moral activity and capable of being set to work, as it was at the end of the century, with economic theories opposed to laissez-faire justifying programmes of State interference.

Mill, then, was a social philosopher—which is something more and something less than a critic of culture. His flat undistinguished tone of voice was quite distinct from the peculiar powers of persuasion that the Victorian sages exercised. Arnold quite rightly claimed for the critic an autonomous mode of discourse. He was for ever wringing his hands at his own lack of erudition, his deplorable incompetence in abstract argument, his inability to be precise or to be a good party man or to grasp the principles of science or theology; and we know, of course, as his good humour bubbles over, that he is delighted to have imposed upon his readers a style of thinking that does not rely for its power on erudition, scientific principle, precision or orthodoxy. So much so that when F. H. Bradley used the techniques of philosophy to dissect Arnold's concepts, we feel that, despite his shrewd blows, he was not moving on the same plane and the brilliant exhibition leaves Arnold untouched. Just so with Mill. The philosopher and political reformer does not have to be a critic of culture. On that score he is immeasurably inferior to Arnold and even to Carlyle. But, in representing the strain of rationalism, he made several notable contributions to the culture his own times that still echo in ours.

Mill's social theory is simple. There is one end in life to which all others are ultimately subordinate, the progress of society— that is to say, the discovery of the laws by which men can realize their better selves. We cannot progress unless we find truth, and we shall not find truth unless we realize that it is clothed in new ideas. It is with these new ideas that men shape history and tame the ethnological and economic forces that in the past have been beyond their control. In modern society truth is discovered by the intellectual élite; they do not govern, they point the way. The force most likely to hamper the élite in their search is society itself—the stupidity, vested interests, shibboleths and bigotry of various classes and groups. That is why intellectual and political liberty are paramount: a free élite is free to disturb the rest of society with its new truths. These truths, if acted upon, will in fact conflict with the selfish private interests of some individuals. Sometimes we must not force individuals to conform to these truths but allow them to continue to act selfishly and foolishly, because it is so important to preserve freedom of conscience and action. At other times the State will be justified in interfering so that society as a whole may benefit. Such interference can be justified on the grounds that no individual shall be allowed palpably to harm others. In other cases individuals will have to be persuaded by education and argument to change their ways. Is there any argument which can persuade a man that this is better than that, or that will disprove Bentham's assertion: 'Quantity of pleasure being equal, push-pin is as good as poetry'? Only the reason that 'it is better to be Socrates dissatisfied than a fool satisfied', and that if the fool is of a different opinion it is because he has experienced only the pleasure of push-pin, whereas Socrates has experienced the pleasure of both push-pin and poetry and knows that the latter is a higher and better form of pleasure.

Out of this theory three notions ought to live for the critic and student of literature: Mill's call to truth, his passion for intellectual freedom and his belief in the clerisy.

Truth for Mill was almost a tangible entity. You feel that for him it was composed of hard, gritty particles which needed to be poured into a centrifuge in order to be redistributed

correctly. Truth in its primitive state was not necessarily
exact. 'Mankind', he said, 'have many ideas, and few words.
Two consequences follow from it; one, that a certain laxity in the
use of language must be borne with, if a writer makes himself
understood; the other that, to understand a writer who uses
the same words as a vehicle for different ideas, requires a
vigorous effort of co-operation on the part of the reader.'[1] At
one time he thought that Truth was sown and germinated in
the mind and was not to be 'struck out like fire from a flint'
by the collision of opinions. Later he came to believe the
reverse, and held that Truth did not always emerge in the right
shape—it had to be hammered until it rang true, it could
'establish itself only by means of conflict.' Truth mounted at
compound interest. 'The progress of opinions is like the
advance of a person climbing a hill by a spiral path which
winds round it, and by which he is as often on the wrong side
of the hill as on the right side, but still is always getting higher
up.'[2] That was why militant discussion was valuable: that was
why Mill argued that a government that suppressed discussion
unjustifiably assumed itself to be infallible; and that was why
he often returned to the deadening effect that custom, convention, taboos and social disapproval can have on intellectual life.

Mill's insistence on the sacredness of truth had the force of a
religious commandment; and it had an immense influence not
only upon his rationalist followers but throughout the Victorian
clerisy. It forced people to consider the grounds for their
beliefs, it compelled them to give reasons for these beliefs
where formerly they had not needed to do so, it put a premium
upon intellectual honesty and scrupulousness. A literary critic
may object that Mill's criteria for establishing truth are excessively scientific; and his criteria, no less than those of Arnold,
have of course dated. So, perhaps, has Mill's hunger for truth.
There are in every academic discipline or activity in life today
innumerable accommodations that enable men to treat other
qualities such as goodness or scepticism as more important.
But during the nineteenth century the notion that truth was

---

[1] 'Review of Use and Abuse of Political Terms', *Tait's Edinburgh Magazine*, I,
(1832), p. 299.
[2] *Letters of Mill*, ed. H. Elliott, vol. II (London, 1910), Appendix A.

tangible and in some degree, however small, attainable was an element in culture. There are novels which owe a direct debt to Mill—Mrs Humphry Ward's *Robert Elsmere* (1888) is certainly a document, and Olive Schreiner's *The Story of a South African Farm* (1883), which is almost a Millite tract, at one point presents Mill's conception of the search for truth in the form of an allegory. But to search for far-fetched examples of Mill's influence is unprofitable. It is much more important for the student of literature to see how the theme of truthfulness—not in regard to abstract beliefs but in personal relations—is handled by novelists such as Jane Austen, Constant, George Eliot, Forster or the great Tolstoy. The theme of untruthfulness and self-deception in the relationship between one person and another is endemic in nineteenth-century literature, with Emma or Adolphe, between Lydgate and Rosamund Vincy, or Dorothea and Casaubon, in the Schlegel family or with poor Ricky, above all between Anna and Vronsky. 'To tell the truth', wrote Tolstoy, 'is a very difficult thing; and young people are rarely capable of it.'

The essay *On Liberty* (1859) is often referred to as a classic defence of individual freedom, yet very few of its arguments stand up to criticism. Only one of them is utilitarian, the others are assertions that a man must always be responsible to himself for his actions—which is a religious notion. Time and again we can think of instances which contradict Mill's reasons—for instance, those who care most deeply about the truth are often those most ardent in suppressing it, because they mistakenly believe that they, and they alone, have attained it. Time and again, to justify freedom today, we would use arguments that Mill would have disliked, such as the argument that good ends conflict, or that diversity of opinions and of moral standards are good in themselves. Time and again we have seen political situations arise that justify the suppression of certain freedoms that Mill thought should never be suppressed. Mill did not appreciate how greatly social factors determined freedom: how freedom in Britain, for instance, rested on the supremacy of the mid-Victorian Royal Navy, and the absence of any internal subversive movement willing to aid an external enemy.

And yet Mill's essay continues to exist as a monument to belief in intellectual liberty. It is a solemn reminder how important it is to keep alive the idea of *negative* liberty, that is to say the right to allow people to go their own way even if it is to hell. For although Mill thought that it was of importance not only what men do but what manner of men they are that do it, he also thought that individual spontaneity had a value in itself and he was not prepared to coerce men to realize their better selves. The Essay burnt itself into the consciousness of each succeeding generation of liberals: whatever else they discarded from mid-Victorian radicalism, they retained the Essay—it troubled the conscience of converted Marxists and mellowed the convictions of British socialists. Its spirit was one of the challenges to the prudery and podsnappery that Thackeray complained hamstrung the novel in England. It still provides some of the standard arguments against censorship and the burning of books, because it insists that the onus of proving that a book or some poisonous opinions will cause irreparable social harm must fall on the prosecution. The prosecutions which were uppermost in Mill's mind were those for blasphemy made in defence of religion; he did not live long enough to see the most notorious ones made against birth-control, a cause which he fearlessly advocated. But the piece of cultural history that is already being forgotten was the series of prosecutions or refusals between 1880 and 1930 to publish poetry and novels on grounds of obscenity that was part of the savage outburst of philistinism and hatred of artists that met the great revolution in the arts. How far it has been forgotten was well shown by the debate that followed the prosecution in 1960 of the publishers of *Lady Chatterley's Lover*. The book there on trial was as much the essay *On Liberty* as Lawrence's novel: and what was interesting was that those who criticized the witnesses for the defence forgot that Mill cared less whether a book was good or bad literature than that its suppression meant suppressing truth—the truth that the conflict of opinion about the merit or worthlessness of the book would throw on sexual love and its portrayal in a novel, and upon Lawrence's status as a novelist. How far Mill's principle of freedom affects the writing of good literature is still almost wholly obscure. We know that much of the greatest art—

certainly nineteenth-century Russian literature, which was the greatest of all national literatures in Mill's lifetime—has been produced under severe censorship. All we know is that artists hate censorship.

Mill's third contribution to culture was his notion of an intellectual élite, which he developed from Coleridge's woolly concept of a national clerisy. It is understandable that he should have created this class in his own image, picturing it as centred educationally on University College London and the dissenting academies rather than on Oxford and Cambridge and the Clarendon schools, and on the high-minded liberal families of the provincial cities such as the Rathbones of Liverpool or the Frys of Bristol. He saw it manning the civil service which, as government became more complex, the aristocracy were unable any longer to treat as a field of patronage, being forced to employ middle-class men of ability such as himself. In the last years of his life he could see representatives of this class gathering to deliver the unsparing anticlerical attack of the seventies. It was natural enough for him to envisage the intelligentsia as a class that would keep their distance from the rulers of the country whom they would chide and guide as occasion saw fit, if only for the fact that as a class it is always separated from the main body of society. Intellectuals create society's art, they make its past explicit, they interpret its religion and morality and customs, they provide it with new political constitutions. It is they who protest in times of revolution or deep political dissatisfaction that the rulers have no legitimate authority to act as they are doing. Society and its rulers are often enraged by them, and their taste conflicts with intellectual expressions in art, religion and politics. The things that intellectuals ask people to believe, respect and enjoy lie outside people's experience, and therefore they will reject these things in times of stress and blame the intellectuals for forcing them to accept them. Similarly, while it is to the advantage of rulers to get the intellectuals on their side, particularly since many of the intelligentsia are bureaucrats or scientists or journalists or manipulators of the mass media that influence public opinion, the rulers' interests will always diverge from those of the intelligentsia. Intellectuals purport to regard their work as concerned with sacred subjects such as truth and goodness; and some even do so regard it. This alienates them from rulers and businessmen, who are interested primarily in whether things will work and who are obliged to compromise and make innumerable political adjustments that seem to the intellectual corrupt and cowardly. This conflict between ideal solutions and practical politics in turn sets up a conflict within the intelligentsia itself—between administrators and those who are divorced from making or executing policy, between churchmen and theologians, labour politicians and socialists, the organizers of science and research scientists, publishers and authors, editors and journalists, or corporations and technologists.

At the same time, although intellectuals are always to some extent opposed to the various forms of social and political authority, it is an error to imagine that they are permanently in revolt. Some of them advise the rulers and their bureaucracy; others, as we have seen, are part of the machine of government; a few may even be politicians, as Mill was in one Parliament. Some kinds of politics, e.g. liberal and constitutional or socialist politics, are the creation of intellectuals, who are therefore deeply implicated in them and have an interest in making them work. Intellectuals never completely reject the central value system of their country. The Marxist conclusion that intellectuals must feel alienated in a bourgeois society is untrue: intellectuals can feel much at home even when sensing the tension between themselves and those who are the guardians of the central institutional system. What is impossible to achieve is a situation (which figures often in intellectuals' dreams) in which the intelligentsia stands quite aside from the vulgar activities of rulers, middle-men and the populace who, however, prove to be docilely willing to accept their prognostications and dictates, to do their best to put them into practice, and meekly to accept criticism of their efforts.

Mill was under no such illusion, but even so he overestimated the independence of the British intelligentsia and underestimated their desire to assimilate and use the reformed ancient institutions of the Establishment, such as Oxford and Cambridge and the public schools. Many of his intellectual élite were only too anxious to ally themselves to the ruling class. There were always sources of radicalism and discontent— collectivist liberalism, anti-clericism, Fabianism, syndicalism, anti-industrialism—but the sources were always drying up and changing, especially in the area in which Mill expected them to gush: the provinces. The intelligentsia as a whole became most disaffected in the period between the two wars, when the revolution in the creative arts went hand in hand with bitter attacks on imperialism and public schools, capitalism and advertising, popular entertainment and suburbanism—indeed on the whole of English society. But this was an interlude, and in the post-war years the intelligentsia has been tamed and has fragmented.

Nevertheless Mill's spirit is still at work among them. There have always been many ready to analyse and reform social evils: if they do not share Mill's faith in the perfectibility of man in its pristine form, they act as if it might be true. Indeed a double portion of his spirit falls on a few, they inherit Mill's moral temperament and, in a new form, his religion of humanity. As Leavis correctly points out, it descended on Beatrice Webb. But the student of literature, as he reflects on the writers of importance during the past hundred years, will come to a melancholy conclusion. They have loathed and rejected Mill's vision of life. Whether it is Tolstoy or Dostoievsky, Flaubert or Proust, Yeats or Joyce, Nietzsche or Rilke, Henry James, Lawrence or T. S. Eliot, none has any love for this abstract description of human behaviour and prediction of moral and material improvement. The only novel of any merit I know which realizes in fictive form some of Mill's emotion is Gorki's *A Confession*: the only outstanding figure whose criticism of progressive humanitarianism shows how much of it an artist in the liberal tradition has to reject is Forster. Nor has the gospel of progress gripped any writer of importance today.

There are many reasons, some of them highly complex, why this should be so. Perhaps something not entirely pleasant, which artists are quick to sense, emanates from high-minded and dedicated human beings such as Mill and Beatrice Webb. There is a censorious, waspish tone of voice, a lack of sympathy and humour, a contempt for living foolish human beings (as distinct from humanity), an inability to see people except as material to be moulded and exploited, a mind which, if at first open to arguments and facts, closes like a rat-trap once it has digested them—a temperament which in fact is at variance with their creed. One remembers Mill's venomous reference to 'that creature Dickens' who had dared to satirize blue-stockings in *Bleak House*. Creative writers, moreover, may also recognize in the social scientists' description of human behaviour something that is a genuine challenge to their art. In Mill's time the method was still crude, but with the revolution in sociology at the beginning of this century their description of human behaviour is more penetrating. As sociologists no longer tried to discover grandiloquent social laws in the style of Mill or Marx, and as they explored how family, class, age-group, occupation and a maze of other social institutions conditioned human behaviour and moulded the morality of society, so a new and no less inimical way of depersonalizing life and discarding the living individual in favour of the group acquired prestige. Yet although sociology abstracts and categorizes life, it also sometimes brings to life the way in which living people describe their style of life and the institutions through which they live. So much so that Lionel Trilling noted that no American novel of recent years had given the sense of actuality that David Riesman's essays were able to convey.[1] Whereas once artists were confident that their vision of life was a whole vision which did not have to break up life into a spectrum as the social scientist did, now their vision is partly focussed by the findings of the social scientists: the Coleridge of today is panting after Bentham. One thing only is certain. We know little about the relation of art to society and practically nothing about the reasons why it flourishes or declines. Dogmatic assertions about the superiority of 'organic' communities are as fanciful as the sketches that Mill's contemporaries made of the Middle Ages. If we see in Mill the ominous portent of a method of looking at society which at the moment coincides with a decline in the arts, we must admit that this method seems the most likely to explain why this decline has occurred.

[1] Lionel Trilling, *A Gathering of Fugitives* (London, 1957), p. 92.

13

MATTHEW ARNOLD AND THE CONTINENTAL IDEA

BY HEINRICH STRAUMANN

To examine the unfamiliar works of an author of repute may often throw light on a number of essential aspects of his work as a whole which might otherwise escape critical attention. At the end of his chapter on Matthew Arnold (1822–1888) in *Nineteenth Century Studies* (1949), Basil Willey has pointed to a case of this sort. Apart, however, from Arnold's religious books, to which Professor Willey especially refers, there are also other essays seldom mentioned by critics because they appear either obsolete, or too technical, or simply irrelevant to the major issues in Arnold's position.

Schools and Universities on the Continent, published in the year 1868, belongs to this category. There are several reasons why this book has been made the subject of the present study. Firstly, it shows Arnold as a remarkably precise observer and careful interpreter of extremely complex material—qualities by no means generally assumed in his case. Again, it contains a number of statements illustrating Arnold's better known critical works, together with an attitude characteristic of his 'divided self'. And finally, it permits me to pursue a subject which through my origin, professional work in literary history and education, and personal attachment to England has always been particularly dear to my heart: Anglo-Swiss intellectual relations.

As the book is nowadays not generally accessible and in fact very little known, it may be well to begin with a brief outline of its contents.[1] At first sight it seems little more than the

---

[1] There is no study specially devoted to *Schools and Universities on the Continent*. There is, of course, W. F. Cornell's full-length and highly instructive analysis *The Educational Thought and Influence of Matthew Arnold* (London, 1950), with many references to the book in question, but with no discussion of it as a whole. Lionel Trilling, in his otherwise comprehensive and penetrating study *Matthew Arnold* (New York, 1939), hardly refers to the problem.

published version of an official report made by Matthew Arnold in his capacity as a Foreign Assistant Commissioner to the School Inquiry Commission which prepared for the new measures associated with the Education Act of 1870. It is the result of extensive investigations made during Arnold's journeyings in France, Italy, Germany and Switzerland from April to October in the year 1865. Of roughly 300 pages of the book, one-third is given to France, one-sixth to Italy, one-fourth to Germany, one-fifteenth to Switzerland and the rest to general conclusions and to the appendix with statistical tables about school expenditures, university lecture lists and the like.

After the preface, the book opens with a brief survey of secondary-school instruction in Europe, with special emphasis on France. There follows a chapter on the organization of French secondary schools from the Ministry of Public Instruction down to the positions and salaries of teachers in a *lycée*, with high praise for the work done at the *École Normale*. After a survey of the subjects taught there, the author proceeds to discuss some of the drawbacks, such as the long working hours, the problem of competitive examinations, private schools and communal colleges, and the nature of the discipline. He is convinced that French teaching of mathematics is vastly superior, that of Latin about equal, and that of Greek inferior to what is being done at an English Public School. Without any negative or positive comment he mentions the 'growing disbelief in Greek and Latin, at any rate as at present taught', and ends up with a brief sketch of French university instruction.

The second part of the book deals with Italy, and again begins with a short history of Italian schools from the Middle Ages to the Union and the Legge Casati of 1859. After pointing out the extravagance of Italy in having a secondary school teacher to every ten pupils, Arnold on the one hand applauds the new proposals, according to which Latin and Greek were 'not to come till the two last years of the gymnasial course'[1] and, on the other, deplores the laxity and indulgence in the practical application of the new measures. Similarly he disapproves of the strong tendency among university students to pursue their

[1] *Schools and Universities on the Continent,* p. 123. Page references hereafter without identification are to this work.

16

studies for predominantly practical reasons, especially medicine and law, whereas he is convinced that 'the prevalence of the study of letters is a good test of a country's general condition of culture and civilization' (p. 130). Italy spends more money on her universities than France or Prussia, and yet, owing to the laxity and want of discipline, it is not turned to the best account, Turin and Naples being commendable exceptions. Sweeping reforms would be necessary and are actually proposed: 'education in Italy needs to be reconstructed from the very bottom' (p. 140).

Part III of the book is devoted to German, or rather Prussian, schools. From the very beginning Arnold frankly declares that 'the school system all through Germany . . . is in its completion and carefulness such as to excite a foreigner's admiration' (p. 155). He proceeds to give an exact description of the types of higher secondary schools in Prussia, especially of the 'Gymnasium' with its *Lehrplan*, or hours of work in each branch of instruction year by year: Latin, Greek, mother tongue, French, mathematics, geography, history, natural sciences in exchange for Greek, drawing, writing and religious instruction, and its aim of the 'formation of the pupil's mind and of his powers of knowledge, without prematurely taking thought for the practical applicability of what he studies' (p. 159). There follows a discussion of the legal basis of the Prussian school system, of the Education Department, and of the important role played by Wilhelm von Humboldt at the beginning of the century, with due stress on the public control of the higher schools through the Provincial School Boards and the Governmental District Boards. Arnold then points out that admission to the universities depends on the leaving examinations of the Gymnasium (*Abitur* or *Maturität*), and that the learned professions can only be reached through the universities. In these examinations 'the total cultivation (*Gesamtbildung*) of the candidate is the great matter' (p. 182), i.e. the training is more important than the examinations. and this applies equally to the so-called *Realschule*, where physics and chemistry replace Greek, and where requirements in Latin are only translation without free composition.

A whole chapter is devoted to the description of the training, examination, appointment and payment of the Prussian school-master, including attendance at a seminar. Arnold is aware that in Prussia 'the schoolmasters should be men who will train up their scholars in notions of obedience towards the sovereign and the State' (p. 196), but he is convinced that the dangers implied in such an attitude are not real in Prussia, for 'the truth is that when a nation has got the belief in culture which the Prussian nation has got, and when its schools are worthy of this belief, it will not suffer for them to be sacrificed to any other interest; and however greatly political considerations may be paramount in other departments of administration, in this they are not' (p. 197). This optimistic view, which was fairly justified up to the beginning of the twentieth century but later came tragically to grief, is supplemented by the remark that 'in France neither the national belief in culture nor the schools themselves are suffici-ently developed to awaken this enthusiasm [viz. in culture]; and politics are too strong for the schools, and give them their own bias' (pp. 197–8)—a rather unexpected statement by the author of 'The Literary Influence of the Academies', but far from being the only one of its kind in *Schools and Universities*. Arnold amplifies his observations on Prussian schools by describing some of the more outstanding ones in detail, especially Schulpforta, for which he has special praise; and he then proceeds to a discussion of the structure of the Prussian universities, stressing their character as state establishments and describing the way in which pro-fessors are appointed by the state authorities at the suggestion of the faculties. He explains the system of the *Privatdozenten* and the importance of the doctorate, and concludes that '*Lehrfreiheit* and *Lernfreiheit*, liberty for the teacher and liberty for the learner, and *Wissenschaft*, science, knowledge systemati-cally pursued and prized in and for itself, are the fundamental ideas of that system' (p. 231). 'It is in science that we have most need to borrow from the German universities' (p. 232).

On the whole the tone of the sections on France, Italy and Germany is pleasantly balanced, praise and blame being ex-pressed with due reserve—an attitude in general, though with notable exceptions, in keeping with Arnold's earlier and later work. Although a surprising amount of Arnold's description of the school organizations of these countries still applies, it is not so much the factual aspects that hold the attention of the modern reader. A first suspicion will be felt when we turn to the one brief chapter on Switzerland (20 pages out of 300), where we seem to notice some kind of a change. There are more evaluative remarks, more personal judgements, more critical estimates and, above all, more comparisons with Britain. It is as if the author felt on safer ground, though there is no sign that he ever feels uncertain in his discussions of other countries or that from his earlier experience he ever thought he knew Switzerland better than her neighbours. One explanation can be found in the opening sentences of the preface. Although the book is essentially devoted to secondary schools and universities, the author makes it plain that owing to the public interest in England in the education of the poor he has given a 'full account of the primary school system in Canton Zürich—a region free like England, industrial like England, Protestant like England' (preface, p. v).

In Switzerland [he says], more than in any other country with which I am acquainted, all classes use the same primary school; and in Switzerland, therefore, I had occasion to touch upon the primary school—the school of the poor—because there this school forms a link in the chain of schools in which the middle and upper classes are educated. . . . School attendance is obligatory there, and the schools are very good. . . . (preface, p. v.)

This passage reveals many of Arnold's methods and concerns. He begins by establishing a similarity, and, for once, fortunately not on ethnological grounds such as Teutonic, Germanic or Saxon, as he might well have done,[1] but based on more tangible elements, political, economic and religious. The word 'free' is especially important here, for it makes the term 'obligatory school attendance' appear in the right perspective, just as the word 'the school of the poor' gives more weight to the statement that the schools are very good. Together with the reference to the middle and upper classes we have here the nucleus of a conception which, if developed, might have led to much farther-reaching conclusions about the enlightenment of

---

[1] A detailed analysis of this aspect of Arnold's work is offered by Frederic E. Faverty, *Matthew Arnold the Ethnologist* (Evanston, Ill., 1951).

populace, philistines and barbarians. As it stands, the statement testifies to Arnold's admiration for something which he considered an unusual achievement: the creation of an educational basis on which higher aims could soundly be developed.

Arnold is convinced that Dutch, German and Swiss schools and their inspection are better than those in England, and that as a result 'the working-class in Zürich or Saxony is, in general, less raw and illiterate than ours' (preface, p. xii). Moreover, 'the compulsoriness is, in general, found to go along with the prosperity, though it cannot be said to cause it; but the same high value among a people for education which leads to its prospering among them, leads also in general to its being made compulsory' (preface, p. xvi). Here Arnold tries to establish a common denominator for compulsory education in *all* classes of the population, their material prosperity and the conduct of the poor, although he carefully avoids suggesting a causal connexion. It is the same principle which made him appeal to the English public to carry out plans for improvements not as isolated operations but 'as parts of a regularly designed whole' (preface, p. xx). The concept of the organic whole, which lies behind this appeal also appears in his repeated statement that a Swiss or German schoolmaster, who enjoys much consideration as one discharging an important function, 'makes his voice heard in the school legislation and school regulations of his country' (preface, p. xiii), whilst in England 'the most important questions of educational policy may be settled without such men being even heard' (preface, p. xxi). This time the problem is really that of the schoolteachers being excluded from their share in helping to find an adequate solution of the very questions with which they seemed most competent to deal.

Altogether, the preface points out some urgent problems in the educational situation of England and explains a good deal of Arnold's particular attitude to Switzerland. The natural affinity which in some respects he obviously felt for the region of Canton Zürich was, with regard to Switzerland in general, shared by many of his contemporaries. Scholars and writers as wide apart as George Grote, Charles Dickens, Leslie Stephen,

John Ruskin[1] could be mentioned in this connexion. Guided by such fundamental sympathy, Matthew Arnold discovered and set forth all those features in Swiss education which were of particular help to him in his general argument, and it must be emphasized that there are hardly any points which he did not see and describe correctly.

At first everything seems to be all praise and plain sailing. He begins with the fact that 'nearly a third of the whole public expenditure of the Canton Zürich is directed to education, and one in five of the population are in school' (p. 236), whilst in England, according to optimistic estimates about which Arnold expressed his doubts, it was only one in seven or eight. He amplifies this later by a striking comparison:

A region [i.e. Canton Zürich] with the population of Leicestershire possesses a university, a veterinary school, a school of agriculture, two great classical schools, two great *real* schools, a normal school for training primary and secondary teachers, fifty-seven secondary schools, and three hundred and sixty-five primary schools; and many of those schools are among the best of their kind in Europe. (p. 253)

It is remarkable that Arnold should lay so much stress on a predominantly quantitative argument. After all, the university, to give only one example, had at that time (1864) not more than 200 students, though it also had twenty-nine professors—a ratio, incidentally, to which one looks back with nostalgia. But the quantitative argument was undoubtedly necessary for the immediate purpose of the investigation, which was to provide the School Enquiry Commission with the necessary material for the discussion of the new Education Bill in public.

Arnold then systematically works his way upward, beginning with a description of the primary day-schools, which were attended by practically all children of all classes; he explains the branches of instruction, the system of checking school absences and the school administration of the commune

---

[1] For a collection and analysis of statements made by Englishmen on Switzerland at that time, see Hans Löhrer, *Die Schweiz im Spiegel der englischen Literatur 1849–1875* (Zürich, 1952).

(*Gemeindeschulpflege*) elected by the commune, the school administration of the district (*Bezirksschulpflege*) with its inspecting duties, and finally the supreme authority, the Education Council (*Erziehungsrat*). The Education Council consists, as it still does today, of its president, who is at the same time Director of Education for the Canton and a member of the government of the canton, and of six other members. Four of these are elected by the cantonal parliament and two by the School Synod, a body consisting of all the teachers of the canton from the primary schools to the university. The business of the Education Council is the supervision and promotion of education throughout the canton. Arnold concludes his survey of the education authorities with the remark that

the spirit in which they have been contrived, balanced, and organised is, as the English reader will perceive, an intensely democratic and an intensely local spirit; yet not insanely democratic, so that the idea of authority, nor insanely local, so that the idea of the State, shall be lost sight of. (p. 243)

It is evident that Arnold feels particularly impressed by the balance between State authority and strictly democratic structure prevailing in the system. What he does not refer to is the way in which this carefully established balance has been achieved in the course of centuries of development; a development, moreover, that definitely had its origin in the political autonomy of the commune, in the innermost centre of a specifically Swiss brand of democracy. There is as yet no word of 'provincialism' here, nothing of 'being remote from a centre'—although such criticism might easily have come from an author who never tired of pointing out the weaknesses of a civilization without a rallying point and who later in the same chapter indicates a real difficulty in the Swiss system.

Before doing so, however, he proceeds to a description of the higher schools such as the higher elementary (or lower secondary schools), where he is 'particularly struck with the thorough way in which French was taught and learnt' (p. 245). He is again especially interested in the structure and aims of the Gymnasium, which has the same subjects as the same type of school in Prussia. There is, however, the essential difference that the Zürich Gymnasium has an immediate connexion with the popular elementary school—evidently an important asset in Arnold's view for the same reasons which called forth his approval of all classes having the same elementary instruction.

But what is most noteworthy is that not only is no Latin or Greek verse done in the Gymnasium at all, but no original Latin or Greek composition in prose is done there; a translation once a week,—into Greek one week and into Latin another,—is all the Greek and Latin composition done; and this translation is little more than a grammatical exercise. (p. 247)

On the basis of this passage alone it would not be easy to decide whether Arnold approves of this arrangement or not. On the one hand it clearly points towards a decrease in the practical command of the two classical languages, on the other towards the possibility of devoting much more time to actual reading. From his 'general Conclusion' it becomes clear that he prefers the latter (p. 262), which is in keeping with his efforts to 'hellenize'. Above all, he wishes to stress the difference from an English Public School.

Arnold also mentions the *Industrieschule*, a school with similar subjects as those of the Gymnasium—Latin and Greek, however, having been replaced by more mathematics and geometrical drawing and with three divisions in the upper form (the mechanical, the chemical and the business line). Similar higher schools, but run on commercial lines, are also to be found at Winterthur, a town of the same Canton, but with its 8,000 inhabitants much smaller than Zürich. 'Winterthur is, I think, for its school establishments, the most remarkable place in Europe. . . . The schools of this small place recall the municipal palaces of Flanders and Italy' (p. 249). It is in remarks of this kind that Arnold betrays his passionate belief in the civilizing power of educational work, and his admiration for the concentrated efforts of a community. After mentioning that the private schools, because of the quality of the state schools, were becoming less and less important, and that even a famous school like Fellenberg's at Hofwyl could no longer successfully vie with the state schools, he briefly discusses the position of the University of Zürich and of the Polytechnicum, now the Federal Institute of Technology.

So far everything is clear, direct—an immediate expression of
Arnold's main concern to promote schools of every kind, whatever their aims in each particular case. There is also that well
known tendency to praise things foreign at the expense of his
own country which irritated Arnold's contemporary critics so
much. But then, on the last two pages of the chapter on Switzerland, he suddenly offers some critical remarks of vital
importance:

The aim which Swiss education has before it, is not I think the
highest educational aim. The idea of what the French call *la grande
culture* has not much effect in Switzerland, and accordingly it is not
in her purely literary and scientific high schools, and in the line of
what is specially called a liberal education, that she is most successful . . . A genuine German, I am told, does not much like the
atmosphere in which he finds himself there; he sighs for the more
truly scientific spirit, the *wissenschaftliche Geist*, of the universities of
his own country, and will not in general stay long in Zürich. The
spirit which reigns at Zürich, and in the thriving parts of German
Switzerland, is a spirit of intelligent industrialism, but not quite
intelligent enough to have cleared itself of vulgarity. (p. 254)

A statement of this sort is all the more impressive because it
comes after so many laudatory remarks. At first sight it seems
to contradict a good deal of what Arnold had set out to explain.
Yet, when seen in a wider context, it is a perfect instance of
that deeper tension between apparently irreconcilable elements
which may be detected in almost everything Arnold wrote or
did.

The most natural question that will be asked first is whether
it is true. As always with generalizations of the sort, the
question itself is only partly relevant. Even if Arnold were
entirely wrong in his pronouncement, it would be essential for
the understanding of his critical purpose and significant as
such. Moreover, the statement belongs to that category of
national or ethnological images which are closer to myths than
to verifiable abstractions. In Arnold's chain of ideas they probably represent the weakest links. Celtic melancholy, German
steadiness, English energy and lack of intelligence, Jewish
morality, to mention only a few—they all sound a little pre-
posterous nowadays. And yet with regard to the statement on

Swiss education it would, even today, be difficult for an in-
formed Swiss to deny it entirely. Absence of *la grande culture*,
intelligent industrialism, a touch of vulgarity in the sense in
which Arnold used the word—it does not seem so wrong, and
one could only take exception to the passage about the Germans
in Zürich, who certainly do not sigh nowadays for the more
truly scientific spirit of their own universities.

But all this is of secondary importance in comparison with
what the statement means in Arnold's own terms. There it is
nothing more and nothing less than what he, often in the same
words, used to say about the English middle classes. By the
absence of *la grande culture* he means the lack of unity of thought
and of a centre of intellectual aspirations which in his opinion
the French possessed and which later he called 'the study of
perfection'.[1] The expression here goes hand in hand with the
idea of the scientific spirit which Arnold chiefly attributes to
higher learning in Germany, with the quest for knowledge and
truth for its own sake, irrespective of any practical utility and
application.

It is surprising that Arnold in this connexion never refers to
Johann Heinrich Pestalozzi (1746–1827), whose ideas were, and
still are, playing such an important part in educational thought.
His name never even occurs in *Schools and Universities*, nor does
it appear to be found in Arnold's other writings, except possibly
in a school report.[2] Yet he must have been aware of Pestalozzi's influence on Swiss education, because he mentions
'Fellenberg's famous school at Hofwyl' (p. 251), and Fellenberg
was and is generally known as one of Pestalozzi's most influential
disciples. One of Pestalozzi's main concerns was to understand
the nature of man, and to find a way that would enable each
individual to overcome the inevitable difficulties in his existence
by means of a clearer perception of the order of the world around
him and at large. It would not be impossible to connect this
with Arnold's ideas of culture as the study of perfection or of
'the high best self'. There is even a passage in *Schools and*

[1] *Culture and Anarchy*, ed. J. Dover Wilson (Cambridge, 1932), p. 45.
[2] W. F. Cornell, in *The Educational Thought and Influence of Matthew Arnold*
(London, 1950), mentions Arnold's indifference to pedagogic doctrines and
methods even when backed by the eminent authority of Pestalozzi: 'It is doubtful
if he ever read any works of educational philosophy' (p. 229).

Universities which sounds extraordinarily like an echo from Pestalozzi: 'The idea of a general, liberal training is to carry us to a knowledge of ourselves and the world' (p. 268). But this seems rather an isolated statement and is not directly brought into the main arguments about the role of culture. It is evident that Pestalozzi's conception is very much more existential and can easily be interpreted along predominantly pragmatic lines, as has often been done in practice. And that was exactly what Arnold in his own theories wanted to avoid, and what he objected to in Swiss education as being less than the highest aim.

On the other hand, Arnold was clearly impressed by the efficiency of the primary and lower secondary schools of Switzerland. 'Meanwhile', he says, 'let us be grateful to any country which, like Switzerland, prepares by a broad and sound system of popular education the indispensable foundations on which a civilizing culture may in future be built' (p. 256). Any broad and sound system of popular education will eventually lead to *la grande culture*. This is hardly in keeping with his statement about the absence of that culture in the aim of Swiss education. In the last analysis the whole difficulty reveals itself as an attempt to have it both ways, and it reappears in the remark about the spirit of intelligent industrialism which, however, is 'not quite intelligent enough to have cleared itself of vulgarity'. Is it possible to have a general system of popular education without any utilitarian or pragmatic touch ? Without something like an affluent society, this is practically impossible. Arnold based his conception of culture chiefly on his intimate knowledge of the positive and negative qualities of the middle and upper classes in England which, at that time, were materially so well off that they could afford an educational system based on Arnold's ideas of culture. For the lower classes, then the immense majority of the population, which still had to struggle hard for the basic means of existence, an educational system without a practical bias and without a fundamental training for some useful occupation was out of the question. If all classes are to use the same primary school, which Arnold approved of so much in the case of Swiss education, a compromise between higher aims and practical considerations is inevitable, and it will necessarily cast its reflexion on the structure and conception of higher schools.

It is difficult to decide whether Arnold was fully conscious of the fatal dilemma in which he found himself. What we know for certain is that by nature and upbringing he instinctively sided with taste and delicacy if confronted with a choice between them and vulgar efficiency, even with a choice between education on the one hand and charming indolence on the other. There is an amusing and highly illuminating passage in a letter written on his arrival in Germany after the journey from Italy across the Eastern Swiss Alps to Coire. He gives a colourful description of his journey from Milan to Como and Chiavenna and across the Splügen pass. In an earlier letter he had vented his impatience with the Italians in the following words:

And the whole lump want backbone, serious energy and power of honest work to a degree that makes one impatient. I am tempted to take the professors I see in the Schools by the collar, and hold them down to their work five or six hours a day—so angry do I get at their shirking and inefficiency. They have all a certain refinement which they call civilisation. . . .[1]

A fortnight later he writes the following to his mother:

There was also a charming Italian family with whom I afterwards travelled from Coire to Nuremberg, and with whom I became great friends. . . . At Coire everything was changed; the inn clean and comfortable, but Swiss Germanic and Bourgeois; and instead of the dark-eyed Roman and Florentine women looking out of their lattices, four German women dressed and hatted as only German and English women of the middle class can dress and hat themselves, sitting at the top of the table, taking tea and talking loud in their hideous language; and when the travellers' book, which they had just signed was brought to me, the last name was, 'Linda Walther, Universitäts Professors Gattin!' You may imagine my feelings, and how my Italian family were a relief to me to break the change; but now I am left alone with this, the most *bourgeois* of nations; that is exactly the definition of them, and they have all the merits which this definition implies. But I cannot write about them now. Their schools are excellent.[2]

[1] Letter to Mrs Forster from Turin, June 1865; in *Letters of Matthew Arnold 1848-1888*, ed. George W. E. Russell (London, 1901, 2nd edition), vol. I, p. 326.
[2] Letter to his mother from Berlin, 5 July 1865; *Letters*, I, 333 and 335.

A bourgeois nation, middle class, impossibly dressed, talking loud in a hideous language, bragging about their titles, the peak of vulgarity—but a nation with excellent schools. On the other hand, high praise for a charming Italian family and romantic associations of an attractive people utterly inefficient in education. There could hardly be a more striking instance of what has been called Arnold's divided self. It is not just a contrast between an emotional and intellectual attitude: the rift goes right through the centre. He really is angry about the ways of Italian professors, and genuinely moved by the quality of German and Swiss schools; nor is the logic of his argument within the narrower field of the improvement of schools faulty or insincere.

The rift is a basic one, a crucial aspect of Arnold's whole existence and, more important, it is the very element of his creative tension. Within the framework of this study it is, of course, not possible to enlarge on the problem. Part of it has been pointed out before.[1] It may suffice to recall a few of the more striking aspects—especially in his poetry, which has been chosen because it is remote enough from his activities as a school inspector to permit direct transference in argumentation. Moreover, the language in poetry is so totally different from that of prose that any similarity in the concept of either must needs be of special significance.[2] In his poetry then, and especially in his best poetry, the themes of departure, separation, longing for a union of irreconcilable elements, a choice between equally unacceptable values, appear so often

[1] Especially by E. K. Brown, *Matthew Arnold: a Study in Conflict* (Chicago, 1948); and to a lesser extent, by William A. Jamison, *Arnold and the Romantics* (Copenhagen, 1958); by D. G. James, *Matthew Arnold and the Decline of English Romanticism* (Oxford, 1961); by Vincent Buckley, *Poetry and Morality: Studies on the Criticism of Matthew Arnold, T. S. Eliot and F. R. Leavis* (London, 1959); more briefly by Florence R. Scott, 'The Duality of Matthew Arnold', in *Personalist*, XXXI (Summer 1950), pp. 304–10; and more recently by Leon Gottfried, *Matthew Arnold and the Romantics* (London, 1963). On the other hand there are several critics who start from the assumption of an essential unity in Matthew Arnold's conception, e.g. John Holloway in his two essays in *The Victorian Sage* (London, 1953), pp. 202–43, and *The Charted Mirror* (London, 1960), pp. 149–63, and J. D. Jump, *Matthew Arnold* (London, 1955).

[2] Arnold's poetry is here referred to entirely on the basis of the problem of education. One of the most detailed and comprehensive studies is by Gerhard Müller-Schwefe, *Das persönliche Menschenbild Arnolds in der dichterischen Gestaltung* (Tübingen, 1955).

.that they cannot be simply ascribed to Romantic traditions. They are obviously an integral part of the poet's main concern and the symbols of an inward division.

The theme of separation sometimes appears as the actual subject and a leading motif, as in 'The Forsaken Merman', and 'Tristram and Iseult'. It may assume the shape of a simple lament over the loss of a highly esteemed person or a friend, as in 'Obermann' or the Arthur Hugh Clough of 'Thyrsis'. The whole group of the Marguerite poems, including the later poem 'The Terrace of Berne', is exclusively conceived as the experience, imaginary or real, of parting, absence, the end and not the flowering of a love relationship, the impossibility of bridging the gulf between the poet and the person addressed.[1] In 'A Southern Night' the subject is the death of an Indian youth on board ship far from his home and his burial at Gibraltar, while the ashes of his young wife will be buried in India. Often the theme is coupled with the hope for some divine enlightenment, as in 'A Summer Night'; or with the idea of living altogether in another world, as in 'The Scholar-Gipsy'.

Even when he makes use of more or less well known myths or legends, as in his longer poems, Arnold chooses those which lend themselves most easily to such themes. In 'Sohrab and Rustum' (1853) there is the tragic conflict between two lives that should by nature be closely connected but which have been separated by fate, while the end of the poem contains the famous image of the majestically flowing river Oxus, split into streams to become a 'foil'd circuitous wanderer' until it is united with the boundless ocean. In 'Balder Dead' (1855) it is the old German myth of the young god who is killed through a ruse of Lok's and can only be restored to life if all that lives and moves upon the earth weeps for him. But the reunion with the gods is not possible, because there is an element which does not comply with this request, and Balder has to remain in Hela's realm amongst the dead until the day of a new creation.

Merope (1858), too, is a tragedy of separation through death

[1] A detailed examination of the Marguerite poems and their implications is given by Paull F. Baum in *Ten Studies in the Poetry of Matthew Arnold* (Durham, N.C., 1958), pp. 58–84. See also Henry Charles Duffin, *Arnold the Poet* (London, 1962), pp. 68–81.

(Merope's husband being killed by Polyphontes), of a union on impossible terms (Merope's marriage with Polyphontes), and of its abrupt end through an act of revenge (Polyphontes being killed by Merope's son). Here, too, elements are brought together which even in their positive aspects make for a combination of forces essentially insecure. The original King's closest adviser is the man who will kill him, the mother by mistake almost slays her own son, and the new rule by mother and son is, above all, a hope of the future.

In the dramatic poem *Empedocles on Etna* (1852) the sage plunges into the crater because, as he says of himself at the beginning of Act II, 'Thou canst not live with men nor with thyself.'

At the end of his preface to *Schools and Universities on the Continent* Arnold points out that one of the obstacles to the consulting of foreign experience in matters of education is 'the notion of the State as an alien intrusive power in the community'. He then continues: 'The other obstacle is our high opinion of our own energy and wealth' (preface, p. xxii). In our age one could not literally subscribe to this statement. Nevertheless it remains true on two entirely different levels. One is the general situation of western civilization which, on account of its energy and wealth, is in danger of disregarding the necessity of continually re-examining the basic educational aims and methods and what 'the best that is known and thought in the world' can possibly be. The other is the personal level. If energy and wealth are taken in an intellectual sense, as activity and the abundance of ideas, then they may actually conceal the very same conflict of values which underlies Arnold's idea of education. Charming indolence or hideous efficiency is, as in his case, the paradox which we increasingly have to live with. We feel it our duty to improve conditions of life and work, to provide the necessary implements, to accept, if not to promote, technical progress in every field— and yet we wish to escape the obvious drawbacks which such improvements necessarily carry with them. We complain about the rush and noise of our daily existence; we disapprove of the excrescences of mass media; we avoid or dislike holiday crowds collecting at points of historical or aesthetic importance, although they try to do exactly what we wish them to do, to 'hellenize' in a twentieth-century style. In this sense more than in many other aspects of his cultural criticism, Matthew Arnold belongs, for better or worse, to our own age.

14

JOSEPH CONRAD:
ALIENATION AND COMMITMENT

BY IAN WATT

The doubts of the critics about the whole history-of-ideas approach are understandable enough: one way of not experiencing *King Lear* is to underline a few passages containing recognizable ideas, and to make the gratifying reflexion that the Great Chain of Being is really there. The search for such portable intellectual contents as can be prised loose from a work of imagination is likely to deflect attention from what it can most characteristically yield, in exchange for a few abstract ideas whose natures and inter-relationships are much more exactly stated in formal philosophy. And if we cannot base our literary judgements on philosophical criteria, we must be equally on our guard against the criteria of the historian of ideas, which naturally place most value on literary works which are ideologically representative; whereas the greatest authors actually seem not so much to reflect the intellectual system of their age as to express more or less directly its inherent contradictions, or the very partial nature of its capacity for dealing with the facts of experience. This seems to be true of Chaucer and Shakespeare; and it tends to become truer as we come down to the modern world, in which no single intellectual system has commanded anything like general acceptance.

All these are familiar objections; and as regards criticism of modern literature they have been reinforced by a new form of philosophy's old objections to the cognitive validity of art—by the symbolist aesthetic's rejection of all forms of abstraction and conceptualization. The ancient notion was that ideas were the natural and proper inhabitants of man's mind; T. S. Eliot's resounding paradox that 'Henry James had a mind so fine that no idea could violate it' transformed them into dangerous ruffians threatening the artist with a fate worse than death.

The alarm, we can now agree, was exaggerated; indeed, the recent tendency for much literary criticism to add moral to formal analysis might well proceed further, and make inquiry into intellectual backgrounds an essential, though not a dominating or exclusive, part of its critical procedure. For instance, an understanding of Conrad's intellectual attitudes, and of their relation to the various ideological battlegrounds both of his own and of our time, seems to me to illuminate several literary problems which have not yet been satisfactorily answered, despite the increasing critical attention which his works have lately received. At the same time, the consideration of these problems seems to indicate that it is not in ideology as such, but in the relationship of systems of ideas to other things, things as various as personal experience or the expectations of the audience, that we are likely to find answers to literary questions.

The position of Joseph Conrad (1857–1924) among his great contemporaries is unique in at least three respects. First, he has a much more varied audience: one finds his admirers not only in academic and literary circles, but among people in all stations of life. Secondly, Conrad's reputation, after a relative decline following his death in 1924, seems to have grown steadily ever since the Second World War; and it continues now, just as one detects a certain mounting impatience, just or unjust, against most of Conrad's literary peers—mainly against Joyce, Pound, and Eliot, but also, to some extent, against Yeats. The reasons for these two features of Conrad's literary appeal seem to be connected with a third and equally well-known matter—his obscurity. For although the charge of obscurity against modern writers is not novel, it takes a very special form in the case of Conrad. E. M. Forster expressed it most memorably when he asked whether 'the secret casket of [Conrad's] genius' does not contain 'a vapour rather than a jewel', and went on to suggest that the vapour might come from 'the central chasm of his tremendous genius', a chasm which divided Conrad the seaman from Conrad the writer:

Together with these loyalties and prejudices and personal scruples, [Conrad] holds another ideal, a universal, the love of Truth. . . . So there are constant discrepancies between his nearer and his further vision, and here would seem to be the cause of his central obscurity. If he lived only in his experiences, never lifting his eyes to what lies beyond them: or if, having seen what lies beyond, he would subordinate his experiences to it—then in either case he would be easier to read.[1]

The continual contradiction which Forster describes between the seer and seaman, between philosophy and experience, seems to offer a key to the three literary problems I have posed. For whereas Conrad's 'further vision' was very similar to that of his great contemporaries, his 'nearer vision', his actual range of experience, was not; and in his works the two perspectives combine in a way which seems directly related to the varied nature of his audience, to the renewed topicality of his view of the world, and to the unresolved conflict of attitudes which underlies his obscurity.

Conrad's further vision was dominated by the characteristic despair of the late Victorian world-view, which originated in all those developments in nineteenth-century geology, astronomy, physics and chemistry which combined with industrialism to suggest that, so far from being the eternal setting created by God for his favourite, man, the natural world was merely the temporary and accidental result of purposeless physical processes. In one letter, written in 1897, Conrad used an appropriately industrial metaphor to express this notion of the universe as a determinist mechanism denying all man's aspirations towards progress and reform:

There is a—let us say—a machine. It evolved itself (I am severely scientific) out of a chaos of scraps of iron and behold!—it knits. I am horrified at the horrible work and stand appalled. I feel it ought to embroider—but it goes on knitting. You come and say: 'This is all right; it's only a question of the right kind of oil. Let us use this—for instance—celestial oil and the machine will embroider a most beautiful design in purple and gold.' Will it? Alas, no! You cannot by any special lubrication make embroidery with a knitting machine. And the most withering thought is that the infamous thing has made itself: made itself without thought, without conscience, without foresight, without eyes, without heart. It is a tragic accident—and it has happened. . . .

[1] 'Joseph Conrad: a Note', *Abinger Harvest* (London, 1946), pp. 136–7.

It knits us in and it knits us out. It has knitted time, space, pain, death, corruption, despair and all the illusions—and nothing matters. . . .[1]

In such a meaningless and transitory universe, there is no apparent reason why we should have any concern whatever with the lives of others, or even very much concern with our own:

The attitude of cold unconcern is the only reasonable one. Of course reason is hateful—but why? Because it demonstrates (to those who have the courage) that we, living, are out of life—utterly out of it. . . . In a dispassionate view the ardour for reform, improvement, for virtue, for knowledge and even for beauty is only a vain sticking up for appearances, as though one were anxious about the cut of one's clothes in a community of blind men.[2]

What had been considered man's most precious gift, consciousness, is really, therefore, a curse:

What makes mankind tragic is not that they are the victims of nature, it is that they are conscious of it. To be part of the animal kingdom under the conditions of this earth is very well—but as soon as you know of your slavery, the pain, the anger, the strife—the tragedy begins.[3]

In *Lord Jim* (1900), Stein contemplates a butterfly, and discourses like a discouraged version of the great evolutionist Alfred Wallace, on whom he was in part based:[4]

'. . . so fragile! And so strong! And so exact! This is Nature— the balance of colossal forces. Every star is so—and every blade of grass stands *so*—and the mighty Kosmos in perfect equilibrium produces—this. This wonder; this masterpiece of Nature—the great artist!'
'. . . And what of man?' [Marlow asks]:
'Man is amazing, but he is not a masterpiece,' he said. . . . 'Perhaps the artist was a little mad. Eh? . . . Sometimes it seems to me that man is come where he is not wanted, where there is no place for him.'[5]

[1] G. Jean-Aubry, *Joseph Conrad: Life and Letters* (London, 1927), vol. I, p. 216.
[2] *Ibid.* I, 222.
[3] *Ibid.* I, 226.
[4] Cf. Florence Clemens, 'Conrad's Favourite Bedside Book', *South Atlantic Quarterly*, xxxviii (1939), pp. 305–15.
[5] Dent Collected Edition (London, 1948), p. 208. Future references from Conrad are to this collection, unless otherwise stated.

Man, in fact, is Nature's permanent alien; he must create
his own order if he can. This, of course, was how the Victorians
had come to think of human destiny; the religion of progress,
in Tennyson's words, called on man to

> Move upward, working out the beast
> And let the ape and tiger die.

But that was not so easy, as Freud was to show; and also, at
much the same time, Joseph Conrad in *Heart of Darkness* (1899).

Kurtz begins as a representative of all the highest aspirations
of nineteenth-century individualism; he is an artist, an eloquent
political speaker on the liberal side, an economic and social
careerist; and his story enacts the most characteristic impulse
of Victorian civilization, combining the economic exploitation
of Africa with the great moral crusade of bringing light to the
backward peoples of the world. But the jungle whispers 'to
[Kurtz] things about himself which he did not know, things
of which he had no conception till he took counsel with this
great solitude' (p. 131). His 'forgotten and brutal instincts'
(p. 144) soon lead Kurtz to outdo the other colonial exploiters
in sordid rapacity; he enslaves and massacres the surrounding
tribes; and he ends up being worshipped as a God to whom
human sacrifices are offered.

At the back of the great nineteenth-century dream was the
assumption that man could be his own God. But to Disraeli's
question 'Is man an ape or an angel?', Kurtz's fate seems to
answer that we are never less likely to 'let the ape and tiger
die' than when we imagine we are angels. Kurtz thought that
'we whites . . . must necessarily appear to [the savages] in the
nature of supernatural beings—we approach them with the
might as of a deity'. But he ends his report to the International
Society for the Suppression of Savage Customs: 'Exterminate
all the brutes!' (p. 118)

For Conrad, then, man's hope for progress ignores the fact
that the ape and tiger are not merely part of our evolutionary
heritage, but are ontologically present in every individual.
This goes beyond the usual assumptions of the most sceptical
of Victorians, and it makes impossible the faith in the development of man's intellectual potentialities through education

which characterized the main spokesman of the Victorian and Edwardian periods. Thus, when his reformer friend Cunninghame Graham wrote that his democratic ideal was the heroic sailor, Singleton, in *The Nigger of the 'Narcissus'* (1898), but a Singleton who has been educated, Conrad retorted:

> I think Singleton with an education is impossible. . . . Then he would become conscious—and much smaller—and very unhappy. Now he is simple and great like an elemental force. Nothing can touch him but the curse of decay—the eternal decree that will extinguish the sun, the stars, one by one, and in another instant shall spread a frozen darkness over the whole universe. Nothing else can touch him—he does not think.
>
> Would you seriously wish to tell such a man 'Know thyself! Understand that you are nothing, less than a shadow, more insignificant than a drop of water in the ocean, more fleeting than the illusion of a dream?' Would you?[1]

Knowledge merely makes the individual more conscious of the terrible disparity between actuality and aspiration: nor does man's love of his fellows afford any more secure a foundation for political and social reform. Such reform represents no more than—as Conrad put it in *Victory* (1915)—the conflict between 'gorge and disgorge' (p. 384); and man's own nature dooms his longing for fraternity; as Conrad asked: 'Frankly, what would you think of an effort to promote fraternity amongst people living in the same street, I don't even mention two neighbouring streets? Two ends of the same street. . . . What does fraternity mean? . . . Nothing unless the Cain-Abel business'.[2]

Conrad, then, shared with the Victorians their rejection of the religious, social and intellectual order of the past, but he also rejected, as completely as Yeats, Pound, Eliot, Joyce, Lawrence or Thomas Mann, the religion of progress with which they and the Edwardians had replaced it. This alienation from the prevailing intellectual perspectives both of the past and of his own time naturally did much to colour Conrad's picture both of his own selfhood and of his role as an author. I use the word 'alienation' because it seems to me the most comprehensive term to describe the two aspects of the process we are concerned

---

[1] *Life and Letters*, vol. I, pp. 214–15.   [2] *Ibid.* I, 269.

with—the external or public, and the internal or private. We have already considered the public, the external ideological vision; but it would, from a literary point of view, remain merely 'notional', as Newman put it, unless it were internalized: that it was in Conrad, we shall see.

The word 'alienation' has been used in a wide variety of ways,[1] but its derivation and early usage make its main meaning reasonably clear. From *alius*, 'another', Latin developed the forms *alienus*, 'belonging to another country', and *alienatus*, 'estranged'. Our word 'alienation' thus bears the constant notion of being or feeling a stranger, an outsider. Alienation, as a translation of the German *Entfremdung*, was given philosophical currency early in the nineteenth century by Hegel, who used it to denote what he thought to be characteristic of the individual in the modern world, his sense of inward estrangements, of more or less conscious awareness that the inner being, the real 'I', was alienated from the 'me', the person as an object in society. Later, Marx transferred the idea to the economic plane; for Marx, man only loses his isolation and realizes himself as a person through his activities, through his work; but under capitalism, since the commodity and its cash value are primary, the individual, no longer in personal control of his labour, feels alienated from his work, and therefore from society and from himself.[2]

Conrad, I need hardly say, was neither a Hegelian nor a Marxist; but all his writings, and especially his letters, make it clear not only that his mind completely rejected the social and intellectual order of the day, but that his whole inner being seemed to have been deprived of meaning. There can surely be few expressions of such total estrangement from the natural world, from other people, from the writing process, and from the self, to equal this Conrad letter to Garnett:

I am like a man who has lost his gods. My efforts seem unrelated to anything in heaven and everything under heaven is impalpable

---

[1] Cf. Herbert Marcuse, *Reason and Revolution: Hegel and the Rise of Social Revolution* (New York, 1941), pp. 34-9, 246-7; Lewis Feuer, 'What is Alienation? the Career of a Concept', *New Politics*, I (1962), pp. 1-19; Melvin Seeman, 'On the Meaning of Alienation', *American Sociological Review*, XXIV (1959), pp. 783-91; and, more generally, Robert A. Nisbet, *The Quest for Community* (New York, 1953).

[2] Marcuse, *Reason and Revolution*, pp. 272-95.

to the touch like shapes of mist. Do you see how easy writing must be under such conditions ? Do you see ?

Even writing to a friend—to a person one has heard, touched, drank with, quarrelled with—does not give me a sense of reality. All is illusion—the words written, the mind at which they are aimed, the truth they are intended to express, the hands that will hold the paper, the eyes that will glance at the lines. Every image floats vaguely in a sea of doubt—and the doubt itself is lost in an un-explored universe of incertitudes.[1]

But alienation, of course, is not the whole story: Conrad also gives us a sense of a much wider commitment to the main ethical, social and literary attitudes, both of the world at large and of the general reader, than do any others of his great contemporaries.

'Commitment' I take to be the secular equivalent of what prize-giving speakers call 'dedication'—a binding engagement of oneself to a course of action which transcends any purely personal advantage. And the question inevitably arises as to how a man with the general intellectual perspective sketched above can possibly commit himself to anything larger than his own personal interests.

The beginnings of an answer are probably to be found in Conrad's life, which made alienation not an endless discovery demanding expression, but merely the initial premise. The initial premise because Conrad was, to begin with, an orphan; his mother died when he was seven, and his father when he was eleven. Then there was his nationality: as a Pole he belonged to a country which no longer existed, and whose people, Conrad wrote, had for a hundred years 'been used to go to battle without illusions'.[2] Adolescence brought further estrangements: in France from 1874 to 1878, Conrad tried to realize his dream of a career at sea, but he achieved only failure, debts, an unhappy love affair, and, it now seems virtually certain, an attempt at suicide. But when, at the age of twenty, Conrad joined the crew of the English freighter *Mavis*, the premise of total alienation began to be undermined. Conrad's successful struggle, under conditions, for the most part, of unbearable physical and psychological hardship, to rise from

---

[1] *Letters from Conrad, 1895–1924*, ed. Edward Garnett (London, 1928), pp. 152–3.
[2] *Ibid.* p. 216.

able-bodied seaman to captain, must have given him a sense of the unexpected possibilities and rewards of individual participation in the ordinary life of humanity. Conrad's years at sea were everything for his career as a writer. Not because they gave him a subject—Conrad would surely be a major novelist quite apart from the sea stories; but because to the earlier perspective of every kind of alienation there was added a foreground of immediate experience which featured a series of the most direct personal and social commitments—to his career, to his fellow-seamen, to his adopted country. These commitments had the most far-reaching effects on Conrad's attitude to his audience, on his role as a writer, and on his understanding of human life; and their importance was not diminished by the fact that they arose from attitudes which were in perpetual opposition to the larger view of the world which Conrad the seer had absorbed from his nineteenth-century heritage.

There is no very specific statement about the conflict in Conrad's letters or essays, but its results appear very clearly in his views of his audience, and of his art, as well as in the novels. In the earliest extant letters alienation is the pervading theme, and there is very little about commitment; where the conflict of the two does occur, it is very much from the point of view of alienation, as in an early letter to Madame Poradowska. We are condemned, Conrad wrote in 1894, to go through life accompanied by

. . . the inseparable being forever at your side—master and slaves, victim and executioner—who suffers and causes suffering. That's how it is ! One must drag the ball and chain of one's selfhood to the end. It is the price one pays for the devilish and divine privilege of thought; so that in this life it is only the elect who are convicts— a glorious band which comprehends and groans but which treads the earth amidst a multitude of phantoms with maniacal gestures, with idiotic grimaces. Which would you be: idiot or convict?[1]

The war within is an internal projection of the external conflict between the uncomprehending multitudes, the idiots, and the convicts whose intelligence and self-consciousness have condemned them to loneliness and alienation. The possibility

---

[1] *Letters of Joseph Conrad to Marguerite Poradowska, 1890–1920*, trans. and ed. J. A. Gee and P J. Sturm (New Haven, 1940), p. 72.

of siding with the idiots, of course, is presented by Conrad only as a rhetorical question. In this, Conrad is echoing, not so much Hegel's picture of alienation, as the familiar romantic dichotomy between the sensitive artist and the crass world outside and, more particularly, its later development, the division of the reading public into highbrow and lowbrow. These divisions must have been much more familiar to Conrad than to many of his English contemporaries, since he read such French writers as Flaubert and Baudelaire very early in his career, and for them the alienation of the writer from the bourgeois public was both more conscious and more absolute than for any English writer of the Victorian period.

Unlike Flaubert and Baudelaire, however, Conrad had no private means, and so as soon as he began his career as an author the problem of finding a public became immediate. When his first literary adviser, Edward Garnett, urged Conrad to follow his own path as a writer and disregard the multitude, Conrad retorted: 'But I *won't* live in an attic! I'm past that, you understand? I *won't* live in an attic!' On the other hand, keeping out of attics unfortunately seemed feasible only for such popular writers as Rider Haggard, and when Garnett mentioned his work, Conrad commented: 'too horrible for words'.[1]

Conrad's financial dependence on public favour must often have reinforced his sense of separateness. On the one hand, he was forced by economic necessity to degrade himself—as he once put it, 'all my art has become artfulness in exploiting agents and publishers';[2] on the other hand, his inner self remained aloof and proudly refused to accept the role of authorship as society defined it. We find Conrad on one occasion declining to send his photograph to his publisher, though he added with sardonic magnanimity, 'if I were a pretty actress or a first-rate athlete, I wouldn't deprive an aching democracy of a legitimate satisfaction'.[3] When, for advertising purposes, Algernon Methuen requested a description of *The Secret Agent*, which his firm was publishing, Conrad replied disdainfully, 'I've a very definite idea of what I tried

[1] *Letters from Conrad, 1895-1924,* p. xiii.
[2] *Ibid.* p. 183.
[3] *Joseph Conrad: Letters to William Blackwood and David S. Meldrum,* ed. William Blackburn (Durham, N.C., 1958), p. 171.

to do and a fairly correct one (I hope) of what I *have* done.
But it isn't a matter for a bookseller's ear. I don't think he
would understand: I don't think many readers will. But that's
not my affair.'[1]

What his readers thought was not his affair. That, at least,
is one of the postures of authorship which Conrad adopted.
But there was another.

How a writer comes to form an idea of his audience is no
doubt a complicated and highly idiosyncratic matter; but the
starting point must always be the people the writer has actually
talked to and heard talk. In Conrad's case, when he became
an author virtually everyone he had heard talk English was a
seaman; and although collectively they were part of the mass
public he scorned, yet many of them were people he respected
as individuals. This may be part of the reason why when
Conrad speaks of the reading public, as in this letter to John
Galsworthy, his sardonic mockery is qualified by the sense that,
however fatuous, the reading public is, after all, composed of
human beings:

A public is not to be found in a class, caste, clique or type. The
public is (or are?) individuals. . . . And no artist can give it what it
wants because humanity doesn't know what it wants. But it will
swallow everything. It will swallow Hall Caine and John Galsworthy, Victor Hugo and Martin Tupper. It is an ostrich, a clown,
a giant, a bottomless sack. It is sublime. It has apparently no eyes
and no entrails, like a slug, and yet it can weep and suffer.[2]

There is no sense here, such as one finds in many other modern
authors, that the writer must make a conscious choice of a
public, and set his sights either at the literary élite or at the
masses who have to be written down to. Conrad the seer
viewed both with the same jaded scepticism, and he chose
neither. Still, the humbler side of his double vision reminded
him that the target of his scorn could also weep and suffer;
and so he retained sufficient faith in a 'direct appeal to mankind' to write for a public comprising readers as different as
his later literary friends and his former shipmates. After nearly
twenty years of discouraging struggle, Conrad's residual com-

---

[1] *Life and Letters*, vol. ii, p. 38.   [2] *Ibid.* ii, 121.

mitment to mankind considered as an audience bore fruit when *Chance* (1913) became a best-seller: this response, Conrad wrote in his 'Author's Note',

gave me a considerable amount of pleasure, because what I had always feared most was drifting unconsciously into the position of a writer for a limited coterie; a position which would have been odious to me as throwing a doubt on the soundness of my belief in the solidarity of all mankind in simple ideas and sincere emotions. . . . I had managed to please a number of minds busy attending to their own very real affairs. (pp. viii–ix)

The checks which the committed seaman imposed on the alienated writer in his attitude to his audience also affected Conrad's general literary outlook; and this despite his awareness, as he put it in the 'Familiar Preface' to *A Personal Record* (1912), that 'as in political so in literary action a man wins friends for himself mostly by the passion of his prejudices and by the consistent narrowness of his outlook'. Most obviously, Conrad's training at sea ran counter to any intransigent expression of his inner alienation. '. . . to be a great magician', he wrote in the same preface, 'one must surrender to occult and irresponsible powers, either outside or within one's breast.' But this direction, he continued, was not for him, because his sea training had strengthened his resolve to 'keep good hold on the one thing really mine . . . that full possession of myself which is the first condition of good service'; and Conrad concluded that the conscience must sometimes 'say nay to the temptations' of the author: 'the danger lies in the writer becoming the victim of his own exaggeration, losing the exact notion of sincerity, and in the end coming to despise truth itself as something too cold, too blunt for his purpose—as, in fact, not good enough for his insistent emotion'.

As for literary doctrine, Conrad's disenchantment with the accepted literary modes was with him from the beginning of his career as a writer. He expressed it most fully and most eloquently in the famous preface to *The Nigger of the 'Narcissus'*. None of the 'temporary formulas of [the artist's] craft' is reliable, Conrad begins: '. . . they all: Realism, Romanticism, Naturalism, even the unofficial sentimentalism (which, like the poor, is exceedingly difficult to get rid of), all these gods must, after a short period of fellowship, abandon him—' (pp. x–xi).

All the conceptual formulae, whether of literature or of science or of philosophy, are much too unreliable a basis for the writer: he must depend on those primary facts of the experience which he shares with mankind at large. So the positives of the nearer vision, of ultimate commitment, some-how enabled Conrad to bypass the findings of the alienated intellect, and to convert the most esoteric of literary doctrines— Art for Art's sake—into the most universal:

> The changing wisdom of successive generations discards ideas, questions facts, demolishes theories. But the artist appeals to that part of our being which is not dependent on wisdom; to that in us which is a gift and not an acquisition—and therefore, more per-manently enduring. He speaks to our capacity for delight and wonder, to the sense of mystery surrounding our lives; to our sense of pity, and beauty, and pain; to the latent feeling of fellowship with all creation—and to the subtle but invincible conviction of solidarity that knits together the loneliness of innumerable hearts, to the solidarity in dreams, in joy, in sorrow, in aspirations, in illusions, in hope, in fear, which binds men to each other, which binds together all humanity—the dead to the living and the living to the unborn. (p. viii)

At this point I can begin to answer the first question: the breadth of Conrad's appeal was made possible by the fact that, almost alone among his great contemporaries, he thought a broad appeal worth making; he was glad, he wrote in the 'Author's Note' to *Chance*, that 'apparently I have never sinned against the basic feelings and elementary convictions which make life possible to the mass of mankind' (p. x). This alone surely does much to account both for Conrad's decline in critical esteem during the twenties, and for the way he acquired wider and more miscellaneous audience than his literary peers. If alienation had been the sum of his subjects and literary attitudes, Conrad might have captured the highbrow vote more quickly; but the wide variety of people whom he respected and admired, and their very various ways of looking at life, were always there as a constant check to the extremes of the vision of the isolated writer. Conrad's writings do not proclaim their author's radical separateness from the rest of mankind; their style does not flaunt his alienation like a banner announcing a certified Dark Knight of the Soul. It was characteristic of Conrad that he should praise the work of his friend Ford Madox Ford on the grounds that 'he does not stand on his head for the purpose of getting a new and striking view of his subject. Such a method of procedure may be in favour nowadays but I prefer the old way, with the feet on the ground.'[1]

On the other hand, of course, the alienation is still there; there is nothing promiscuous about Conrad's commitment; he is very far from what D. H. Lawrence called 'the vast evil of acquiescence'; and even in his most affirmative works the heroic, romantic or popular elements are always qualified by the general atmosphere—an atmosphere, to use Conrad's own phrase, of 'cold moral dusk'.[2] The tone of desperate alienation which one finds in Conrad's early letters is not directly expressed in the novels; but one can often recognize its muffled presence, whether in the defeated cadences of his rhetoric, or in the tendency of the narrative progress to seem under the constant threat of enveloping torpor. Nevertheless, it seems broadly true that, in Conrad's most characteristic work, the negative voices of alienation are confronted and largely overcome by the possibilities of commitment, or, in Conrad's term, of solidarity.

What Conrad meant by solidarity is sufficiently evident from the preface to the *Nigger of the 'Narcissus'*. In the terms of our argument we can see it as an intangible and undemonstrable but existent and widespread acceptance of common human obligations which somehow transcend the infinite individual differences of belief and purpose and taste. It is not a conscious motive, and it rarely becomes the dominating factor in human affairs; its existence seems to depend very largely upon the mere fact that, in the course of their different lives, most individuals find themselves faced with very similar circumstances; nevertheless, it is solidarity which gives both the individual and the collective life what little pattern of meaning can be discovered in it. Conrad's own experience, of course, tended to confirm this view of solidarity; and his most typical

---

[1] *Letters to Blackwood*, p. 114.
[2] 'A Glance at Two Books', *Last Essays*, p. 135.

JOSEPH CONRAD   271

writing is concerned to present its achievements, to enact its discovery, or to assay its powers.

The theme of solidarity is most obvious in what are surely Conrad's most perfect, if not his most important works, in *The Nigger of the 'Narcissus'*, *Typhoon*, *The Shadow-Line*. But in some form it also controls most of the other novels, which characteristically present the movement of the protagonist towards another person or persons; the movement is often incomplete, or too late to succeed; but, from Marlow's involvement in the fate of Kurtz and Lord Jim, to the sexual relationships of *Chance* and *Victory*, the reader's attention is usually engaged in following the fortunes of an isolated and alienated character towards others; and this quest eventually assumes both for the character and for the reader a much larger moral importance than that of the personal relationship as such.

In *Lord Jim*, for example, Marlow is presented with an apparent breakdown of his unquestioned belief in the values of solidarity when an unknown first mate, a young man, 'one of us', deserts his post and leaves the 800 passengers on the *Patna* to their fate; for no apparent cause Marlow discovers that his deepest being demands that he know:

Why I longed to go grubbing into the deplorable details of an occurrence which, after all, concerned me no more than as a member of an obscure body of men held together by a community of inglorious toil and by fidelity to a certain standard of conduct, I can't explain. You may call it an unhealthy curiosity if you like; but I have a distinct notion I wished to find something. Perhaps, unconsciously, I hoped I would find that something, some profound and redeeming cause, some merciful explanation, some convincing shadow of an excuse. I see well enough now that I hoped for the impossible—for the laying of what is the most obstinate ghost of man's creation, of the uneasy doubt uprising like a mist, secret and gnawing like a worm, and more chilling than the certitude of death—the doubt of the sovereign power enthroned in a fixed standard of conduct. (p. 50)

The doubt can never be set at rest; but the concern remains, not only in *Lord Jim*, but in most of Conrad's novels. Of course, it takes different forms. In Conrad's later works, for example, the protagonist is often closer to our sense of the younger, the more sceptical, Conrad, as with Decoud, for example, or Heyst. There the concern for solidarity tends to an opposite pattern: the protagonist's moral crisis is not that the fixed standard of conduct is challenged, but that, to his surprise, the alienated protagonist encounters its overwhelming imperatives.

This movement from alienation towards commitment is rather rare in the other great modern writers. They tend, indeed, to equate the achievement of individuality with the process of alienation; the poetry of Eliot and Pound, for example, typically leads us away in revulsion from contemporary actuality; while the novels of Joyce and Lawrence tend to focus on the breaking of ties with family, class and country: both poets and the novelists leave us, not with a realization of man's crucial though problematic dependence on others, but with a sharpened awareness of individual separateness.

It is here, of course, that we may find one reason for the renewed interest in Conrad. For since the Second World War, the experience of a whole generation has brought it close to Conrad's personal position; partly because world history has played over so many of his themes in deafening tones; and partly because our habituation to alienation, reinforced by the vision of the other great modern writers, has inevitably brought us back to the dominating question in Conrad: alienation, yes, but how do we get out of it?

One can observe the recent convergence on this typical Conradian preoccupation in many different intellectual areas. Most directly, it can be seen in recent Conrad criticism, which, since Morton Dauwen Zabel's article 'Chance and Recognition' in 1945,[1] has concentrated on Conrad as the master of the process of moral self-discovery leading to human commitment; most widely, we can turn to the extremely close parallel between this aspect of Conrad and the main philosophical and literary movement of the last two decades, Existentialism.

Existentialism, like Conrad, rejects all traditional philosophy as too theoretical, too concerned with cognitive problems treated in isolation from the actual personal existence. It attempts instead a full understanding of the individual confronting life; and this, as in Conrad, involves much attention

---

[1] *Sewanee Review*, LIII (1945), pp. 1–23.

to such themes as death, suicide, isolation, despair, courage and choosing to be. In each case the starting point is the alienated man who, believing, in Sartre's words, that 'there can no longer be any *a priori* good',[1] or in Conrad's that there is 'no sovereign power enthroned in a fixed standard of conduct', concludes that the whole external world and man's attempt to establish a valid relationship to it are equally absurd. The way out of the dilemma, apparently, is that, at a certain point, the existential hero, realizing that 'he is free *for nothing*',[2] comes out on the other side of despair to discover a more realistic kind of provisional commitment.

There are, of course, vital differences. Conrad does not see commitment as a single willed reversal occurring with dramatic clarity and violence in the individual consciousness; for him it is, rather, an endless process throughout history in which individuals are driven by circumstances into the traditional forms of human solidarity: are driven to accept the position that fidelity must govern the individual's relation to the outside world, while his inner self must be controlled by restraint and honour. This conservative and social ethic is certainly very different from the existentialist position, and embodies the main emphases of the most widely shared secular codes of behaviour over the ages. It is also rather closer to the philosophical materialism of Marx than to the basically subjective metaphysic of Existentialism, since Conrad sees solidarity as an eventual consequence of corporate activity. Thus Conrad begins his essay on 'Tradition' by quoting Leonardo da Vinci's 'Work is the law', and comments:

From the hard work of men are born the sympathetic consciousness of a common destiny, the fidelity to right practice which makes great craftsmen, the sense of right conduct which we may call honour, the devotion to our calling and the idealism which is not a misty, winged angel without eyes, but a divine figure of terrestrial aspect with a clear glance and with its feet resting firmly on the earth on which it was born.[3]

The origins of solidarity, then, are derived from the economic

---

[1] *L'existentialisme est un humanisme* (Paris, 1946), p. 35.
[2] *Le sursis* (Paris, 1945), p. 286: 'Je suis libre pour rien.'
[3] *Notes on Life and Letters*, p. 194.

necessities to which men find themselves involuntarily but inexorably exposed: as Conrad writes elsewhere:

Who can tell how a tradition comes into the world? We are children of the earth. It may be that the noblest tradition is but the offspring of material conditions, of the hard necessities besetting men's precarious lives. But once it has been born it becomes a spirit.[1]

It is surely remarkable that Conrad's way of looking at the conditions of positive individual commitment would have such strong affinities with three such contradictory ideologies—the conservative, the existentialist and the Marxist. It helps, of course, to explain the present width of his appeal, but we are bound to return to Forster's view of the discrepancies between Conrad's nearer and his further vision, and to wonder if there is not some radical confusion in a position which leads in three such different directions; whether, in fact, Conrad's obscurity may not be an unavoidable result of his failure to establish any real connexion between the alienation he felt and the commitment he sought.

Conrad would probably have answered that his outlook was based on common elements of experience which were more enduring than any particular social or economic or intellectual system. He thought of his own age, he wrote in *Victory*, as one 'in which we are camped like bewildered travellers in a garish, unrestful hotel' (p. 3); and the best we could do at any time was to assume that in any given circumstance the direction of individual commitment would be sufficiently clear to anyone who, like Axel Heyst in *Victory*, finds that he cannot scorn 'any decent feeling' (p. 18). This, indeed, was close to the teaching of his uncle and guardian, Thaddeus Bobrowski, who once wrote to him: 'I have taken as my motto "*usque ad finem*", as my guide, the love of duty which circumstances define.'[2]

The way people actually react to the circumstances of their lives—such seems to be Conrad's only justification for his view of solidarity. We would no doubt like more; but it is only fair to observe that the logical difficulties of demonstrating the

---

[1] 'Well Done', *Notes on Life and Letters*, p. 183.
[2] *Life and Letters*, vol. i, p. 148.

validity of any ethical system are just as great either in traditional philosophy or in Existentialism; so that we must be careful not to condemn Conrad because his working assumptions echo the greatest of English empiricists, who in *Twelfth Night* gave Sir Andrew Aguecheek the immortal words: 'I have no exquisite reason for 't, but I have reason good enough.'

The reason good enough, we might now be tempted to add, is that the way things are with our poor old planet, the time has come for bifocals. Such, it appears, was Conrad's view, and he once justified the patent irrationality of this dual perspective on the simple grounds that it reflected the facts of common human experience:

Many a man has heard or read and believes that the earth goes round the sun; one small blob of mud among several others, spinning ridiculously with a waggling motion like a top about to fall. This is the Copernican system, and the man believes in the system without often knowing as much about it as its name. But while watching a sunset he sheds his belief; he sees the sun as a small and useful object, the servant of his needs. . . sinking slowly behind a range of mountains, and then he holds the system of Ptolemy.[1]

In the perspective of the history of ideas, the wheel has indeed come full circle: Conrad seems to accept an impasse to which his great contemporaries, more ambitious, and perhaps less deeply alienated from the possibilities of belief, tried to find solutions. Most of twentieth-century literature, for example, may, broadly speaking, be said to have an implicit programme; it urges a direction which, to put it simply, is based on an adherence to the ideology either of the future, or of the past, or of the supernatural world. But Conrad, as we have seen, had no belief in liberal reform, in the politics of the future to which Shaw, Wells and Galsworthy devoted so many of their writings; and he had equally little interest in the backward look, in the utopianism of the past which, in various forms, can be found in the thought of Yeats, Joyce, Pound and Eliot: Conrad speaks, for example, of 'the mustiness of the Middle Ages, that epoch when mankind tried to stand still in a monstrous illusion of final certitude attained in morals, intellect

[1] 'The Ascending Effort', *Notes on Life and Letters*, pp. 73–4.

and conscience'.[1] Nor, finally, did Conrad find any appeal in supernatural transcendence: his objection to Christianity combined a Voltairean rejection of myth, superstition and hypocrisy, with a primary emphasis on the impracticality of Christian ideals; as he once wrote to Garnett:

I am not blind to [Christianity's] services, but the absurd oriental fable from which it starts irritates me. Great, improving, softening, compassionate it may be, but it has lent itself with amazing facility to cruel distortion and is the only religion which, with its impossible standards, has brought an infinity of anguish to innumerable souls— on this earth.[2]

Conrad the seaman, then, could not allow the seer to make that leap out of the chaos of immediate reality which must precede the construction of any system. More willingly than most of his contemporaries, he followed Heyst in *Victory* and entered 'the broad, human path of inconsistencies' (p. 176). We, surely, can join Thomas Mann in admiring the 'refusal of a very much engaged intelligence to hang miserably in the air between contraries',[3] and to concentrate not on the illogicality, but on the achievements, of men who live their lives according to Ptolemy's erroneous notion that man is the centre of the universe. To do this, Conrad seems to argue, we must not be too demanding about the intellectual foundations of human needs; Marlow, for instance, probably speaks for Conrad when he says of Jim's need for a truth, or an illusion of it, to live by: 'I don't care how you call it, there is so little difference, and the difference means so little' (p. 222). In *Heart of Darkness* Marlow's final act is even more explicit: when he preserves the 'great and saving illusion' about the dead Kurtz which is enshrined in the Intended's 'mature capacity for fidelity' (pp. 159, 157), he enacts the notion that, once we have experienced the heart of darkness, we may be driven to the position that, in cases where fidelity is in conflict with truth, it is truth which should be sacrificed.

Commitment to human solidarity, of course, also implies that

[1] 'The Censor of Plays: an Appreciation', *Notes on Life and Letters*, pp. 76–7.
[2] *Letters from Conrad, 1895–1924*, p. 265.
[3] 'Joseph Conrad's *The Secret Agent*', in *Past Masters and Other Papers*, trans. Lowe-Porter (New York, 1933), p. 247.

whatever disgust and doubt we experience at the spectacle of history, we must nevertheless feel that in some sense the past and the future of mankind are a part of ourselves; not as nostalgia, and not as programme, but as experienced reality, the kind of reality expressed by Emilia Gould in *Nostromo*, who thought that 'for life to be large and full, it must contain the care of the past and of the future in every passing moment of the present' (pp. 520–1). Conrad's pessimism about the direction of contemporary history, shown in *Heart of Darkness*, for example, or in *Nostromo*, was logically incompatible with any optimism about the future of man; and yet even here the gloom was pierced by a moment of Ptolemaic affirmation.

In 1950 Conrad's greatest literary descendant, William Faulkner, seems to have had a passage of Conrad obscurely in mind when he declared in his Nobel Prize Address:

It is easy enough to say man is immortal simply because he will endure; that when the last ding-dong of doom has clanged and faded from the last worthless rock hanging tideless in the last red and dying evening, that even then there will still be one more sound: that of his puny inexhaustible voice, still talking. I refuse to accept this. I believe that man will not merely endure: he will prevail.

The Conrad passage this seems to recall comes from a 1905 essay on Henry James; in it Conrad's further vision cannot but foresee disaster, and though the nearer vision appeals against the verdict, it does so in terms so qualified by the ironic distance of the seer that they underline how Faulkner, yielding to his own insistent emotion, finally protests too much:

When the last aqueduct shall have crumbled to pieces [wrote Conrad], the last airship fallen to the ground, the last blade of grass have died upon a dying earth, man, indomitable by his training in resistance to misery and pain, shall set this undiminished light of his eyes against the feeble glow of the sun. The artistic faculty, of which each of us has a minute grain, may find its voice in some individual of that last group, gifted with a power of expression and courageous enough to interpret the ultimate experience of mankind in terms of his temperament, in terms of art ... whether in austere exhortation or in a phrase of sardonic comment, who can guess?

For my own part, from a short and cursory acquaintance with

my kind, I am inclined to think that the last utterance will formulate, strange as it may appear, some hope now to us utterly inconceivable. For mankind is delightful in its pride, its assurance, and its indomitable tenacity. It will sleep on the battlefield among its own dead, in the manner of an army having won a barren victory. It will not know when it is beaten.[1]

---

[1] 'Henry James: an Appreciation', *Notes on Life and Letters*, pp. 13-14.

15

ENGLISH AND SOME CHRISTIAN TRADITIONS

BY JOHN HOLLOWAY

There is no doubt that readers of this book, if only through their knowledge of the life, writings and teachings of him whom it seeks to honour, must know that the religion of the English people has left its mark deeply on their literature. A number of scholars, from G. R. Owst to Miss Helen Gardner, have illuminated the connexion; even so, it has often been given insufficient weight. Moreover, since these essays are collected under the name of one who is both scholar and teacher, it is pertinent to add that in the world of English teaching the connexion still does not receive the emphasis it should. Several British universities, for example, permit their students of English literature to give detailed study to English philosophy; but none appears to do as much for our religion.

Yet the student of literature—who, turning to philosophy or to religion, in either case goes beyond his own specialism—cannot but find the excursion into philosophy the more difficult and precarious of the two. After all, the English philosophers were usually dealing with sophisticated problems of a directly professional kind: the perennial 'problems', in other words, of philosophy at its most rigorous. Indeed, this has been more typical of them than of their continental colleagues: a Plotinus, a Schopenhauer, a Bergson, a Croce are not easily paralleled in English. Locke's views on moral principles raise the whole problem of synthetic *a priori* knowledge. Berkeley's account of matter, Hume's (to speak in shorthand) of the nature of obligation, are part and parcel respectively of their views on mathematics, and on causality and the existence of external objects. Both raise the issue of philosophical analysis and its proper nature and extent, and I doubt are to

be easily understood by one who has not studied this fundamental issue in a fundamental way.

Religion, of course, has its intricacies too; or else theology
would not exist. But at this very point comes the sharp contrast. Berkeley's Philonous is at pains to explain to the good
Hylas why his account of physical objects abandons nothing
of the plain man's ways of speaking or acting. It is simply a
subtle insight, or deeper clarification, for the refined and
sophisticated mind. Hume more than once insists that he leaves
his philosophy behind him when he shuts his study door, that
we must 'think with the learned and act with the vulgar'.
Descartes meticulously directed himself not to suffer his
systematic 'philosophic' doubt to influence his daily conduct.

There is reason why the student of literature should actively
misunderstand at this point; he has learnt, within his own field,
that what has deep and direct communion with life is fruitful,
while what has none is arid. At precisely this point, therefore,
will he find an open road in religion take the place of an
obstacle in philosophy; for the essence of any religious speculation is that it is not remote from daily experience, but immediately and transformingly bound up with it. Pascal's challenge
to the *honnête homme* that he rank eschatology alongside dice,
cards and horses, and see what the stakes ought to be, is merely
the wittiest and catchiest of illustrations to what every theologian who has ever lived would have endorsed. Religious
thought which does not come home to men's business and
bosoms is nothing; and so—to take the argument a stage
further—nothing is more natural than that it should touch,
intimately and comprehensively, what men have written about
life: which is their literature.

This is a matter of history, not of truth. I mean that to admit
the pre-eminent impact of Christianity on the daily life of the
English people for the millenium and more which is represented by their literature, to recognize that (by contrast with
philosophy) it is of the essence of religion to have this pre-
eminent impact, is to leave quite open that question of whether
Christianity is true or not. It is doubtless necessary for each
man to settle this question of truth; but there are many questions which it is necessary for men to settle, yet not as part of

their English studies. The point is of importance because the student of literature who gives his attention to religious traditions will see concepts of nature, impressions of life, views of the nature of man, moving as the centuries pass from religion into literature, and sometimes moving into religion from literature or branches of thought associated with it. But, for the student of literature as such, it remains an open question whether these fundamental attitudes to nature, man and society receive their full and authentic formulation in Christianity alone, and merely an insecure and derivative one when they occur in literature without Christianity; or whether they stand in their own right as interesting and tenable views of man and the world, and receive from Christianity a particularization and justification which are not intrinsic to them.

An open question vexes some as much as an open window. But the study of literature cannot be seen as a series of invitations to agree or disagree. Its purposes do not include the decisive fixing of the moral imagination, but only its enlargement. This is achieved in part by presenting the student with those clashes and divergencies necessary to intellectual health in any society or at any time; but largely, by presenting him with works that embody a sense of man, life and the world remote from his own, because they originated in a society remote from his own time. To this study, the study of Christian tradition is nothing short of integral.

Consider the word 'mortified'. That its traditional meaning was not of mere disappointment, but of such a disillusionment with worldly things as helped one to prepare for death and the world to come, has its link with a point of view expressed perennially by our writers. Chaucer's outburst at the close of *Troilus and Criseyde*

> O yonge fresshe folkes, he or she . . .
> Repeyreth hom fro worldly vanyte

strikes many modern readers as abrupt and unintegrated with the rest of the tale. The closing fragment of Spenser's Mutabilitie Cantos is sometimes seen as in stark contradiction with the main idea of the whole section; with which, in fact, it stands in a beautiful and traditional logic. The Duke's 'Be absolute for death' speech to Claudio[1] has been taken by a prominent Shakespeare critic as a mark of his inadequacy. Clarissa's elaborate preparations when she felt her life drawing to its close are now usually felt to be sentimental and morbid; and in the verse of Hopkins or Eliot which 'turns away from life' there is diagnosed, respectively, a tragic partial obduracy of vocation, or a regrettable inadequacy of character.

These findings may or may not be valid. But the tendency is to reach them on too easy terms; because present-day Christianity, optimist and activist, encourages both Christian and non-Christian to overlook one of the great contours, or perhaps I should say panoramas, of Christian development in the past. The dying Addison's summoning of a young relative to his bedside, in order to 'see how a Christian can die', may strike us as typical Addisonian smugness; but it filled Edward Young forty years later with astonishment and reverence at its resolute piety.

Sketching this contour or panorama backward into the past (and here it can be no more than sketch) might commence with Newman's superb 'General Answer to Mr Kingsley':

Starting then with the being of a God . . . I look out of myself into the world of men, and there I see a sight which fills me with unspeakable distress. . . . I look into this busy living world, and see no reflexion of its Creator. . . . I am far from denying the arguments in proof of a God . . . but they do not warm me or enlighten me; they do not take away the winter of my desolation. . . . The sight of the world is nothing less than the prophet's scroll, full of 'lamentations, and mourning, and woe'. To consider the world in its length and breadth . . . is a vision to dizzy and appall. . . .

Almost exactly two centuries before, Richard Baxter carries back the tradition in a way that takes from Hamlet's

> Or that the Everlasting had not fix'd
> His canon 'gainst self-slaughter

its seeming petulance, and suggests its conventionality instead:

O, if we did but verily believe . . . sure we should be as impatient of living, as we are now fearful of dying . . . we should . . . hardly

[1] Shakespeare, *Measure for Measure*, III, i, 5.

refrain from laying violent hands on ourselves . . . what would a serious Christian belief do, if God's law against self-murder did not restrain ?[1]

The traditions of Christianity are at this point ample and complex: but this aspect of them goes back far beyond Baxter, for example to More's *Dialoge of Comfort against Tribulacion* (1553):

Now because that thys world is as I tell you not oure eternal dwelling, but oure lyttle whyle wandryng, God would that we should in such wyse vse it, as folke that were wearye of it, and that we should in this vale of laboure, toyle, teares and myserye, not looke for reste and ease, fame, pleasure, wealthe and felicity. For they that do so fare lyke a fonde felowe, that goyng towards hys owne house, wher he should be wealthie, woulde for a tapsters pleasure become an hostler by the waye, and dye in a stable, and never come at home. (I, 13)

and two centuries before More, to Walter Hilton's *Ladder of Perfection*:

I am convinced that anyone who could once have a little insight into the spiritual dignity and beauty which belong to the soul by nature, and which it may retain by grace, would loathe and despise all the joy, love and beauty of the world as he would the stench of corruption. (ch. 46)

In the great pre-Conquest divines, the sense of life and the world is the same; and the eschatology which explains and warrants it is clear:

Men stand in need of God's laws above all at this time which is the time of the end of this world; and many are the perils which men stand in before the end comes. . . .[2]

Good people, learn the truth: this world is in haste, and draws nigh its end. And so, in the world, the longer things go, the worse they become: and so it must needs be, from bad to worse and worst, day by day, for men's sins, till the coming of Anti-Christ; and then indeed will it be a day of wrath, and a day of dread, far and wide.[3]

Perhaps the decisive thing is to sense how these convictions,

[1] *The Saints' Rest* (1650), Part IV, ch. 2.
[2] Aelfric, preface to the *Homilies*; modernized versions of Old or Early Middle English passages are my own.
[3] Wulfstan, *Address to the English*.

and others that go with them, have sunk over centuries and almost over millennia into the English mind in its most solemn moments; so that Wulfstan's celebrated 'a swa leng swa wyrse', is paraphrased in the 'Reeve's Tale' and almost paraphrased in the *Faerie Queene*; and when Donne speaks in a letter of 'this sickly dotage of the world, where vertue languisheth in a banishment' he is employing the same idea. In Shakespeare the tradition sometimes lies a mere hand's breadth behind the text: 'We have seen the best of our time: machinations, hollowness, treachery and all ruinous disorders follow us disquietly to our graves.' Gloucester's catalogue, just before this, of the ruinous disorders themselves, reads almost like a free paraphrase of Wulfstan. That, of course, it is not: the likeness comes from drawing on one enduring side of human life, and having contact with the perennial tradition—a Christian tradition—which put it into words. But the great earlier tradition was never far away. Innocent III's *De contemptu mundi* was indeed paraphrased by George Gascoigne in 1576, the very year of the opening of the Elizabethan theatres. Later, this sombre and solemn note tended to fade away. But 'mortification' in the older sense is a key to the dénouement of *Rasselas* (1759), and Cowper's 'Retirement' ('Hackney'd in business, wearied at that oar . . .') is a remarkable fusion: its protagonist is an almost Horatian Maecenas-figure, but his 'retirement' is to prepare for death in the full Christian sense.

Perhaps, at this point, another of the more minatory convictions of earlier Christianity should come to mind. Hell, which was such a stumbling-block for the religious consciousness of the nineteenth century, seems now in large part to have gone by default. The World's Classics translator of Dante's *Inferno* (1921) suavely says: 'It must never be forgotten that all the physical imagery of Hell is the Poet's only means of vividly figuring the tortures of self-condemnation.' Given a really living consciousness of how religious writers have treated Hell, this falls dramatically short of self-evidence. The point might be followed up in innumerable authors, from Baxter's *Saints' Rest* to the *Old English Homilies* of the twelfth century:

. . . after that he showed him high trees, burning at hell-gate, and on those trees he showed him the souls of the damned, hanging

some by the feet, some by the hands, some by the tongue, some by
the eyes. . . . Next he showed him an oven . . . and many were the
wicked souls hung inside it. Again, he showed him a fountain of
fire, and twelve Prince Devils guarded the fountain to torment the
wretched guilty souls inside it. After that he showed him the sea
of hell. In that same sea were nameless creatures, some with four
feet, some with no feet at all; and their eyes were all like fire, and
their breath was alight, like lightning in thunder. And day and
night, without ever stopping, they struck down the wretched bodies
. . . some of those men wept bitterly, some bit their own tongue for
grief; and all their tears were like burning coals trundling down
over their faces.[1]

With these facts in mind, Claudio's celebrated speech takes on
a new complexity and sharpness:

> Ay, but to die and go we know not where:
> To lie in cold obstruction and to rot;
> This sensible warm motion to become
> A kneaded clod; and the delighted spirit
> To bathe in fiery floods, or to reside
> In thrilling region of thick-ribbed ice;
> To be imprison'd in the viewless winds,
> And blown with restless violence round about
> The pendent world; or to be worse than worst
> Of those that lawless and incertain thoughts
> Imagine howling: 'tis too horrible!
> The weariest and most loathed worldly life
> That age, ache, penury and imprisonment
> Can lay on nature is a paradise
> To what we fear of death.[2]

Isabella's 'alas, alas!' at this is not mere distress at the hard-
ness of her task of persuasion. It releases a deeper embarrass-
ment and grief: that of the young religious who detects how her
condemned brother is totally and sorrily unprepared; who
responds, as it were, to the skill with which Shakespeare, while
leaving his hero free from any taint of active Pyrrhonism, yet
reveals him, in his ambiguous 'go we know not where' and
'uncertain thoughts', his casual 'worldly', his disordered
jumbling of the future of the soul with that of the body, as one
whose faith is unthought and unstable: who, in his youth and
spirits, has not even begun to learn the lesson that still had

[1] *In Diebus Dominicis*; abridged.   [2] *Measure for Measure*, III, i, 118 f.

meaning for the eighteenth century, which could find it (as the seventeenth could not) in Browne's *Christian Morals*: 'Measure not thyself by thy morning shadow, but by the extent of thy grave'.

Awareness of these sterner and now largely interred traditions of Christianity opens up whole provinces of English literature, and minister to the essential task of the specialist: to set aside general impressions in favour of controlled complexity and comprehended depth. But to this process, other and happier traditions of Christianity have no less relevance. 'Traditions of Christianity' is a valid expression here, although it points to movements of thought which spread wider than Christianity, and further back in time. Arthur O. Lovejoy, in his classic book, has shown how the European traditions of both immanence and transcendence are present and wedded together in Plato.[1] That God is present in the life, beauty and richness of his creation is already clear from the earliest times of English poetry: 'Great are the powers of Christ; fate the swiftest, winter the coldest, spring the frostiest, and lasts cold the longest, summer the sunniest, and the sky hottest, autumn the splendidest, bringing to men the fruits of the earth that God is sending them'.[2] In this sense of God-in-his-creation there is nothing, of course, alien to the mysticism of the fourteenth century— and by the very nature of metaphor it is implicit in a fourteenth-century lyric like

> I sing of a mayden
> That is makeles.

Although it is not easy to find an English medieval mystic who actively and repeatedly celebrates it, that very fact affords an opportunity to enlarge the horizon once again, and recall how 'St Dionysius' (as the author of *The Cloud of Unknowing* calls him) stands as a major influence behind all medieval mysticism, and behind him, in turn, stands the incomparable Plotinian marriage of immanence and transcendence:

... soul is the author of all living things, ... it has breathed life into them all, whatever is nourished by earth and sea, all the creatures

---

[1] *The Great Chain of Being* (Cambridge, Mass., 1936), ch. i.
[2] *The Ways of Creation*, II, 4–9.

of the air, the divine stars in the sky; it is the maker of the sun; itself formed and ordered this vast heaven . . . Into that heaven, . . . let the great soul be conceived to roll inward at every point, penetrating, permeating, from all sides pouring in its light. As the rays of the sun throwing their brilliance upon a lowering cloud make it gleam all gold, so the soul entering the material expanse of the heavens has given life, has given immortality. . . .[1]

Christianized, this spiritual worldliness, this faith scintillating with the light of reality, is nowhere so eloquently and yet discriminatingly expressed as in Traherne. 'Discriminatingly' is essential. True, the visionary immediacy of Traherne's childhood experience, sustained by his writing into adult life, is sometimes breathtaking in its pristine clarity. His corn that never should be reaped, nor was ever sown, his maids 'strange seraphic pieces of life and beauty', his boys and girls at play that were moving jewels, belong to our poetry as much as to our prose. But the literary readers to whom these phrases mean so much do not always have in mind how small they bulk in the *Centuries of Meditation* as a whole.

In the first place, Traherne is scrupulous in finding a place for *de contemptu mundi*. 'To *contemn* the world and to enjoy the world are things contrary to each other. How then can we contemn the world, which we are born to enjoy? Truly there are two worlds.' Traherne presses the traditional art-nature contrast into service, in order to dismiss everything made by man ('Invented Riches, Pomps and Vanities, brought in by Sin'). It is the frontier in Traherne's sensibility where argument takes over from vision; and for English poetry it was of great significance. Moreover, limpid and glowing as are Traherne's visionary phrases about the beauty of the natural world, they express what in the whole edifice of his thought has no large place. The world is 'the beautiful *frontispiece* of Eternity' (I, 20); 'O what a world of *evidences*! We are lost in abysses, we now are absorpt in wonders, and swallowed up of demonstrations. Beasts, fowls and fishes teaching and evidencing the glory of their creator' (II, 22) [my italics]. The major part, in bulk, of each of the *Centuries* is devoted to the nature of the soul, or of God, or of that Love which is their

---

[1] *Enneads*, v, i. 2; trans. S. MacKenna, vol. iv (London, 1926).

proper inter-communion; and the matter of subordination is perfectly clear:

. . . the idea of Heaven and Earth in the Soul of Man is more precious with God than the things themselves, and more excellent in nature. . . . As much . . . *as the end is better than the means*, the thought of the World whereby it is enjoyed is better than the World. (II, 90)

At this point, perhaps may be seen one of the most interesting lights thrown by the study of specifically Christian writing upon the development of English literature as a whole. Traherne seems to be the last writer in English in whose work may be found both a visionary sense of the numinous everywhere in creation, and a severely orthodox submission of this aspect of world-experience to something intrinsically superior, viz. spiritual experience. Milton indeed sees God as triumphantly and self-vindicatingly present in his creation; and there are passages in Book VII of *Paradise Lost* which can well stand beside Traherne, or anyone else, for immediacy of apprehension. But here Milton is writing of the actual moment of God's creating the world; and his more usual—in a sense, one might add, his more considered and more deeply felt sense of God as present throughout the world—is different in kind. In fact, it decisively reflects the Protestant transformation of Christianity; though its penetration of literature came more slowly than its ecclesiastical dominance. For Milton, God is present in Nature not by contrast with, but by means of, the works of man. He is manifest above all in human achievement: achievement made possible, no doubt, by grace, but operating also through the superb quality of great human virtues: proper pride, courage, resolution, steadfastness. Adam and Eve wiping their tears and setting off to inhabit a new world, Milton's very Arian Christ holding out against Satan, Samson's 'new acquist'—God is immanent through some intense and splendid effort of the individual, the decisive earnestness of his wrestle with evil and his ultimate success.

This distinctively Protestant modulation had of course its connexion, as Professor Ian Watt has pointed out, with the novel; and it is apt to notice that in the period when the first major English novels were being written, Milton's narratives, widely known and revered as they already were, constituted (Chaucer being unavailable) almost the only models of integrated narrative in English. The obvious alternative is *The Pilgrim's Progress*, and from the Christian standpoint this may very well be regarded as an immediate sequel to *Paradise Lost*. In fact, it is not difficult to see two major lines in English fiction extending from Milton's two basic types of narrative. First would come the spiritual-picaresque, as one might put it; which emerges from *Paradise Lost*, running on through such works as *Joseph Andrews*, *Waverley*, *David Copperfield*, *Portrait of a Lady*, *Jude the Obscure*, *Sons and Lovers*. The basic mode of these works is a kind of journeying through the world by the hero or heroine, seeking above all spiritual success, establishment as a morally adequate individual. Second would come what might be termed the anti-picaresque novel: that not of the wayfaring but of the abiding individual, whose task is not to find himself or herself as morally adequate, but to preserve integrity in a world of un-integrity: *Clarissa*, *Persuasion*, *The Heart of Midlothian*, *Jane Eyre*, *Tess*, *The Wings of the Dove*, *Victory*.

The point is not, of course, that Milton with his two kinds of narrative must really be seen as the direct father of the English novel. It is simply that his work helps one to register how English fiction, over its whole development, has moved either explicitly within, or over the purlieus of, the world of Protestant Christianity. The point becomes clearer, for example, if one notices how the English *Bildungsroman*, insofar as that term has meaning, is overwhelmingly a moral and not an intellectual or cultural one. The contrast with *Wilhelm Meister* is decisive; and the rarity of such works as *The Mill on the Floss* or *Portrait of the Artist*, where other sides of the individual's development creep in, and the modest degree to which they do so, set the matter beyond doubt. Again, the popularity in translation of the *Thousand Nights and a Night* is a well-known fact about the earlier eighteenth century, in England as elsewhere throughout Western Europe. It is, of course, a work wholly unrelated to the tradition of Christianity and Protestantism. But there are only two works of any significance which show its influence, *Vathek* and *Rasselas*; and of these the first stands completely alone, and

19

the point about the second is precisely that it is a fantasy which
begins as Oriental and ends as Protestant: the journey of the
individual towards moral adequacy.

Thus the Protestant-Christian emphasis, that God shows in his
creation through the decisive acts of virtuous men, lies behind
much of English fiction; though after the inescapably christianized drama of Richardson's work it becomes more secularized
and generalized. Traherne's dominant consciousness, however,
was of the numinous everywhere in created nature; and this
led forward into the development of English poetry. The
overtly religious content progressively disappears, but certain
of the original contours remain. Pope says that the body nature
is, and God the soul; Thomson, in his Hymn concluding the
Seasons, that the round of the year is 'but the varied God'. In
both cases, however, this religious dimension is by way of an
addition to the main body of the work, an after-word if not an
afterthought. It may ring sincerely enough, but the writer's
imagination, his creative power generally, is absorbed with the
spectacle of creation precisely as in Traherne it was not. In
the early Wordsworth, the Wordsworth of 'Tintern Abbey' or
the 1805 version of the *Prelude*, there is a further development:
the numinous at the heart of nature is as emphatically non-
Christian as it is indisputably numinous.

Yet there are substantial continuities. One of them is the
very distinctive and by no means self-evident conviction that
nature exerts on those who deeply sense her quality an influence
which pre-eminently is a moral and character-building influence. Here the continuity from Thomson through Akenside
to Wordsworth is particularly plain. Moreover, it is a
Protestant kind of character-building: nature makes men
serious, steadfast, thoughtful, plain-living, high-minded. Another continuity with the antecedent Christian tradition shows
in Wordsworth's firm insistence on the primacy, over and above
the poet's feeling for nature, of man himself. Wordsworth, as
is now recognized, is no nature-poet:

> . . . the Mind of Man—
> My haunt, and the main region of my song.[1]

---

[1] *The Recluse*, I, quoted in the preface to *The Excursion* (London, 1814).

That is how he expresses the matter himself; and the point is a vital one. Secularized, Wordsworth's order of priorities follows the lines of Traherne's.

Another aspect of the same matter is that the English romantic poets, even including Keats, preserved the art-nature contrast of the earlier tradition. On the evidence at least of their poems, they do not see in painting, sculpture, music, the deeper radiance that comes to them from scenery or from men. 'Ozymandias' reflects the recent discovery of Egyptian megalithic sculpture, but little of its quality. *Endymion* reflects Keats's knowledge of Greek fifth-century sculpture, but it seemed natural to his imagination to transform the stone into living persons in a quasi-human drama. He does much the same in the 'Grecian Urn'. Perhaps this poem, with his sonnet on the Parthenon Marbles, may be taken as the beginning of a change. But English poetry had no Gautier. Throughout the nineteenth century—Shelley, Hopkins, Hardy, Patmore all come to mind—there was in the poet's interest in style and the arts a hint of the surreptitious; it got into their prose and letters, not their verse; and it was not until Yeats and Wallace Stevens that this frontier seems finally to have been crossed.

Again, from Akenside's *Pleasures of Imagination* through Beattie's *Minstrel* and Blake's *Thel* to the *Prelude* itself, we find a certain recurrent mode in which poetry is written; and (compare the trend in fiction) it is the Protestant archetype of the individual, this time through his contact with nature, striving to make progress towards moral and human adequacy. The later romantic poets, in most other respects, broke with the Christian background. In *Childe Harold* the character-building powers of Nature are barely in question, in 'To Autumn' Keats seems to be seeking the quality of the natural world as it is in itself, and the 'power' which Shelley tries to identify in 'Mont Blanc' is not a numinous power at all. Nevertheless, although these poets moved further from the Christian patterns, the poetic structure they employ is still frequently that of the individual's lonely, Lutheran struggle, or attempted struggle, from inadequacy to adequacy. This does not apply to Byron. But clearly it is the basis of *Alastor*; and in Keats it is present not only in *Endymion* and the famous opening section of the *Fall of Hyperion*, those two documents which virtually open and close his poetic life, but also in the whole 'Vale of Soul-Making' of the letters themselves.

If Traherne was indeed the last major religious visionary in English, this cannot but be associated with the way in which, with the coming of Protestantism, it was natural for the tradition of Christian writings to become more emphatically an argumentative and ratiocinative tradition. Needless to say, medieval mysticism was not the only or even the most prominent side of medieval Christianity. It is something of an accident that, apart of course from Langland, the two aspects of medieval Christianity best represented in English are mysticism and what I might call the pre-Protestantism of Wiclif. With the Reformation, what happened was that the idea of 'evidences', in Paley's sense instead of Traherne's, moved slowly into the dominant position. But it did so through a complex pattern of change, in which things opposite in fundamental tendency seem sometimes to come together.

As a first approach, one may say that the primacy of argument brought Protestants together even when they argued for very different things. Hooker in the *Laws*, and Baxter in *The Saint's Rest*, both give the main place to methodical proof and evidence, but Baxter sees his task as establishing the definitive authority of scripture, and Hooker sees his as proving that it has only its proper place in an ordered hierarchy of law where the ultimate judge is natural reason. Yet from the point of view of temper the upshot is the same. Both give the primacy of place to rationality, to systematic marshalling of evidence, argument and proof; and in fact, at this point we witness the formation of something which came to have great and permanent importance in the English intellectual tradition. For Hooker the light of reason, because it is a natural light, is also both a moral light and an easy light. 'That light of Reason, whereby good may be known from evil,' he firmly says. Since he never questions whether men genuinely do have knowledge of good and evil, the next step follows. Perhaps men, in their perverse ingenuity, can make the work of reason difficult, but in itself it is easy:

The main principles of Reason are in themselves apparent. For to make nothing evident of itself unto man's understanding were to take away all possibility of knowing any thing.

The next step is easy too:

The general and perpetual voice of man is as the sentence of God himself . . . the Law of Reason is such that being proposed no man can reject it . . . there is nothing in it but any man (having natural perfection of wit and maturity of judgement) can by labour and travail find it out. And to conclude, the general principles are such that it is not easy to find men ignorant of them.

—and the next:

. . . the greatest moral duties we owe towards God or man may without any great difficulty be concluded; . . . the greatest part of the moral law being *so easy* for all men to know. (I, viii, 5–11)

The innate conservatism of this viewpoint need but be touched on in passing, as also the difficulty which Hooker creates when soon afterwards he writes, 'laws politic . . . are never framed as they should be, unless presuming the will of man to be inwardly obstinate, rebellious, and averse from all obedience . . . in a word, *unless presuming a man to be in regard of his depraved mind little better than a wild beast* (I, x, i). We need only observe that the paradox of which Shakespeare was able to make *Hamlet* or *Lear* lends itself to drama more easily than to logic.

Hooker's affinities—at first glance improbable enough— with the Empiricists now emerge. For Locke too the basic principles of morals were 'so easy' for men of perfected wit and mature judgement. Consisting simply of 'relations between ideas', they could not but be 'apparent' unless the natural light of men's reason were artificially clouded. Reference to Baxter makes the point clearer. He, in the *Autobiography*, also 'discerns the necessity of a methodical procedure in maintaining the doctrine of Christianity', finds the results 'so consonant to the law of nature', asks for 'no more credit from the reader than the self-evidencing light of the matter, with concurrent *rational* advantages . . . shall constrain him to', and finally, inclines to the view that what is essential is also easy:

In my youth I was quickly past my fundamentals and was running up into a multitude of controversies, and greatly delighted with metaphysical and scholastic writings. . . . But the elder I grew the smaller stress I laid upon these controversies and curiosities, . . . as finding far greater uncertainties in them than I first discerned . . . and now it is the fundamental doctrines of the Catechism which I highliest value and daily think of, and find most useful to myself and others. (I, x, 3)

Baxter's link with the Empiricist tradition from Bacon to Hobbes is inescapable:

At first the style of authors took as much with me as the argument . . . but now I judge of truth not at all by any such ornaments or accidents, but *by its naked evidence.* (I, x, 13)

My certainty differeth as the evidences differ. . . . (I, x, 5)

I am more and more sensible that most controversies have *more need of right stating* than of debating; and if my skill be increased in anything it is in that, in narrowing controversies by explication, and *separating the real from the verbal,* and proving to many contenders that they differ less than they think they do. (I, x, 36)

Besides this, his temper of mind is important to one of our major intellectual traditions, both religious and secular. The key lies in phrases like 'the truth is . . . to give them their due'; 'the true moderate healing terms'; 'seasonably and moderately'; 'the poor Church of Christ, the sober, sound religious part, and like Christ that was crucified between two malefactors; the profane and formal persecutors on the one hand, and the fanatic dividing sectary on the other hand'. The link between Baxter's temper of mind (or the not dissimilar temper of Hooker) and the political or ecclesiastical necessities of the age lies outside this essay, and is in any event not unfamiliar. But with these two religious thinkers, one can trace emerging an attitude of mind which was to have a long history. The focal points of it seem to be these: that truth is separable from error by reasonable thought; that reasonable thought is easy for anyone who will satisfy certain simple conditions (which are, keeping the mind free from anger or prejudice on the one hand, and verbal confusion on the other); and that those who succeed will think, and write, with sobriety, levelheadedness, and amiability.

Here the tradition of Hooker, Baxter and Tillotson shades into that from Bacon to Hume, though Hume takes delight in making these eminently respectable methods issue in out-rageous paradox, and is in fact disrupting the tradition he inherited. It also, however, shades into the main line of English 'prose of thought': Swift, though 'amiability' must in his case be understood within the complex frame of irony; Bishop Butler; Johnson; Burke; Newman; Mill; Matthew Arnold. 'Everything is what it is, and not another thing'; 'you must clear your mind of cant'; 'to think a little more, and bustle a little less'. It would be an interesting though large enterprise to trace out some of the interactions between this urbane and predominantly Anglican tradition, and that of the plain and simple style—as life—in which Bunyan, for all his intensity of feeling, has his place, and after him Defoe, Cowper, Cobbett and (with a difference) George Eliot. This is, of course, a familiar strand in English letters, and so is the fact that it has drawn, over a long period, on the way of life of English non-conformity. In the sixteenth century, when the Anglican church still had its Puritan wing, this did not apply: Bishop Jewel is among the first to demand complete simplicity of style. George Herbert too must be understood in this context; and the Anglican tradition of plain living and writing continues—though by the early eighteenth century the Church of England could not keep him—with William Law's *Serious Call* (1729).

At first sight, Law seems to speak with an authentic earlier voice. He laments living in 'the dregs of time', when one sees 'no real *mortification* . . . no true contempt of the world':

all Christians as such have renounced this world . . . for an eternal state of quite another nature, they must look upon worldly employ-ments, as upon worldly wants, and bodily infirmities; things not to be desired but only to be endured and suffered, till death and the resurrection have carried us to an eternal state of real happiness . . . what a strange thing it is, that a little health, or the poor business of a shop, should keep us so senseless of these great things that are coming so fast upon us! (chh. iv, iii)

Yet renunciation and mortification now mean new things; not a total and deeply felt withdrawal from the world, but a kind of sober and virtuous continuing in its very midst:

You say, if you was to imitate cleanly plainness and cheapness of dress, you would offend your husbands.

. . . if your husbands do really require you to patch your faces, to expose your breasts naked, and to be fine and expensive in all your apparel, then take these two resolutions:

First, to forbear from all this, as soon as your husbands will permit you.

Secondly, to use your utmost endeavours to recommend your selves to their affections by such solid virtues as may correct the vanity of their minds. (ch. ix)

If a merchant, having forbore from too great business, that he might quietly attend on the service of God, should therefore die worth *twenty*, instead of *fifty* thousand pounds, could anyone say that he had mistaken his calling, or gone a loser out of the world ?

If a gentleman should have killed fewer foxes, been less frequent at balls, gaming, and merry meetings, because stated parts of his time had been given to retirement, to meditation, and devotion, could it be thought, that when he left the world, he would regret the loss of those hours ? (ch. xx)

This is no mere accident, because Law is writing on the active not the contemplative life. Nor is the main point even that the religious classic of this age should be a treatise of the active life, while the other tradition is unrepresented. Its essence lies in the whole temper with which Law saw Christianity; and here it is the accents of Hooker and Baxter that we hear once again. What Law condemns is 'every temper that is contrary to *reason and order*': and it is the reason of Butler, not that of Boethius. Virtue is natural to man, and the natural is the reasonable. The principles of conduct for a 'reasonable life, and a wise use of our proper condition' (the sobriety, the level-headedness, are unmistakable), 'are not speculative flights, or imaginary notions, but are plain and undeniable laws, that are founded in the nature of rational beings' (ch. v). If Law's starting point seems like that of the *Ladder of Perfection*, his final position approximates to Butler's *Sermons* (1726); and his sketches of unobtrusively virtuous persons within the daily round of Augustan society bring to mind *The Spectator*.

One group of Christians did not endorse either the primacy of reason, or—at least in its early vigour—the good-humour and amiability of temper which have gone with that. Baxter indicates them: '. . . the *Quakers*, who were but the Ranters turned from horrid profaneness and blasphemy to a life of extreme austerity on the other side. Their doctrines were mostly the same as with the Ranters. They make the light which every man hath within him to be his sufficient rule. . . .' We know how much Blake owed to the Ranters and to other small but remarkable sects of the same kind. The connexion between our romantic poetry and the Methodist Revival, and its affinity with Traherne, have also been dealt with.[1] Methodism, distinctive in its organization and in its position with regard to the established church, is distinctive above all for sustaining the idea of a sudden coming of insight which brings with it a total regeneration of the man. This goes back, of course, to the beginning of Protestantism, and in a more general way to St Augustine's 'Thou wert more inward to me, than my most inward part' (Confessions, III, vi), or indeed to Saul on the road to Damascus. But regeneration as a complete spiritual transmutation has also its literary side. It is central and recurrent in Blake (The Four Zoas) and is in fact nothing other than the victory of 'Innocence' over 'Experience' which he sees as the concluding phase of his myth of history.

In fact, regeneration is one of the recurrent patterns of English writing in both prose and verse from the mid-eighteenth century, and in this context it has no loose meaning, it is no mere remedying of some defect, nor ἀναγνώρισις of a general kind. It means that there comes a brief and decisive time when it is as if the scales fall from the eyes of the protagonist, and he sees the world and himself as if he were re-born into wholeness and integrity. The climactic phase of the Prelude records just such an experience: 'Imagination and Taste, how Impaired and Restored' is Wordsworth's suavely eighteenth-century way of expressing it, but what he is recording is the evanescence, and re-birth, of essential human quality. In 'The Ancient Mariner' and the first version of the Dejection Ode, the initial phase of Coleridge's spiritual death, sudden illumination, and final reborn condition, are also clear. So they are in The Fall of Hyperion. The whole experience is what these poems are about.

---

[1] Cf. A. L. Moreton, The Everlasting Gospel: a Study in the Sources of William Blake (London, 1958); and F. C. Gill, The Romantic Movement and Methodism (London, 1937), especially pp. 46–71, 129–59.

To apply these ideas to English fiction is more dubious, but I cannot regard it as fable. The Christian analogues nearest to *Lear* or *The Winter's Tale* are pre-Protestant: purgatory, penance, atonement. But novels as varied as *Pride and Prejudice, Northanger Abbey, Jane Eyre, Hard Times, Adam Bede, The Lost Girl,* and *A Passage to India,* all seem to have something of a common basic pattern: the climax of the book is a relatively brief but traumatic experience of the protagonist, when he learns what is vital to life, and in learning is renewed, re-invigorated, re-born. The pattern, that is (though secularized and generalized), of revivalism; or more exactly, since this is something far older than Wesley, of one great variety of Protestant conversion. To use a now fashionable terminology: Protestantism may well lie behind one of the recurrent 'myths' of the English novel.

The case of Lawrence is of special interest. His defence, recently, as a 'Puritan' is well known.[1] The traumatic moment of conversion is not dominant in his work, but the contrast between the elect and the damned, in a sense which it is perfectly right to call spiritual, and the conviction that the state of election is one in which the 'more inward to me, than my most inward part' at last flows freely to the surface, are certainly dominant. That word 'inward', moreover (Augustine's Latin is 'tu autem eras interior intimo meo') gives a further clue. 'Inward' is one of the keys to Quakerism; and to read Fox's *Journal* (1694) is to find oneself in an astonishingly Lawrentian atmosphere. In the first place the language of Lawrence, as of those who in criticism or in general social and moral thinking start from Lawrence, is largely the language of the Quakers. 'Inward' is one of Fox's words, and so is 'tender' ('I met with a tender people'; 'a very tender young man'). So is the very distinctive use of 'moved' which is much favoured by Lawrentian critics ('I was moved to go to them again, and . . . many of them were brought to the Lord', Fox writes). So above all, is the free use of the word 'life':

> when I stood among the people the glory and *life* shined over all.
> a great flock of sheep hath the Lord in that country, that feed in his pastures of *life*.

[1] *Regina* v. *Penguin Books Ltd.; The Times* (20 October 1960), p. 10.

so if any *have a moving* to any place, and have spoken what they were *moved of the Lord*, let them return to their habitation again . . . and live in the pure life of God . . . so will ye be *kept in the life*—in the solid and seasoned spirit.

This community between Lawrence and the Quakers is no matter only of vocabulary alone, however. What most distinguishes Lawrence is the way in which his marvellous receptivity and openness combined with, was genuinely inseparable from, a wholly sincere but angry and ungracious contentiousness and censoriousness. It is a psychologically remarkable combination; but Fox's exactly. 'I was moved to tell him he was a dog'; 'I told him his heart was rotten.' And Fox makes plain why, for both men, the self-righteous anger and visionary aliveness had to go together. 'His words were like a thistle to me'; 'I told him it *struck at my life*.' For one whose openness to life has this glowing, incandescent, in the end obsessive integrity, it is mere prevarication to be tolerant, to be easy-going; even— this marks the limit of its validity—to be tender.

'Wholeness' (ferocious or otherwise) has been a keynote to English criticism at least since Johnson wrote: 'there is always an appeal open from criticism to nature.' This point of view criticism partly owes to Christianity, and more especially to Protestantism. 'The poet . . . brings the whole soul of man into activity', wrote Coleridge. 'The whole man moves', Newman said of conversion; and if Newman was much indebted to Coleridge, as he acknowledged, and a Catholic by the time he wrote those words, he started life as a nonconformist, and the *Grammar of Assent* (1870), from which the phrase is taken, is exceptional and not altogether acceptable as Catholic apologetics. The tradition is emphatically present in those arch-protestants, Ruskin and Carlyle; and Carlyle's essay on Burns is a *locus classicus*:

he does not write from hearsay but from sight and experience, it is the scenes he has lived and laboured amidst, that he describes. . . . Let a man but speak forth with genuine *earnestness* the thoughts, the emotions, the actual condition of his own heart; and other men . . . will find some response within which must and will give heed to him.

Fully to work out the affiliations of this emphasis on the 'whole man', it would be necessary to trace the influence on both

Carlyle and Coleridge of the thought and criticism of the other
great Protestant nation, Germany, and also to notice how
clearly the same standpoint emerges in the work of the French-
Swiss Protestant critics like Montégut and Edmond Schérer,
whom Matthew Arnold saluted in his essay 'A French Critic
on Milton'.[1]

Nothing is further from the truth than the still much-favoured
idea of the nineteenth century as a period of 'divorce' between
thought and feeling. On the contrary, our modern stress on
unity of being and integrated sensibility is the culmination of
thinking over that very period. A few pointers must suffice:

the mind, strong in reason and just feeling united. . . . (Coleridge,
The Friend)

but whatever of sensation enters into the feeling must not be local
. . . it is a condition of the whole frame, not of part only . . . it
pervades the entire nervous system. States of feeling which thus
possess the whole being are the foundations of that which we have
called the poetic. (J. S. Mill, 'On Poetry', 1859 version)

thought and feeling in their lower degrees antagonize, in their
higher harmonize. (Mill, *Diary*, 1854)

Earth's . . . two-sexed meanings . . . wed the thought and felt.
(Meredith, 'The Woods of Westermain')

[In] the highest, purest poetry of love in English literature . . . the
claims of the whole being, body and spirit, are admitted to the
utmost. (Joseph Jacob, obituary on Browning)

. . . no divorce of heart from brain. (Patmore, *The Angel in the
House*, x, b, 4)

But to dismiss that error is a mere preliminary to noticing how
the movement of critical thought belongs to a more general
movement.

No work helps one to see how this movement was Christian
in general and Protestant in particular as much as what will
one day unquestionably be recognized as a classic: *Lux mundi*
(1889), a collection edited by the modernist theologian Charles
Gore. This momentous work marks the decisive recovery of

---

[1] My attention was first drawn to the interest of this group by Mrs J. Gooder.

Protestant Christianity, as a viable system of thought and life, from the assault of mid-nineteenth century scientism. J. R. Illingworth's contribution, 'The Incarnation and Development', triumphantly assimilates Darwinism, and in so doing re-shapes the vision which Blake shared with Traherne:

The kind of design in nature which first arrested earlier thinkers was its usefulness to man . . . they came to look upon all natural phenomena as having for their final cause the good of man. . . . This was not an untrue conception; . . . but it was partial and inadequate, as Bacon and Spinoza shewed. And we have now come to regard the world not as a machine, but as an organism . . . whose primary purpose is its own perfection, something that is contained within and not outside itself, an internal end. . . . When we look at nature in this way, and watch the complex and subtle process by which a crystal, a leaf, a lily, a moth, a bird, a star realize their respective ideals with undisturbed, unfailing accuracy, . . . when we further find that in the very course of pursuing their primary ends, and becoming perfect after their kind, the various parts of the universe . . . with infinite ingenuity of correspondence and adaptation subserve not only one but a thousand secondary ends, linking and weaving themselves together by their mutual ministration into an orderly, harmonious, complicated whole, the signs of intelligence grow clearer still. And when, beyond this, we discover the quality of beauty in every moment and situation of this complex life; the drop of water that circulates from sea to cloud, and cloud to earth, and earth to plant, and plant to life-blood, shining the while with strange spiritual significance in the sunset and the rainbow and the dewdrop and the tear; the universal presence of this attribute, so unessential to the course of nature, but so infinitely powerful in its appeal to the human mind, is reasonably urged as a crowning proof of purposeful design.

This passage has been abridged, but its relevance to earlier parts of the present essay is inescapable. Similarly with H. Scott Holland's essay entitled 'Faith' in the context of the integrated sensibility. Quotation can barely show how this is inspired with a conviction that every important aspect of life draws its importance from the inexpugnable wholeness of man:

Faith is not to be ranked by the side of the other faculties in a federation of rival powers, but is behind them all. It goes back to a deeper root; it springs from a more primitive and radical act of the central self than they. It belongs to that original spot of our being, where it adheres in God . . . Out from that spot our powers divide, radiating into separate gifts—will, memory, feeling, reason, imagination, affection; but all of them . . . run back into that home where faith abides.

Faith springs from a source anterior to the distinct division of faculties . . . acts of faith are more radical than those of reason, and . . . they belong to the entire man acting in his integrity . . . faith is the primal act of the elemental self, there at the root of life, where the being is yet whole and entire. . . .

The promulgations of Lawrence, the intimations of Eliot, underlying the whole modern approach to literature and to criticism, seem here present and fully articulate.

This essay has sometimes been discussing what cannot be denied as the legacy of Christian tradition in our literature; but sometimes too discussing what, in varying combinations, have been simply communions of outlook and response, issuing ultimately from the whole mental life of the English, and the continuing corpus of their traditions and culture. It is a corpus in which Christianity in general, Protestantism in particular, and literature in addition, have played unusually prominent roles. That there should be a complex story of their interconnexion, incompletely sketched here, is natural enough.